FIVE
VIEWS
ON

THE CHURCH
AND POLITICS

Books in the Counterpoints Series

Church Life

Evaluating the Church Growth Movement
Exploring the Worship Spectrum
Remarriage after Divorce in Today's Church
Understanding Four Views on Baptism
Understanding Four Views on the Lord's Supper
Who Runs the Church?

Bible and Theology

Are Miraculous Gifts for Today?
Five Views on Apologetics
Five Views on Biblical Inerrancy
Five Views on Law and Gospel
Five Views on Sanctification
Five Views on the Church and Politics
Four Views on Christian Spirituality
Four Views on Divine Providence
Four Views on Eternal Security
Four Views on Hell
Four Views on Moving Beyond the Bible to Theology
Four Views on Salvation in a Pluralistic World
Four Views on the Apostle Paul
Four Views on the Book of Revelation
Four Views on the Historical Adam
Four Views on the Role of Works at the Final Judgment
Four Views on the Spectrum of Evangelicalism
Genesis: History, Fiction, or Neither?
How Jewish Is Christianity?
Show Them No Mercy
Three Views on Creation and Evolution
Three Views on Eastern Orthodoxy and Evangelicalism
Three Views on the Millennium and Beyond
Three Views on the New Testament Use of the Old Testament
Three Views on the Rapture
Three Views on the Doctrine of the Trinity
Two Views on Women in Ministry

FIVE
VIEWS
ON

THE CHURCH
AND POLITICS

J. Brian Benestad

Robert Benne

Bruce L. Fields

Thomas W. Heilke

James K.A. Smith

Amy E. Black, general editor
Stanley N. Gundry, series editor

ZONDERVAN

Five Views on the Church and Politics
Copyright © 2015 by Amy E. Black, J. Brian Benestad, Robert Benne, Bruce Fields,
    Thomas W. Heilke, and James K.A. Smith

This title is also available as a Zondervan ebook. Visit www.zondervan.com/ebooks.

Requests for information should be addressed to:
Zondervan, 3900 *Sparks Drive SE, Grand Rapids, Michigan* 49546

Library of Congress Cataloging-in-Publication Data

Five views on the church and politics / Thomas W. Heilke, Robert Benne, Bruce L.
    Fields, James K.A. Smith, J. Brian Benestad ; Amy E. Black, general editor.
        pages cm. — (Counterpoints: Bible and theology)
     Includes bibliographical references and index.
     ISBN 978-0-310-51792-4 (softcover)
  1. Christianity and politics. 2. Theology, Doctrinal. I. Black, Amy E., editor.
BR115.P7F58   2015
261.7 — dc23   2015030120

Cover design: Tammy Johnson
Cover photography: © *Travel Pictures Ltd/SuperStock.com*
Interior design: Kait Lamphere

Printed in the United States of America

HB 11.01.2023

CONTENTS

CHRISTIAN TRADITIONS AND POLITICAL ENGAGEMENT

AMY E. BLACK

Christians throughout the centuries have asked questions about how to interact with governing authorities and the broader culture. Followers of Christ owe ultimate allegiance to God, yet they also have rights and responsibilities as earthly citizens.

The Pharisees and Herodians even tried to drag Jesus into political controversies of his day. Knowing that either answer would very likely cause him trouble, they hoped to trick Jesus into making a dangerous statement, asking, "Tell us, then, what is your opinion? Is it right to pay the imperial tax to Caesar or not?" (Matt. 22:17).

Unwilling to take their bait, Jesus responded with a command and a question. First, he told them to show him the coin used to pay the tax, and then he asked them whose image it bore. When they answered that the coin bore the image and inscription of Caesar, he offered this enigmatic response: "So give back to Caesar what is Caesar's, and to God what is God's" (Matt. 22:21). With this reply, Jesus refused to take a side in the fierce political debate of his day over the poll tax and "implied that loyalty to a pagan government was not incompatible with loyalty to God."[1]

Much as in Jesus' own time, political debates today on a wide range of issues divide people, including those in the church. And Christians

---

1. Gordon J. Wenham et al., eds., *New Bible Commentary: 21st Century Edition* (Leicester, England, and Downers Grove, IL, USA: InterVarsity Press, 1994), 933.

still debate what it means to give back to Caesar what is Caesar's and to God what is God's. Historical traditions have offered varying interpretations of the extent to which followers of Christ should engage with governing powers and what it means to be faithful citizens. Yet many Christians are unaware of how these rich traditions can guide them to think more deeply about the relationship between their faith and politics. This book introduces five of these historic traditions of Christian political thought: Anabaptist, Lutheran, Black Church, Reformed, and Catholic.

Five Traditions in Conversation

Not every theological tradition has a robust and distinctive set of teachings that we might call a "political theology," but four in particular (Catholic, Reformed, Lutheran, and Anabaptist) stand out for their enduring influence on conversations about church and state over many centuries. A fifth tradition, that of the Black church, is specifically rooted in the United States and represents a distinctive theological perspective, not to mention forms of communal practice, that is too often discussed in isolation or simply ignored.

This book places these five approaches in conversation with one another, aligning them along a spectrum representing the extent of their Christian political engagement. Borrowing terms from H. Richard Niebuhr's classic *Christ and Culture*,[2] the essays in this book outline five different views on church and politics.

The Christian traditions represented in this volume are rich and diverse. Although most are historically centered on the work of a particular individual or small group of thinkers, each has developed and changed over centuries. Modern Lutheran denominations, for example, draw deeply from ideas presented in Martin Luther's writing and teaching. At the same time, they have developed doctrines and practices that address situations and contexts incomprehensible in Luther's era and

---

2. Niebuhr's account has been criticized in many circles, especially by those who claim his descriptions of various traditions are unfair in favor of his transformationist perspective. Even though many of these critiques have merit, his descriptive terms are familiar to many and provide a useful basis for our spectrum of views. He admits that his types are oversimplified, but he demonstrates how they connect us to key motifs that often reappear in the basic decisions people make about how to relate the Bible to culture.

veer far from what Luther could have imagined. The endurance and adaptation of each of the traditions in this book, despite vastly changing political contexts, highlight their value for understanding present and future contexts, not just the past.

Each of the contributors to this volume writes from within a particular tradition and with keen awareness of its variations, strengths, and weaknesses. The authors do not intend to speak for the entirety of their traditions. Instead, they write from their own perspectives and offer insights into ways that their historical traditions inform thinking about the relationship between Christian faith and politics. Their essays and responses to one another provide a rich introduction to ways in which Christians across time and traditions have understood both the relationship between church and state and the rightful place for individual and collective political participation.

To prepare for the detailed accounts from our contributors, I will briefly describe here some of the basic stances of the different views. Like the essays that follow, I will begin with the Anabaptist tradition, which advocates the strictest churchly separation from secular politics, continue with each view across the spectrum, and end with the Catholic tradition, which is most open to churchly engagement in political life.

The Spectrum of Views: Introductory Descriptions

Anabaptist Political Thought

On the side of the spectrum advocating the most limited possible Christian involvement in politics are Anabaptists. This tradition arose in the sixteenth century when a group of "Radical Reformers" including Menno Simons spoke against the infant baptism characteristic of state churches at the time, teaching that baptism is reserved for adult believers. Early Anabaptists faced intense suffering, persecution, and even execution because of their beliefs, a legacy that has deeply shaped Anabaptist political thought.

When introducing the Anabaptist tradition, I find it helpful to mention briefly how Anabaptists differ from modern Baptists. Anabaptists trace their roots to a radical reform movement in sixteenth-century Switzerland. Although the history is still somewhat debated, many historians trace the emergence of modern Baptists to movements arising out of English Puritanism and Separatism in the seventeenth century.[3]

The two largest streams that emerged, General Baptists and Particular Baptists, differed over their views of atonement but shared commitments to believers' baptism, congregational autonomy, and religious freedom. Anabaptist thought has clearly influenced the Baptist movement, but the two traditions are quite distinct. The Baptist tradition emphasizes the individual, whereas Anabaptists focus on community. Although modern Baptists have tended to advocate for separation of church and state, they have not adopted nonviolence or the distinctive Anabaptist practice of abstaining from government interaction such as serving in the military, running for public office, or taking public oaths.[4]

The Anabaptist tradition emphasizes the life and teaching of Jesus, expressed most fully in his Sermon on the Mount. Jesus explicitly taught what it means to prioritize forgiveness and grace — even to the point of loving our enemies. Jesus personified this teaching by rejecting the violent tendencies of the Zealots, by refusing to resist his own death, and by giving his life as a ransom for others.

As a result, Anabaptists take a posture of nonviolence; they do not endorse use of lethal force or coercion, whether at the hands of individuals or the government. This commitment to pacifism includes rejecting violence even for self-defense, recognizing that suffering and pain could ensue: "For Anabaptists, nonresistance was not a calculated survival strategy but a principle for Christian life and conduct; an assumed nonpolitical kingdom ethic revealed by Christ."[5] Such a stance calls for radical peacemaking in a violent age.

Because governmental actions are tainted so much by violence, Anabaptists have an uneasy relationship with politics. They strongly affirm that the church should lead the way in modeling the actions of Jesus. For many in this tradition, such a stance leads to complete separation from the work of the state and the belief that individuals should not participate in the government because of its coercive power.

---

3. W. David Buschart, *Exploring Protestant Traditions: An Invitation to Theological Hospitality* (Downers Grove, IL: IVP Academic, 2006), 146.

4. Glen H. Stassen, "Anabaptist Influence in the Origin of the Particular Baptists," in *Mennonite Quarterly Review* 36, no. 4 (October 1962): 34f.

5. Werner O. Packull, "An Introduction to Anabaptist Theology," in *The Cambridge Companion to Reformation Theology*, ed. David V. N. Bagchi and David Curtis Steinmetz (Cambridge: Cambridge University Press, 2004), 209.

Other Anabaptists permit some forms of political involvement, expecting that Christian presuppositions will shape all political interactions and believers will oppose violence in every form. They realize that this stance is unlikely to lead to political success, and they grapple with the fact that nonviolence could entail greater oppression. Through all of these actions, they point to the witness of Jesus, who suffered and calls his followers to do the same.

Instead of looking to government as an agent of change, Anabaptist thought emphasizes the centrality of the church and her call to serve as an alternative community that embodies the truths of the gospel. The church should not seek to influence the broad social and political realms as much as it should *be* a distinctive social ethic that prefigures the kingdom of God in all its Christ-like particularity. Thus, the church simply cannot engage in politics or in violence on the world's terms. Love of God and neighbor must permeate every Christian and church in every context. This requires a countercultural voice and a unified community that lives in light of Jesus' radical commands.

Lutheran Political Thought

The Lutheran tradition stems largely but not exclusively from the teachings of Martin Luther. Core elements of the Lutheran tradition include emphases on justification by faith alone, the reality of human sinfulness, the significance of the Word and sacraments, the "two-kingdoms doctrine," and vocation.

Lutherans differentiate between life in society, the order of creation for all people, and the gospel order of redemption that is given to the people of God. God has chosen to rule the earthly kingdom through universal principles and laws that can be rightly regulated through governmental institutions. But human effort and laws cannot redeem sinful hearts. Good works should be a response to God's love, not efforts to merit salvation.

The Lutheran tradition warns against the dangers of conflating these two systems — the kingdom of creation and the kingdom of redemption. People can wrongly look to law as a means to salvation or turn God's love into an earthly ethical norm.

According to Lutheran teaching, the state resulted from the effects of humanity's fall into sin, but it exists in order to fulfill the

God-ordained purpose of restraining evil, protecting citizens, and seeking justice, which sometimes entails the legitimate use of force. Christians can participate in government because government is the means by which God governs a fallen world, and Christians can fulfill their call to love their neighbors by helping the government effectively pursue justice and punish wickedness.

The church as an institution is called to maintain its focus on the gospel of redemption, preaching the Word of God and administering the sacraments instead of placing definitive hope in the temporal and limited power of government or cultural transformation. Thus, the institutional church refrains from direct involvement in politics, focusing instead on molding the hearts of Christians to love and serve people well. Christians, moreover, bear the power of Christ wherever they live or work, so no activity or job escapes the powerful influence of the gospel.

The Lutheran doctrine of vocation places sacred importance on any occupation, activity, or sphere of life. Some individual Christians will be called to share the church's social concerns with the world and "translate the concerns of God's Word into arguments appropriate for civil government."[6] Therefore, Christians are able to act in partnership with non-Christians while also sometimes disagreeing on political matters with other believers.

Political Thought of the Black Church

In the middle of our spectrum stands the Black church. Unlike the other four traditions discussed in this book, the Black church is distinctly American. Transcending common denominational boundaries, this tradition is rooted in the response of African-Americans to their tragic history. For much of American history, whites sought to dominate all aspects of black lives, including their religious practice. Historically black denominations emerged from this oppression, creating safe spaces for African-Americans to worship freely and independently.

Given this complex history, the Black church is best placed in the middle of our spectrum. African-Americans' historical experiences have

---

6. "Render unto Caesar ... and unto God: A Lutheran View of Church and State," in *A Report of the Commission on Theology and Church Relations of the Lutheran Church—Missouri Synod* (St. Louis: The Lutheran Church—Missouri Synod, 1995), 67.

indelibly shaped how they view the church, government, and broader society. Having faced great oppression yet also borne distinctive witness to some liberation, this tradition is well aware of the potential benefits and shortcomings of governmental action.

At the centerpiece of this tradition stands the cross, a reminder to view human suffering in light of the One who faced the greatest suffering to free others from it. With the cross and the harsh realities of life in mind, the Black church emphasizes God's heart for the marginalized, the downcast, the "least of these." Attuned to the sin and suffering that invade the people and institutions of this world, this tradition speaks truth to power with a prophetic voice.

The goal of the Black church in politics—and the rest of life—is the relentless pursuit of liberation, justice, and reconciliation. The tradition has a mixed view of the role of government. On the one hand, it emphasizes the positive role that government can play in serving justice, seeking the good of all people, and promoting reform and reconciliation. At the same time, the Black church is acutely aware that power can be a means of oppression, because her people have faced it firsthand.

The Black church tends not to view the church or politics in an individualistic sense: Life is a communal endeavor, and everyone must play a part. The church is thus meant to seek holistic justice as a community and serve as a unified voice for peace. This communal outlook calls attention to institutional wrongdoing and systemic sins, especially evidenced in racism, and seeks the transformation of social and political institutions. Corporate sins require structural changes, instituted through political means. Thus, a central part of the church's mission is to be a voice for such communal reform.

In the work to apply the heart of the gospel to the messy places of human life and associations, the Black church advocates on behalf of the poor and marginalized, with the hope that redemption and reconciliation can be accomplished by God's grace. Here the church is more politically active than in the Anabaptist or Lutheran traditions, but less comprehensively or optimistically than the Reformed or Catholic tendencies. Above all else, the Black church places her final hope in the eternal kingdom of God, where peace and justice will ultimately reign, and all things will be made right.

Reformed Political Thought

The Reformed tradition developed from sixteenth-century Protestant Reformers including Ulrich Zwingli, John Calvin, and John Knox. This tradition emphasizes God's supreme sovereignty over all things, including people, the church, and governments. Nothing lies outside God's sustaining providence, and nobody else deserves to receive the ultimate glory due to God. At the center of the Reformed tradition is the narrative of creation, fall, and redemption, a perspective that helps Christians understand God's relation to humanity.

Reformed thinkers emphasize that God created the world very good, bestowing beauty and granting humans the ability and responsibility to fill the earth and multiply the good in it. However, humans bear the scars of the fall—the wounds of depravity that affect every aspect of life, including politics. In his mercy, God allows sinners outside of Christ to do good through common grace—a gift that enables wicked people to live rightly and receive earthly blessings, "to develop many virtues and express many truths."[7]

God's particular grace in Christ provides the only way to attain right standing before God. This kind of grace brings the most complete manifestation of God's redemption in this world. It allows individuals to find union with Christ and forgiveness of sins. By contrast, common grace gives rise to the possibility of institutions such as government that can act for the good of the people. While total redemption is not possible in earthly life, Christians should be agents of renewal and restoration, even as they yearn for the complete harmony and glory that will come in eternity.

Government is thus a good gift from God that, along with other fundamental societal institutions such as schools, churches, families, business, and labor, can be an agent of transformation. Because God instituted government, obedience to government is an expression of obedience to God. On the other hand, "to despise human government is to despise the providence that set that government in place."[8]

---

7. Corwin Smidt, "Principled Pluralist Perspective," in *Church, State, and Public Justice: Five Views*, ed. P. C. Kemeny (Downers Grove, IL: IVP Academic, 2007), 131.

8. David C. Steinmetz, *Calvin in Context* (New York: Oxford University Press, 1995), 204–5.

Christians are called to engage the world in all its dimensions, to spread the transforming power of the gospel into each area of life, and to let the light of Christ shine more and more brightly in society at large.

From this theological perspective, it follows that the church can advocate explicitly for beliefs and policies in the public realm, with the recognition that success cannot be forced or guaranteed. Christians can love all people in all places while fully realizing that only the cross of Christ has the power to save. Government should promote justice and the common good, and Christians should have tempered expectations of what government can and cannot do.

Catholic Political Thought

The opposite end of the spectrum is anchored by Catholic political thought, the oldest tradition discussed in this book. The core of this tradition centers on the unity and mission of the church, with emphasis on the incarnation and the sacraments.

Catholics emphasize that the incarnation of Jesus Christ highlights the dignity of humanity by God's Son taking on human form. Just as Christ came to earth and lived among us, so God designed all people to live in deep communion, taking responsibility for the needs of each other and God's created world. The sacraments physically connect Christians with Christ as the center of life in the church. They also provide regular rhythms of shaping our perspective around Christ and the church.

These principles help undergird some core elements of Catholic Social Teaching (CST), a tradition that lays out fundamental principles for engagement with society. CST identifies seven central themes for the church's posture toward the world: the dignity of all human life; the call to family, community, and participation; rights and responsibilities; preferential care for the poor and vulnerable; the dignity of work; solidarity; and care for God's creation.[9]

Because humans are created in the image of God, human life is sacred. All people and institutions should protect human life and uphold human dignity. God created humanity to live and flourish in

---

9. "Seven Themes of Catholic Social Teaching," US Conference of Catholic Bishops. http://www.usccb.org/beliefs-and-teachings/what-we-believe/catholic-social-teaching/seven-themes-of-catholic-social-teaching.cfm (accessed April 27, 2015).

community, beginning with the foundational relationships of marriage and family and extending outward to other forms of community. Rights and responsibilities indicate the way in which justice ought to govern life on earth. Special concern for the poor is modeled after Christ's sacrificial love and care for the "least of these." The dignity of work and the rights of workers give meaning to life in a fallen world by upholding central ways of participating in creation. Solidarity binds the members of communities together in a mutual commitment to the common good.

Finally, the Catholic Church teaches care for creation; humans have the responsibility to be good stewards of the world God made.

Informed by the teaching of Thomas Aquinas (and, through him, Aristotle), Catholic political thought recognizes the essentially political nature of human life, while highlighting the responsibility of the state to cultivate the common good. In holding to both of these ideas, this tradition upholds the God-given nature of governmental institutions and views the state through the lens of human flourishing, which has both individual and communal dimensions. Thus, the church encourages citizens to participate in government as a means of furthering the common good of all people. The *Catechism of the Catholic Church* outlines three specific obligations of all Christian citizens: voting, defending one's country, and paying taxes.[10] Duty to country extends beyond national borders to the entire world community, especially to the goal of promoting peace.

Although the Catholic tradition sees many ways in which church and state can and should work together to achieve common goals, it now also advocates that the two should remain separate to protect religious freedom. Above all, the church has a transcendent purpose only she can fill—to follow Christ and further the gospel. Government has a necessary and important role, but it cannot meet all societal needs on its own. The principle of subsidiarity upholds the value of other institutions and associations—like churches, families, and community groups—to perform their own respective roles at the most local levels appropriate to meet societal needs. Thus Christian engagement in politics is held in tension with a commitment to a sacramental life shaped by the church.

---

10. *Catechism of the Catholic Church*, 2nd ed. (Washington: US. Conference of Catholic Bishops, 1997), 540.

Organization of the Book

The chapters that follow will describe each of these traditions in richer detail. The authors have been asked to focus on several important elements as they introduce their traditions.

First, they all briefly trace the historical developments of their tradition, noting some foundational principles and theological distinctives.

Each chapter also considers the tradition's view on the role of government: Is it primarily optimistic, emphasizing the ways in which government promotes human flourishing and contributes to the common good; pessimistic, focusing on the need for government to restrain the effects of sin; or a mix of the two?

The authors also demarcate the extent to which individual Christians should participate in government and politics, as well as the role churches should play in addressing political questions.

Engagement with these questions helps outline the hallmarks of each perspective, but it focuses primarily on the theory animating each view. To help the reader understand more about how these different traditions have put their political thought into practice, each chapter ends with a short case study that illustrates how its perspective informs policy debates about domestic poverty.

After each author presents his own tradition, the other authors will offer short responses to further the conversation by identifying points of agreement and disagreement.

The book concludes with reflections that help situate each of these historic traditions in the context of contemporary American politics.

In these complex political times, it is easy to lose sight of important principles that can provide a helpful foundation for meaningful Christian political engagement. The five traditions presented in this volume have spent centuries wrestling with questions about the proper role of government, the rights and duties of citizens, and the place of individual Christians in politics and government.

I invite you to learn from this history and explore these different frameworks, looking for points of agreement and disagreement that can help shape your own understanding of the relationship between church and politics.

THE ANABAPTIST (SEPARATIONIST) VIEW

THOMAS W. HEILKE

Introduction

In 1994, Richard J. Mouw, then-President of Fuller Theological Seminary, wrote a foreword to a collection of essays by Mennonite theologian John Howard Yoder. He suggested that—thanks in good part to Yoder's work—adherents of the Reformed, Lutheran, or Roman Catholic traditions could no longer either ignore or politely condescend to the claims, arguments, and practices of the Anabaptist tradition.

Professor Mouw's observation was a remarkable and generous nod to Yoder's theological project, and perhaps a confirmation of a growing assertion among Mennonite theologians and historians that Anabaptists do have "modern relevance."[1] But the descendants of the early Anabaptists make up today, as they did five centuries ago, an exceedingly small portion of global Christianity: "Anabaptism forms but a rivulet in the stream of Christian tradition."[2] Nevertheless, Mouw argued that Christians who are not of this tiny minority should pay attention to what it has to say. Why?

In this book, five scholars have been asked to explicate five Christian views of politics. Along with at least two other traditions represented in this book, the Anabaptists arose in the early sixteenth century, a

---

1. See, for example, several of the essays in Guy F. Hershberger, ed., *The Recovery of the Anabaptist Vision: A Sixtieth Anniversary Tribute to Harold S. Bender* (Scottdale, PA: Herald Press, 1957).

2. Thomas N. Finger, *A Contemporary Anabaptist Theology: Biblical, Historical, Constructive* (Downers Grove, IL: InterVarsity Press, 2004), 562.

European era of vigorous and widespread political, economic, and religious disruption and dissent. Modern-day groups that trace their heritage or origins to the Anabaptists include Mennonites, Swiss Brethren, Amish, and Hutterites. When Anabaptism has been recognized at all, it has traditionally been "for its ethics."[3]

Politics is perhaps at the pinnacle of "applied ethics," but the "separationist" political ethic that has generally been attributed to Anabaptists would seem to exclude them from seriously addressing political problems with anyone outside their tradition. I will suggest, however, that the Anabaptist "radical wing" of the Protestant Reformation offers a clear alternative to those Christian traditions in the West that are situated in some more or less recognizable "Magisterial" stream. Perhaps the Anabaptist movement — with all its flaws — expresses an ever-present possibility of the Christian gospel that is gaining traction as the magisterial churches are becoming gradually "disestablished" and therefore find themselves confronting a world in which their sociopolitical status looks increasingly similar to that of minority groups like the Anabaptists in what was once Christendom.[4]

Aspects of the Anabaptist movement have been multiply expressed in other movements from some of the traditions identified in this book (for example, in the simple asceticism and missionary impulse of St. Francis of Assisi, or the emphasis on ethical probity in the Lutheran pietism of Nicholaus Ludwig von Zinzendorf, or the missionary impulse of early Calvinism). But does Anabaptism, broadly speaking, really possess distinctive characteristics that together form a coherent body of thought concerning political questions that deserves the kind of consideration implied in Professor Mouw's praise for Yoder's work?

The early Anabaptists never produced a coherent work of "political thought," and neither are their modern-day heirs generally noted for

---

3. Ibid., 562. High personal and communal ethical standards as part of their call to church renewal were distinguishing characteristics of early Anabaptists, for which even their enemies noted them.

4. See, for example, the argument of Stanley Hauerwas and William H. Willimon in *Resident Aliens: Life in the Christian Colony* (Nashville: Abingdon Press, 1989); Thomas Finger, *Anabaptist Theology*, on baptism, 170–75; and the first four essays in Andrew Walls, *The Cross-Cultural Process in Christian History* (Maryknoll, NY: Orbis Books, 2002). This possibility is stated in especially pointed form in John H. Yoder, "The Kingdom as Social Ethic," in *The Priestly Kingdom: Social Ethics as Gospel* (South Bend: Notre Dame University Press, 1984), 80–101.

such. Nevertheless, I will argue that the early Anabaptists did leave deep traces of political thought. General impressions notwithstanding, a number of contemporary authors who are self-described heirs of the Anabaptists have produced substantive, engaged, practically minded accounts of social and political life. The work of Yoder, to which Mouw was responding, is the most widely known of this group. Other authors include Duane Friesen, Ron Sider, and more narrowly, John Redekop,[5] along with the Mennonite fellow traveler and Methodist theologian Stanley Hauerwas.[6]

Anabaptist Beginnings

Anabaptism began more or less as a recognizable movement on January 21, 1525, when Conrad Grebel, the son of a Zurich patrician, baptized ("re-baptized")[7] George Blaurock, a Roman Catholic priest, at the Zurich home of Felix Manz. This "rebaptism" had profound ecclesiastical—and therefore political—implications, and the participants were aware of those possibilities. Several of these soon-to-be Anabaptists belonged to the circle of friends and students around the Zurich reformer Huldrych Zwingli, who swiftly condemned the baptism.

Zwingli's opprobrium became part of a complex of persecution and condemnation such that, within ten years of this first baptism, nearly the entire first generation of Anabaptist leaders had been executed. It was from this group that an initial political theology, or even a general tradition of political-theological inquiry, gradually arose. Robert Friedmann points out, in his search for a core Anabaptist theology with which to account for Anabaptist distinctives, that "[i]t is clear that

---

5. Duane K. Friesen, *Artists, Citizens, Philosophers: Seeking the Peace of the City* (Scottdale, PA, and Waterloo, ON: Herald Press, 2000); Ronald J. Sider, *Rich Christians in an Age of Hunger: Moving from Affluence to Generosity* (1977; reprint, Nashville: W Publishing Group, 2005); John Redekop, *Politics under God* (Scottdale, PA, and Waterloo, ON: Herald Press, 2007).

6. "I am, after all, a (Southern) Methodist of doubtful theological background ... who believes that the most nearly faithful form of Christian witness is best exemplified by the often unjustly ignored people called anabaptists [sic] or Mennonites. In short my ecclesial preference is to be a high-church Mennonite." Stanley Hauerwas, *A Community of Character: Toward a Constructive Christian Social Ethic* (Notre Dame: University of Notre Dame Press, 1981), 6. Throughout his career as a teacher of Christian theological ethics, Hauerwas has been clear concerning his debts to Anabaptist traditions.

7. The German *Wiedertäufer* or "re-baptizer" is rendered in the Greek as "Anabaptist," which gradually became the accepted designation for them. Since the Anabaptists disputed the legitimacy of the "first" (infant) baptism universally practiced by Roman Catholics and nearly all Magisterial reformers, the title of *Wieder-* or "re-" or "Ana-" was itself an unfriendly epithet.

besides Balthasar Hubmaier (d. 1528), who was a doctor of theology (from a Catholic university), there were no trained theologians in the broad array of Anabaptist writers and witnesses."[8] In Franklin Littell's assessment, however,

> Although the best-educated leadership was martyred during the first years, the early leaders—Grebel, Hubmaier, Denck, Hetzer—were men of marked accomplishment in the university world, a world inspired by the new Humanistic studies.[9]

Michael Sattler was a prior of a Benedictine abbey before his conversion to Anabaptism, and Menno Simons was a Catholic priest. Both had received theological training. Nevertheless, neither a definitive political-philosophical treatise nor a strong tradition of articulated political thought emerged from the work of the early Anabaptist leaders.

As the Anabaptist movement developed, most of the disparate groups identified under that label continued to encounter a hostility often connected to a well-tuned violence that offered little leisure in which to formulate a coherent, systematic, and focused theology. Anabaptists tended to focus on personal ethical behavior ("discipleship") and a corresponding unity and purity of the community of believers. Both emphases derived from Anabaptist emphasis on the life and example of Jesus as the model for Christian behavior individually and communally, with a diminished focus on traditional political-philosophical questions of who should rule, in what manner, with regard to what ends, and why.

Beyond questions of Christian behavior and several of the usual doctrinal questions in dispute during the sixteenth century, the next and largely pragmatic concerns of Anabaptist leaders had to do with the survival of the community of believers.[10] Ongoing persecution that forced the dispersion of Anabaptist leaders and believers into various parts of Europe initially enhanced Anabaptist proselytizing tendencies,

---

8. Robert Friedmann, *The Theology of Anabaptism: An Interpretation* (Scottdale, PA: Herald Press, 1973), 19.

9. Franklin H. Littell, *The Origins of Sectarian Protestantism* (New York: Macmillan, 1964), 61, cited in Benjamin Wirt Farley, trans. and ed., *John Calvin: Treatises Against the Anabaptists and Against the Libertines* (Grand Rapids: Baker, 1982), 36n8.

10. Menno Simon's career is typical in this regard. See Harold S. Bender, "A Brief Biography of Menno Simons," in J. C. Wenger, ed., and Leonard Verduin, trans., *The Complete Writings of Menno Simons* (Scottdale, PA, and Kitchener, ON: Herald Press, 1984), esp. 15–29.

but eventually forced a policy of "withdrawal" as a matter of survival, diminishing any nascent theological activity out of which might arise something resembling a coherent body of political thought.

Anabaptist Identity(s)

Political thought as traditionally understood is usually undertaken by people who can imagine themselves in positions of power or in positions to influence those who wield power. It has been undertaken much less often by people whose very existence is under threat and whose chances of proximity to power are nil.[11] Both political thought and political theology are activities of reflection that require *schole*, or leisure,[12] preceded in nearly all cases by the luxury of extensive education.

The first circumstance is unlikely under conditions of persistent suppression and persecution, and the second—at least after the early generation of leaders had been killed—was not a common characteristic of those who joined the Anabaptist movements. Thus, as Mouw rightly points out, a weakness developed in Anabaptist theology from the start: "historical and biblical studies have often been preferred over systematic theology among the Mennonites and their kin."[13]

Those Anabaptists who, like Pilgram Marpeck, were afforded these two luxuries and not killed early in their careers, were either not trained in theology (Marpeck, for example, was a highly skilled engineer), or—like Menno Simons (who had rest from persecution for brief periods)—were concerned overwhelmingly with a specific set of doctrinal questions that formed the loci of attacks on them, or with matters of personal ethics, and with the preservation of their harassed communities of believers. Nevertheless, the Anabaptists recognized the political realm of human activity, and they articulated a general set of attitudes toward it that we can tease out with confidence.

A second difficulty attends the problem of an abbreviated political vision: The beginning of Anabaptism was a relatively amorphous undertaking of disparate movements, with various groups more or less identified as Anabaptist arising in several northern cantons of

---

11. See Yoder, *Priestly Kingdom*, 154.

12. Cf. Hannah Arendt, *The Human Condition* (Chicago: University of Chicago Press, 1958), 14–16.

13. Mouw, "Foreword," in Yoder, *Priestly Kingdom*, viii.

Switzerland, a number of southern German polities, and the Low Countries. The result of this dispersion of origins and developments is that Anabaptist identity cannot be easily established around some set of doctrines or ideas—including political ones. Along a register of doctrines and orientations, we see a wide diversity of perspectives, developments, and settlements in the so-called Radical Reformation; of its many movements, Anabaptism is perhaps the widest and certainly the most important surviving thread, but it is itself a thread of many smaller filaments.[14] This characteristic of Anabaptist multiple origins (polygenesis) is not a mere methodological dispute; in regard to political life, it will influence how we read the "separationism" of Anabaptism.[15]

For purposes of this essay, I will describe Anabaptists as Peter Gay characterized the philosophers of the Enlightenment: They were a grouping of the like-minded with what Ludwig Wittgenstein might have called a "family resemblance."[16] Their articulations of theological, political, economic, and ecclesiological perspectives, doctrines, or ideas should be understood *not* as expressions of "Platonic ideas," but rather as "baskets collecting significant similarities."[17] It is from those baskets that we can draw something of enduring value to reward the charity Mouw expresses.

The heterogeneity of Anabaptist thought is rendered less unusual or even "foreign" if we consider that magisterial reformation thought, too, is not entirely unitary. There is, for example, development in Lutheran and Reformed thought after Luther and Calvin. Consider the names Philip Melanchthon, John Knox, and Abraham Kuyper. In the Roman Catholic tradition, the works of Thomas Aquinas were under severe

---

14. See especially George Huntston Williams, *The Radical Reformation*, 3rd ed. (Kirksville, MO: Truman State University Press, 1992). Thomas Finger (*Anabaptist Theology*, 17–93) provides an abbreviated account of specific developments and incidents that give a flavor of the nearly chaotic diversity of early Anabaptist history. Nevertheless, he finds that "three stable communions emerged from the cacophony and continue today," and that these communions were "guided by deep, interrelated convictions that formed at least implicit theologies" (46). He then follows with a survey of contemporary approaches to historic Anabaptism that provide us with a set of family characteristics.

15. For an early, sensitive treatment of the various historiographical and interpretive problems, see Franklin Hamlin Littell, *The Anabaptist Vision of the Church: A Study in the Origins of Sectarian Protestantism* (Boston: Starr King Press, 1958), esp. 43–45.

16. Ludwig Wittgenstein, *Philosophical Investigations* (London: Blackwell Publishing, 1953).

17. Peter Gay, *The Enlightenment: An Interpretation. The Rise of Modern Paganism* (New York: Random House, 1966), x, 3–8.

attack for a period of time. The existence of conflict, amendment, and creative re-working indicates a vital, living tradition, of which deep-seated disagreement is but one feature.[18] At the same time, Luther, Calvin, Augustine, and Aquinas all set in motion broad patterns or even schools of thinking, so that to speak of each of them as a fountainhead is not simply mythmaking. The influence of neo-Platonism and pagan administrative practices on Augustine, of Aristotle and Averroes on Aquinas, of Occamite nominalism on Luther,[19] and of Stoicism and a particular interpretation of Augustine on Calvin, not to mention the influence on all four of specifically classical Greek philosophical modes of inquiry,[20] established specific vocabularies of thought, inquiry, and doctrine in all four cases. These traditions therefore appear at their origins less "basket-like" than Anabaptism, but it is not entirely clear whether the assumption of consequently greater cohesion or even coherence is in all cases warranted.[21]

Because Anabaptism was an amorphous, lay-led *movement*—rather than an agenda of reform headed by a single, identifiable individual in a specific city or territory where he enjoyed some level of official protection or at least toleration—the fragmented and not unitarily representative character of the Anabaptist movement can make a discussion of "Anabaptist thought" on any matter at times frustratingly fraught with pitfalls.[22]

---

18. See Alasdair MacIntyre, *Whose Justice? Which Rationality?* (Notre Dame: University of Notre Dame Press, 1988), 164–82.

19. Cf. "An Appeal to the Ruling Class of German Nationality as to the Amelioration of the State of Christendom," III.25, in John Dillenberger, ed., *Martin Luther: Selections from His Writings* (New York: Doubleday, 1961), 470–71; Heiko A. Oberman, *Luther: Man between God and the Devil*, trans. Eileen Walliser-Schwarzbart (New Haven: Yale University Press, 2006), 122; see also the second, third, and fourth essays in Heiko Oberman, *The Dawn of the Reformation: Essays in Late Medieval and Early Reformation Thought* (Grand Rapids: Eerdmans, 1992).

20. I am thinking here, for example, of the occasionally arcane debates concerning the metaphysics of the Lord's Supper.

21. See, for example, the overview of scholarly evaluations of Luther's political thought in "Luther's Theory of Temporal Government," in Jarrett A. Carty, *Divine Kingdom, Holy Order: The Political Writings of Martin Luther* (St. Louis: Concordia, 2012), 3–26.

22. "Mennonite scholars do not try to publish articles on the differences between Anabaptists and Mennonites. It is foolhardy to try to define those differences, because so much of what one says cannot be demonstrated clearly to the satisfaction of oneself and others.... Whatever one publishes ought to be properly seasoned with caveats...." (John S. Oyer, *They Harry the Good People out of the Land: Essays on the Persecution, Survival and Flourishing of Anabaptists and Mennonites*, ed. John D. Roth [Goshen, IN: Mennonite Historical Society, 2000], 49).

Anabaptist Theological Distinctives

With appropriate caveats in place, let us nevertheless propose that the several "baskets collecting significant similarities" among the Anabaptists included three distinctives that are pertinent to political-theoretical concerns.

First, *Jesus is the central focus*. In the words of contemporary Anabaptist writer Stuart Murray, Jesus is "example, teacher, friend, redeemer and Lord." For sixteenth-century Anabaptists (and for their various modern heirs), Jesus is to be not only worshiped or admired, but followed. He is "the central reference point for [Anabaptist] faith," for its understanding of the church, and its point of entry for engaging with the surrounding society.[23] This centrality could also be identified in the claim that "Jesus is the focal point of God's revelation." Reading and interpreting the Christian Bible and understanding its implications for individual and communal existence begins with placing the Jesus revealed there in the center of all interpretive implications for the life and practice of individual believers and the community of believers alike.

Second, Anabaptists hold to an ecclesiology that affirms a "priesthood of all believers" and emphasizes lay leadership, even while acknowledging ministers, missionaries, and other designated leaders. The *community of believers* exists for the purpose of mutual spiritual, economic, and moral support and discipleship. Anabaptists therefore insist on a separation of ecclesiastical affairs from the oversight of political authorities. Christian communities of believers are independent of any political authority, and membership is based on confessed belief in the God and the theological principles around which the believing community is formed. It is for this reason that Anabaptists, to express it negatively, are universally anti-pedobaptist: Infants and children cannot voluntarily join the community upon a confession of their own faith.

Third, Anabaptists have a general *inclination toward nonviolence* that is usually expressed in forms of pacifism, including a refusal to serve in the military or to swear oaths of loyalty to a particular regime. The Anabaptist rationale for this principle was essentially the one that Luther and Augustine and a host of other Christian thinkers had previously

---

23. Stuart Murray, *The Naked Anabaptist: The Bare Essentials of a Radical Faith* (Scottdale, PA, and Waterloo, ON: Herald Press, 2010), 45.

identified: The use of violence and divided loyalties are inconsistent with the teachings and practices of Jesus. The Sermon on the Mount has been an especially important source for such arguments.[24]

In these three broad distinctives we can also see three ways that polygenesis affects Anabaptist beliefs, doctrines, and intentions. First, most of these distinctives were in some dispute in the early years of Anabaptist development. The basic distinctives that I have listed here — limited to those doctrines and practices that have a discernible influence on Anabaptist thought, practice, or doctrine concerning politics — are more or less "settled" within, if not among, modern Anabaptist groups.[25] Second, Anabaptist polygenesis has also meant that the *meaning* of these distinctives has been in some dispute among scholars.[26] The implications for political thought and practice are therefore unlikely to be certain until the meaning — again — is "settled," at least provisionally, within that group. Finally, and closely related to the second consideration, these distinctives may have different implications at different times for any specific concerns regarding Christian behavior and access to the political realm.

Can anything even vaguely like a coherent political doctrine — let alone a political philosophy — grow from this woven container that is Anabaptism? For an answer, we must consider distinctive Anabaptist political thinking in its historical and contemporary contexts.

---

24. Cf. Martin Luther, "Secular Authority: To What Extent It Should Be Obeyed," in John Dillenberger, ed., *Martin Luther: Selections from His Writings* (New York: Doubleday, 1961), 378–82; Aurelius Augustine, Letter CXXXVIII, in *The Confessions and Letters of Augustine, With a Sketch of His Life and Work*, in Philip Schaff, ed., Vol. 1, *Nicene and Post-Nicene Fathers, First Series* (Peabody, MA: Hendrickson, 1944 1888.), 481–88; Pilgram Marpeck, "Judgment and Decision," in William Klassen and Walter Klassen, eds., *The Writings of Pilgram Marpeck* (Scottdale, PA: Herald Press, 1978), 332.

25. For introductions to the polygenetic and polymorphic character of these and other distinctives, see the essays by James M. Stayer, Martin Haas, Werner O. Packull, and Albert F. Mellink in Hans-Jürgen Goertz, ed., *Umstrittenes Täufertum, 1575–1975: Neue Forschungen*, 2nd ed. (Göttingen: Vandenhoeck & Ruprecht, 1977). Accessible English-language introductions that treat the topic of polygenesis with appropriate sensitivity include William R. Estep, *The Anabaptist Story: An Introduction to Sixteenth-Century Anabaptism*, 3rd ed. (Grand Rapids: Eerdmans, 1996); C. Arnold Snyder, *Anabaptist History and Theology: An Introduction* (Kitchener, ON: Pandora Press, 1995); and Susan Biesecker-Mast and Gerald Biesecker-Mast, eds., *Anabaptists and Post-Modernity* (Telford, PA: Pandora Press, 2000).

26. A helpful introduction to the debate may be found in John D. Roth, "Recent Currents in the Historiography of the Radical Reformation," in *Church History* 71 (2002): 525–35; see also the Appendix ("A Review of Anabaptist Historiography") in Snyder, *Anabaptist History and Theology*, 397–408, and his summary of "Radical Reformation" doctrines, 43–49.

Early Anabaptist Political Thought

Two characteristics of political philosophy set the context for Anabaptist political thought. A version of the political philosophy and virtue ethics of Aristotle — mediated through Thomas Aquinas and other scholastics — and an unpolished version of Augustine's subtle analysis of human affairs offered the Reformation (and Counter-Reformation) thinkers alternative constructs for reflecting on the purposes and possibilities of politics. Roman Catholics and Protestant reformers alike wrestled with the tension: Does government exist to construct and protect a realm of human flourishing, or does it exist essentially to restrain evil? And, following from that tension, what is the role and place of the church?

The Anabaptists were obliged, like all other reformers and social or political thinkers of the time, to work through these questions. That working through took place against the background of social, political, and economic upheaval and crises that included most immediately for the Anabaptists the widespread peasant uprisings of 1524–25 in the German-speaking territories of central Europe.

The Brotherly Union (Schleitheim Confession)

The statement of faith known as the *Brotherly Union*, which emerged from the Anabaptist conference at Schleitheim, Switzerland, in 1527, remains a prominent *locus classicus* for understanding in summary form Anabaptist thought and practice concerning politics. It was penned in February 1527 by Michael Sattler, an early Swiss Anabaptist leader.[27] Both Zwingli (in 1527) and Calvin (in 1544) wrote detailed treatises against it.[28] The *Brotherly Union* consists of seven "articles" concerned, in order, with the following: "baptism, ban, the breaking of bread, separation from abomination, shepherds in the congregation, the sword, the oath."[29]

---

27. For a brief biography containing all that is known about Sattler's life, see "Introduction," in John Howard Yoder, trans. and ed., *The Legacy of Michael Sattler* (Scottdale, PA, and Waterloo, ON: Herald Press, 1973), 10.

28. Ulrich Zwingli, "Refutation of the Tricks of the Baptists," in Samuel Macauley Jackson, ed., *Ulrich Zwingli: Selected Works* (Philadelphia: University of Pennsylvania Press, 1972), 123–258, esp. 117–219; John Calvin, "Brief Instruction for Arming All the Good Faithful Against the Errors of the Common Sect of the Anabaptists," in Farley, *John Calvin: Treatises*, 36–158.

29. All translations from the *Brotherly Union* are taken from the text found in Yoder, *The Legacy of Michael Sattler*, 34–43.

The document confronts a student of political thought with two immediate problems. First, it would be easy to extract the specifically "political" pieces from the rest and closely probe them in isolation. Such a procedure is illegitimate; the political doctrine articulated in the *Union* is an outflow of the logic of the document as a whole, contained in the vision of a faithful and visible practicing Christian community that informs the document from beginning to end. The political "theory" of the document is completely subordinate to its vision for the church, which is understood as discipleship of Jesus. Accordingly, the *Brotherly Union* is one of the earliest Anabaptist articulations of the first two theological distinctives I listed previously: the centrality of Jesus and the priesthood of all believers.

Second, Gerald Biesecker-Mast's careful reading of the *Brotherly Union* has shown that there are substantial internal tensions in the *Union*'s political theory, demonstrated in its ambivalent rhetoric concerning the political realm and the orientation of the Christian to that realm. In this ambivalence, the document uncovers a fundamental tension in the first Anabaptist distinctive. On the one hand, it presents in Article IV ("separation from abomination") a call to separation from the world:

> Now there is nothing else in the world and all creation than good or evil, believing and unbelieving, darkness and light, the world and those who are [come] out of the world, God's temple and idols, Christ and Belial, and none will have part with the other.[30]

This claim "is the framework within which nearly all of the remaining articles establish their distinctive formulas for the Christian practices of the Swiss Brethren and within which appeals to unity are made throughout the document."[31] The rhetorical position of this separation is not quietism or placid withdrawal from the world, however, but antagonism against it; the document seeks "to negate, to reject and to make the condemned practices mutually exclusive from the Christian identity established by the Schleitheim *Brotherly Union*."[32] Moreover, this antagonistic stance arises not from pure theological

---

30. Yoder, *Legacy*, 38; Gerald Biesecker-Mast, *Separation and the Sword in Anabaptist Persuasion* (Telford, PA: Cascadia Publishing House, 2006), 102.

31. Biesecker-Mast, *Persuasion*, 102.

32. Ibid., 103.

principle, but from a failure of Anabaptists and their opponents to continue in dialogue:

> The *Brotherly Union* ... stands as a statement of protest against the religious and cultural and political establishment associated with the status quo in Switzerland and South Germany. It represents the outcome of failed discussions, disputations and exchanges between Anabaptist leaders and the political and ecclesiastical authorities of Christendom. It is the product of engagement, not withdrawal. The argument for separation is thus more like a boycott of the religious establishment, in both its "popish and repopish" forms, than an apolitical or sectarian argument.[33]

That failure is amply illustrated in an extensive documentation of the initial development of the Anabaptist movement in and around Zürich and the official responses to it of persecution and suppression from roughly 1523 onward.[34] It is equally illustrated in later Anabaptist attempts at dialogue with similar, often lethal results.[35]

The Brotherly Union calls for political separation in response to setbacks and persecutions, but such separation is difficult to maintain along the stark, simplistic lines of the nearly Manichean binary oppositions between church and world, darkness and light, etc., in Article IV. Article VI opens with an appreciably more complex contrast concerning the use of violence: "We have been united as follows concerning the sword. The sword is an ordering of God outside the perfection of Christ."[36] This "ordering" takes form not in the stark contrasts of Article IV, but in a political theology reminiscent of Luther and the early Augustine:

---

33. Ibid.

34. See the remarkable philological work of Leland Harder, ed., *The Sources of Swiss Anabaptism: The Grebel Letters and Related Documents* (Scottdale, PA, and Kitchener, ON: Herald Press, 1985).

35. For an Anabaptist plea for dialogue written in the "second generation," in 1552, see Menno Simons, "Brief Defense to All Theologians," in *Complete Works*, 535–40. The analysis of Marin Haas in this regard is instructive: "Der Weg der Täufer in die Absonderung: Zur Interdependenz von Theologie und sozialem Verhalten," in Goertz, *Umstrittenes Täufertum*, 50–78, especially the summary at 76–78, which includes the observation that Anabaptist separation was open to reversal "wenn die Verhältnisse sich änderten" ("if/when the circumstances changed").

36. Yoder, *Legacy*, 39; Biesecker-Mast, *Persuasion*, 104.

Two orders of preservation and redemption exist together under the same God. In one of them the sword has no place, due to the normativeness of the work of Jesus Christ, whereas in the other the sword has a limited legitimacy, which is tested precisely at the point of its ability to keep itself within limits.[37]

Given these two orders and the legitimacy of both, can a Christian not participate in both? The article answers in four separate points. In each, it cites an example of Christ (here, again, the first Anabaptist distinctive) to answer in the negative: Christians cannot participate in imposing the death penalty; Christians should not participate in adjudicating worldly disputes; Christians cannot be magistrates; and, Christians—echoing the "two cities" political theology of Augustine—belong not to the kingdom(s) of this world, but to the kingdom of heaven.[38]

The rhetorical logic of this argument is unstable. It moves from an antagonistic "mutual exclusivity" in Article IV to a less stark "legitimate difference" in Article VI. Then it moves back again to a newly stated antagonism at the end of Article VI. These two approaches do not come to a resolution.[39] This instability (or irresolution) of the argument arises out of the second Anabaptist distinctive—the desire to be a "visibly distinctive and unified body that function[s] as a concrete, alternative Christian community." This desire explicitly rejects "the popular Protestant construal of Christ's body as invisible," which therefore denies these Anabaptist believers "the option of making the outward witness a secondary and imperfect representation of the inner, purer identity."[40]

The question that engenders the tension in the overall approach is this: How, then, do we live in the world, separate yet in it, rejecting the coercion and violence associated with governance, and "struggl[ing] ... to be separate, vulnerable, and visible Christians while at the same time civil, peaceful, and law-abiding subjects"?[41] Amidst new fragmentation

---

37. John H. Yoder, "'Anabaptism and the Sword' Revisited: Systematic Historiography and Undogmatic Nonresistants," *Zeitschrift für Kirchengeschichte* 85 (1974), 135; quoted in Biesecker-Mast, *Persuasion*, 104–5.

38. Yoder, *Legacy*, 39–41.

39. Biesecker-Mast, *Persuasion*, 106.

40. Ibid., 107.

41. Ibid.

and also new creativity, this new ecclesiological reality gives rise, ever afresh and all the way into the contemporary era, to Anabaptist efforts to resolve the tension of the Schleitheim *Brotherly Union*.

In this struggle for resolution, early Anabaptists experienced at least five political arrangements in their first decade. First, Balthasar Hubmaier for brief (and exceedingly rare) intervals appears to have established a form of Anabaptism as the official religion in two small cities in central Europe, Waldshut and Nicholsburg. Second, Anabaptists suffered immensely under the imperial Hapsburg policy of absolute intolerance expressed in a persecution of Anabaptists to the utmost of the empire's abilities. Third, they were politically sheltered outside the imperial sphere under the declared "zero tolerance" of German territories that was coupled with "an unofficial policy of not looking for trouble," so that Anabaptists could survive underground, fitfully and precariously. Fourth, they flourished for a time under an official and open toleration during the sixteenth century only in Moravia, but this model of welcoming hard-working Anabaptist settlers for the sake of economic (primarily agricultural) development was adopted in other parts of Europe in succeeding centuries. Finally there was the millenarian kingdom of the German city of Münster, to which we briefly turn.[42]

The Münsterite Kingdom

A second, hardly less influential *locus classicus* for referencing Anabaptist political thought is not a text, but a historical episode that is the seeming antithesis of the church envisioned in the *Brotherly Union*, namely, the Münsterite "kingdom" of John of Leyden in 1535–36. It began with the checkered career of Melchior Hoffman, whose teachings influenced a significant number of Anabaptist groups in north-central Europe.[43] Those who followed his teachings ("Melchiorites") tended to distinguish themselves from other Anabaptists and emphasized a spiritualized, apolitical form of apocalypticism with a strong sense of "apocalyptic mission."[44]

---

42. Snyder, *Anabaptist History and Theology*, 181–83.
43. James M. Stayer, *Anabaptists and the Sword* (Lawrence, KS: Coronado Press, 1972), 205.
44. Ibid.

Hoffman's political doctrine, therefore, tended toward an apolitical nonresistance that resembled the nonresistance of the *Brotherly Union*,[45] but he appears to have followed Luther (whose reformation he had actively advocated in the early 1520s) in arguing for the right of a Christian to wield power in the service of political authority.[46] In contrast to the *Brotherly Union*, Hoffman's apoliticism seems to have been "conditioned by his eschatological expectancy." In this, too, he partially echoed Luther, who believed he was living in the endtimes, but was inclined to resignation "in the face of God's inscrutable grace combined with human depravity."[47]

Jan Matthijs concretized the spiritualist apocalypse of Hoffman to provide yet another option. In the midst of the religio-political conflict taking place in Münster, he and his soon-to-be successors embarked on a millenarian revolution in the spring of 1534. It culminated in fantastical abuses and even political terror before being brought to an end by starvation and by a coalition of Lutheran and Catholic forces retaking the city in June 1535 and massacring most of its remaining inhabitants. The revolution had ripple effects as far away as Amsterdam, where a small uprising of armed Anabaptists loosely allied to the Münsterites was put down in May 1535.[48] An unmitigated disaster in nearly all respects, this millenarian adventure ended in complete failure for its participants, in an intensified persecution of Anabaptists throughout northern Europe and in a nearly irredeemable suspicion, frequently repeated, that Anabaptism was *Schwärmerei*—irrational enthusiasm and fanaticism.

The shadow of Münster looms over many discussions of Anabaptism to this day. In Mennonite and other Anabaptist circles, sympathetic historians have essentially disavowed all connection to the so-called "Münsterites," while popular accounts of Anabaptism continue to

45. Ibid., 213.
46. Ibid., 215.
47. Roland H. Bainton, *The Reformation of the Sixteenth Century* (Boston: Beacon Press. 1952), 115.
48. For detailed recountings of the Münster story containing difference emphases and conclusions, see Stayer, *Anabaptists and the Sword*, 205–305; Norman Cohn, *The Pursuit of the Millennium*, 2nd ed. (Oxford: Oxford University Press, 1970), 252–86; Anthony Arthur, *The Tailor King: The Rise and Fall of the Anabaptist Kingdom of Münster* (New York: St. Martin's Press, 1999).

hang the Münsterite tag on the movement in general. Both positions are erroneous, and for the same reason. Münster is a cautionary tale,[49] not merely about Anabaptism, but about Christianity and its secular derivatives more generally: Millenarianism in a wide variety of forms is a constant that arises from Christian eschatology itself.[50]

Toward Contemporary Anabaptist Engagements and Conversations

In between the extremes of these two *loci classici* of either a complete withdrawal from the evils of the world or of a millenarian revolution that used the means of civic force ("the sword") to terrorize the internal population and to prosecute a "crusade of the last days"[51] lies the dominant Anabaptist reality. This dominant reality is embodied in the communal practices of a range of groups, including the Hutterites, Amish, Swiss Brethren, Mennonites, and Church of the Brethren. As Anabaptists gradually coalesced around several European groupings, leaders like Menno Simons and Pilgram Marpeck determinedly disavowed Münsterite sympathies while developing theologies and practices recognizably aligned with the basic tenets of Schleitheim,[52] often with Melchiorite theological characteristics remaining in evidence.

Organized on the model of independent believers' churches, contemporary Anabaptists do not have central, institutional, top-down, guiding forms of authority like those that developed in the magisterial church organizations of the Lutheran and Calvinist reformations. The struggle for a coherent and sustainable articulation of principles regarding the participation of Christians in political affairs and the use of coercion and violence can be traced through a number of Anabaptist

---

49. The cages in which the bodies of the three executed Anabaptist leaders were displayed as a warning to other would-be rebels continue to hang from the spire of the St. Lamberti Cathedral in Münster to this day. See Scott Holland, "When Bloch Pointed to the Cages Outside the Cathedral," in Biesecker-Mast, *Anabaptists and Post-Modernity*, 149.

50. Readers may wish to consult Cohn's *In Search of the Millennium* as an introduction to this argument. The observation of Karl Barth that "Ethics can no more exist without millenarianism, without at least some minute degree of it, than without the idea of a moral personality," directs us to a pertinent element of consideration. See Karl Barth, "The Problem of Ethics Today," in *The Word of God and the Word of Man*, trans. Douglas Horton (Boston: Pilgrim, 1928), 158. Cited in Helmut Thielicke, *Theological Ethics, Vol. 2: Politics*, ed. William H. Lazareth (Grand Rapids: Eerdmans, 1979), 502.

51. Stayer, *Anabaptists and the Sword*, 255.

52. Menno Simons, "The Blasphemy of John of Leiden," in *Complete Writings*, 33–50; Marpeck, "The Admonition of 1542," in *Writings*, 209.

"confessions" and other documents and testimonies from Schleitheim to the Dordrecht *Confession* of 1632, through to the Ris *Confession* of 1766 and beyond into the twentieth century.[53] There are, however, two "family resemblances" that extend into our time and with which I will conclude: community and political economy alongside withdrawal and engagement. By tracing briefly these two conceptual pairings, we will make our way back to Professor Mouw's invitation.

Community and Political Economy

A critique leveled against the ecclesiologies of both Luther and Calvin is that they tend—in somewhat different ways—to be individualistic, stressing the individual sinner before God even in the context of congregational life. Whatever the merits of this criticism, Anabaptists tended strongly in the opposite direction, stressing, as already evident in the *Brotherly Union*, the communal aspects of Christian belief and practice. In this approach we begin with ecclesiological practice and ask ourselves what the relationship of the church to other social forms and institutions should be. Thus, Thomas Finger argues that in Anabaptist theology, political questions receive consideration in light of missional concerns, bringing to the surface specific community practices emerging from those concerns.[54] One might, then, nearly reject the idea of "Anabaptist political thought" and ask instead: What are the consequences of Anabaptist ecclesiology for engaging in political life?

Strict separation in the style of Schleitheim led the Anabaptists not merely to an ecclesiology of political separation, but also to a strong doctrine of proper church practices and disciplines that developed into a new vision of political economy.[55] Among noncommunistic Anabaptists, this vision strained against an overemphasis on strict separation, and it included practices of sharing and other thinking about economics that can be interpreted as implicit critiques of certain Christendom political-economic modes.[56] The visible, disciplined com-

---

53. Biesecker-Mast artfully traces this history in *Anabaptist Persuasion*, 108–160, 170–231.
54. Finger, *Anabaptist Theology*, 255–323.
55. See the summary remarks of John Dillenberger and Claude Welch, *Protestant Christianity Interpreted Through Its Development* (New York: Charles Scribner's Sons, 1958), 64–7.
56. Thomas Heilke, "Locating a Moral/Political Economy: Lessons from Sixteenth-Century Anabaptism," *Polity* 30, no. 2 (Winter 1997): 199–229.

munity practice of Anabaptists was not a separable, specific doctrine, but an integrated part of a conceptual and practical whole. Care for the poor, for example, was an integral part of church order that was at times closely linked theologically to the Lord's Supper. For many Anabaptists, that observance was understood in intimate relation to the self-sacrifice of Jesus and to the unity of Christian love that his disciples were to demonstrate in response. Such unity was further demonstrated in the Christians' material care for one another at any time and in their care for their nonbelieving neighbors.

Anabaptist churches provide witness as communities of faith whose members live out the gospel in their individual behavior and in Christian community. In so doing, they seek to build communities of moral excellence that can be understood on Aristotelian/Thomistic grounds,[57] even if they are not explicitly conscious of this philosophical heritage. As we see in *Brotherly Union*, this emphasis on community witness sprang out of their understanding of New Testament possibilities for forming communities of character. Were they always successful, thriving, and attractive to outsiders? No: abuses, missteps, and failures are an important part of the Anabaptist story. However, they *were*—and understood themselves to be—Christian communities before the watching world.[58]

Anabaptists resist a unity between church and society at large; they see these two kinds of community as radically distinct. In this they follow Luther, but they do not follow him in overlapping the two communities in the heart and mind of the individual believer; instead, the "good city" of political philosophy becomes the church, and the Christian believers are its citizens. Departing from Augustine, the Anabaptists staunchly defend and exhibit the visibility of the City of God as revealed in the concrete practicing community of believers.[59]

---

57. Alasdair Macintyre, *After Virtue: A Study in Moral Theory*, 2nd ed. (Notre Dame: University of Notre Dame Press, 1984), esp. 109–20, 181–243, 256–63; Stanley Hauerwas, *Character and the Christian Life: A Study in Theological Ethics* (San Antonio: Trinity University Press, 1985).

58. I echo, of course, the title of John Howard Yoder's *Body Politics: Five Practices of the Christian Community Before the Watching World* (Scottdale, PA: Herald Press, 1992).

59. Yoder, *Priestly Kingdom*, 135–41.

Engagement and Withdrawal

More radical than separation is nonresistance, the principle of not using force to protect oneself or one's rights, derived from Jesus' injunctions in the Sermon on the Mount to "turn the other cheek" or "walk the extra mile." It, too, precedes the Anabaptists. Both Augustine and Luther, for example, had taught nonresistance and referred to the New Testament teachings to do so. Before he reversed himself on practical grounds, Augustine argued that New Testament principles forbade Christians from using force to oppose schism or heresy, so that "toleration for the sake of peace" and nonviolent persuasion were the only remedies for disagreements.[60] For Luther, nonresistance was to be the posture of Christians in their private affairs (with their neighbor), whereas in their role as citizens, they were encouraged to use all the tools available to them to serve in the role of enforcing justice and the security of the community. Christians operate simultaneously in two distinct ethical realms.[61]

Departing from this conception, Calvin conceived of a divine commonwealth in which there was no dualism, and the standard of ethical performance was the one demanded by good public order and defense as needed. He and Luther stood in contrast to the Roman Catholic conception of a division of society into two classes of people, with saints and professional religious at one level of ethical performance and the great masses of society performing at a basic level of natural justice that can be known apart from any revelation.[62]

Unique to the Anabaptist approach, therefore, was not the conception of either withdrawal or nonresistance, but the need to exemplify both of these practices in and from a visibly distinct community of believers over against the surrounding world. Augustine's "Kingdom of God" was, for the Anabaptists, neither socially or socio-politically integrated into that world.

Almost every Christian political-ethical position that Anabaptists encountered took for granted a common assumption: The moral problem of political participation is the "moral of an entire society without considering faith as a decisive dimension."[63] Seeing it as a political-

---

60. Augustine, Letter XLIII, 276–80; Letter LXXXVII, 365–69.
61. Luther, "Secular Authority," 370–75.
62. See Thomas Aquinas, *Summa theologiae* I-II, Q 90–97.
63. John Yoder, *The Christian Witness to the State*, 2nd ed. (Harrisonburg, VA: Herald Press, 2002), 69.

ethical principle, Anabaptists questioned that assumption. They did believe, however, that they could speak to political authority on the basis of some universally understood standard that accepted a behavioral norm "below" that of the gospel norm that Anabaptist communities sought to achieve. In this way, and, more or less in agreement with Roman Catholic, Lutheran, and Reformed views, the traditional Anabaptist approach has assumed that there exists an "independent standard [of behavior], which can be both known and attained apart from Christ...."[64] The source of this ethical standard can be variously located and discovered, but the result is always that this standard "is challengeable not only because it raises a claim to be revelation outside of Christ but also because it doubts the biblical affirmation that God in Christ is 'Lord' over the world."[65]

In John Yoder's assessment, this stance needs revising. Rather than appealing to a separate standard, Christian believers can use their own language or that of the (unbelieving) addressee, appealing simply to the claims those in power like to make with regard to justice, security, social order, and the like.[66] This approach acknowledges that when Christians call upon political authorities to do better, they recognize "the necessity for [political authorities] to work on a lower level [of ethical performance] than that of *agape*."[67] Yoder proposes that perhaps

> the Christian can speak to the statesman, without failing to take account of their differing presuppositions, using pagan or secular terminology to clothe his social critique without ascribing to those secular concepts any metaphysical value outside of Christ.[68]

As already revealed in the *Brotherly Union*, this bicameral division between "those who are and are not church members or are or are not in the world" can have a second deficiency, often revealed in post-Reformation Anabaptist life:

---

64. Ibid., 71.
65. Ibid.
66. Ibid., 72–73. For a contemporary example of the challenges involved, even in a liberal democracy, see the dialogue in Robert Audi and Nicholas Wolterstorff, *Religion in the Public Square: The Place of Religious Convictions in Political Debate* (Lanham, MD: Rowman and Littlefield, 1997).
67. Yoder, *Christian Witness*, 71.
68. Ibid., 73. See especially Yoder, *Priestly Kingdom*, 160–66, where he discusses the substance and form of such conversations.

> If ... the diversity of standards between the two realms is strongly emphasized, the temptation becomes very strong to "stiffen" the line between the two realms, thinking of the ins and the outs socio-logically or even geographically, weakening both the missionary imperative and the relevance of a witness to the state.[69]

In other words, it becomes the stance, not of mere separation, but of disengagement. Thus, Anabaptists were inclined at times toward a kind of discipline that encouraged mediocrity in their communities and was "often linked with an artificial sense of superiority over and an unrealistic sense of separation from the 'world.'" Part of the impetus to "separationism" continued to be survival and cohesion in the face of intense persecution, but an absence of exchange proved disadvantageous for Anabaptist communities in the longer term.[70]

Other Modes of Engagement

Critique and separatist criticism are not the only modes of engagement. It is possible to participate in the life of the surrounding community, but with limitations (no swearing of oaths, no taking up of arms, and the like). In a Christendom context in which mandatory membership in both church and society was understood to be required for social order, such limitations proved difficult. With the waning of the Christendom order or when Anabaptists emigrated from jurisdictions that strictly enforced such an order, other modes of life—more socially, economi-cally, and even politically engaged—also became available to them. A well-known example, much examined and discussed, is the Mennonite experience in the Netherlands over the course of three centuries. In some cases, initially separated Mennonite communities eventually lost their Anabaptist identity and were largely assimilated.[71] In others, a thriving, distinct Anabaptist identity was tolerated by the surrounding community and sustained by faithful practices.

An instructive case for this consideration is the Mennonite experi-ence in Russia and Ukraine. At the invitation of Catherine II in 1787,

---

69. Yoder, *Christian Witness*, 71.

70. Finger, *Anabaptist Theology*, 209–10.

71. Alastair Hamilton, Sjouke Voolstra, and Piet Visser, eds., *From Martyr to Muppy: A Historical Introduction to Cultural Assimilation Processes of a Religious Minority in the Netherlands: The Mennonites* (Amsterdam: Amsterdam University Press, 1994).

large numbers of Mennonites emigrated from the Danzig area to what is now the Ukraine. Further migrations of Mennonites followed in the early to mid-eighteenth century. An estimated 2,500 families totaling more than 10,000 Mennonites may have emigrated from 1788 to 1859. By the end of the First World War, natural growth had made the total population of Mennonites in Russian territories about 5 percent (100 to 120 thousand) of the roughly two million people stemming from German origins. The Russian government granted these immigrants special privileges, including exemption from military service, freedom of religious worship, and ample land to farm.[72]

The attraction to the Mennonite Anabaptists was obvious. When those privileges were threatened in the latter part of the nineteenth century, large numbers of Mennonites emigrated to the United States and Canada. Cornelius Krahn's evaluation of the Mennonite settlement suggests that one successful "mission" of the Russian Mennonites was to "show the surrounding Slavic and nomadic population an exemplary Christian life in family and community and model methods of tilling the soil." More importantly, "the Evangelical movement of Russia was influenced strongly by the Mennonites for nearly a century."[73] So, too, was the case in the extensive, contemporaneous Mennonite settlements in Ukraine, where

> the threat to the principle of nonresistance had alarmed the Mennonites and caused some to leave the country and others to grow into a more active participation and sense of responsibility in the affairs of the country in which they lived.[74]

Krahn paints a picture in which for a century and a half, Mennonites in Ukraine engaged closely with their neighbors in "an environment [that] offered unusual opportunities for economic and cultural pioneering," in which Mennonites shared "agricultural methods" and other practices, and in which there was frequent close congregational cooperation with their non-Mennonite Christian neighbors.[75]

---

72. Much of this information is taken from "Russia," in *The Mennonite Encyclopedia, Vol. IV*: O–Z (Scottdale, PA: Mennonite Publishing House, 1959), 381–93.

73. Ibid., 392.

74. Ibid., "Ukraine," 766.

75. Ibid., 769.

Nonresistance, pacifism, and a desire for religious freedom do not, therefore, equate to quietism, self-segregation, and nonparticipation in society. Just as, in the tradition of political philosophy, Socrates had to develop from his philosophical vision the terms under which he might participate in Athenian civic life, so the Mennonites and other Anabaptist groups have had to do from their theological vision.[76]

In recent decades, various Anabaptist authors and sympathizers have addressed the question of engagement anew. For example, John Redekop has explored the boundaries of specifically democratic participation from an Anabaptist perspective, including issues of political party membership, participation, and even formation; public policy debates and formulation; civil disobedience; analysis of the purposes of government; and the meaning of an Anabaptist theology of the lordship of Christ in that context. Duane Friesen has attempted a broader sweep, examining from an Anabaptist perspective several kinds of cultural, philosophical, and political engagement in the context of late-twentieth-century America. Stanley Hauerwas and John Howard Yoder have both vigorously defended Mennonites and Anabaptists against charges of "sectarianism," outlining in detail the ways in which a church of the kind that Anabaptists have envisioned and sought to instantiate can in fact "be of great service in liberal societies" without assuming the absolute truth of liberalism or liberal democracy.[77] Yoder has written in considerable detail concerning the "Christian's positive duty to wider society and the state."[78]

One example of such engagement in the United States is the Civilian Public Service. During the First World War, elements of the US government did not respond favorably to requests for conscientious objectors of whatever denominational background to be exempted from military service. In one case, a foursome of Hutterites, for example, was

---

76. See Plato's *Apology of Socrates*.

77. Hauerwas, "Why the 'Sectarian Temptation' Is a Misrepresentation: A Response to James Gustafson (1988)," in John Berkman and Michael Cartwright, eds., *The Hauerwas Reader* (Durham, NC: Duke University Press, 2001), 90–110, at 96; Yoder, *Priestly Kingdom*, 151–71.

78. Hauerwas, "Sectarian Temptation," 97. Hauerwas footnotes Yoder's *Christian Witness to the State*. We can add *Priestly Kingdom* and this quotation from Yoder's *For the Nations: Essays Evangelical and Public* (Grand Rapids: Eerdmans, 1997): "Each of the following essays argues, though each in a somewhat different key, that the very shape of the people of God in the world is a public witness, or is 'good news,' for the world, rather than first of all rejection or withdrawal" (6).

imprisoned for refusal to serve. The men were treated so severely at Alcatraz and then Leavenworth that two died during confinement.[79] In response to US federal demands of conscription and with the clear sense by the 1930s that further large wars were likely, a group of peace churches petitioned the US and Canadian governments for consideration. In 1940, US legislation established the Civilian Public Service (CPS) in response. Conscientious objectors were conscripted into alternative service work that did not require taking up arms or directly supporting those who did. The camp assignments included soil conservation work, forestry maintenance and development, firefighting, staff work in mental facilities, and volunteering for medical experiments.[80]

Reflecting on his experiences in the CPS, John Oyer argues that this model provided a means of "peace testimony" to the wider society, not only in the sometimes unpleasant and uncompensated work (in contrast to military conscripts and even POWs who were paid) that service conscripts performed in various communities, but also in the wider effects that the service had in the communities. For example, "the idea and practice of alternative service were to spread to other Americans— Christian or not—and also to people in other countries that had not permitted alternative service." Similarly, the work of the men and women in CPS "gave an enormous impetus to mission activities overseas and at home" in a wide range of denominations, and it "energized" church-based service organizations of various kinds.[81] Thus, the pacifist witness of Anabaptists and others had beneficial social and ecclesial leavening effects that were neither planned nor anticipated.

The Problem of Poverty

Contemporary Anabaptist responses to poverty are a direct descendant of sixteenth-century Anabaptist practices. Care for the poor, I have pointed out, was a core church practice for Anabaptists, at times closely associated theologically with the Lord's Supper. The primary focus was

---

79. Guy F. Hershberger, *War, Peace, and Nonresistance* (Scottdale, PA: Herald Press, 1946), 119–24.

80. "Civilian Public Service," in *Global Anabaptist Mennonite Encyclopedia Online* (accessed at http://www.gameo.org/index.php?title=Civilian_Public_Service); Oyer, *They Harry the Good People*, 159–80.

81. Oyer, *They Harry the Good People*, 160–61.

on members of the congregation, but it could be expanded to those outside the community. In circumstances in which membership in an Anabaptist congregation could lead to exclusion from whatever support networks might be available in the larger society, it was not surprising that Anabaptists quickly saw the necessity for providing support to needy members, nor was it surprising that they did so following New Testament patterns.

One widespread method for dealing with questions of need and poverty was the "common purse," later known as "mutual aid." In this form of sharing, too, Anabaptists were not unique; both Luther and Calvin expressed concern for the poor or needy and implemented measures to aid them. The Anabaptist distinction was that they "worked with the needy in a direct and mutual relationship, while [Luther and Calvin] extended aid through the channels established by civil authority."[82]

It was common in interrogations of suspected Anabaptists to ask about their communistic practices. While the groups who became known as Hutterites did practice communal ownership of property, most Anabaptist groups did not, and they were keen to defend themselves against the accusation, even while acknowledging and defending their practice of sharing goods freely with one another or of maintaining a common congregational purse for alms.[83] Mutual aid is widely considered among Anabaptist scholars as a core characteristic practice of the Mennonites and other modern Anabaptist groups.[84] Hutterites remain practitioners of a form of Christian communism, the Amish practice mutual aid amongst themselves, and the Church of the Brethren has developed practices similar to those of the Mennonites, including close cooperation with various Mennonite groups around certain pan-church relief organizations.

In contemporary North America, especially as they have themselves prospered economically, many Anabaptist congregations have come to find and treat poverty less in their immediate surroundings than in

---

82. C. J. Dyck, "Mutual Aid in a Changing Economy," in H. Ralph Hernley, ed., *The Compassionate Community* (Scottdale PA: Association of Mennonite Aid Societies, 1970), 170–72.

83. See Oyer, *They Harry the Good People*, 261, 288, 294.

84. *Proceedings of the Study Conference on the Believers' Church* (General Conference Mennonite Church, 1955), 87.

generations past, often turning more attention to identified needs in the distance than locally. The model of congregational autonomy that is part of the Anabaptist tradition has not prohibited pan-congregational organizations from developing, but like many contemporary nonprofits and NGOs, such organizations are not tightly coordinated or directed from a central, denominationally controlled office. Instead, on a "para-church" model, they have relied on the voluntary benevolence of independent congregations and individuals while engaging wider problems.

The best-known of the Anabaptist relief agencies, Mennonite Central Committee (MCC), began in 1921 "as a strictly emergency type of service to feed starving Mennonites and non-Mennonites in Russia." It has developed from that specific and typically Anabaptist purpose to "administering a large ongoing program in a wide variety of services in a world-wide ministry."[85] According to its statement of purpose:

> Mennonite Central Committee (MCC), a worldwide ministry of Anabaptist churches, shares God's love and compassion for all in the name of Christ by responding to basic human needs and working for peace and justice. MCC envisions communities worldwide in right relationships with God, one another and creation.[86]

The stated priorities of MCC "in carrying out its purpose are disaster relief, sustainable community development and justice and peace-building," which it indicates in a listing of various completed projects in its annual report.[87] Thus, MCC strives to be identified as broadly "Anabaptist," not narrowly "Mennonite," and it explicitly appeals to its Anabaptist heritage both in its purpose and in its priorities. According to its 2014 financial statement, MCC received USD $60.55M in cash gifts from a combination of US and Canadian sources, accounting for over half of its FY13/14 income of USD $117.5M. Smaller relief agencies include Mennonite Disaster Service (MDS), which, insofar as the impoverished are often unequally affected by natural disasters, can be understood in part as a poverty relief agency.

---

85. Ibid., 176.
86. "MCC's Principles and Practices" (accessed at www.mcc.org, February 9, 2015).
87. Ibid.

Apart from statements issued at various conferences and from various works of theologians and other scholars (who may or may not be widely known as Anabaptist), there are no explicitly Anabaptist statements concerning poverty from ecclesiastically identified spokespersons or in the manner of papal encyclicals. Perhaps the single best-known contemporary instance of treating the problem of poverty more widely in an Anabaptist mode is Ron Sider's *Rich Christians in an Age of Hunger* (1977). In a manner that one might characterize as typically Anabaptist, Sider does not emphasize systemic social or political reform, nor does he attempt to speak truth to power. Instead, he addresses Christian believers, focusing on their (individual) Christian behavior and calling for reformed lives through mechanisms such as the graduated tithe and less conspicuous consumption, thereby enabling a greater sharing of resources with those who have few of them.

Conclusion

Anabaptist beginnings can be understood as a pragmatic theological effort to evaluate and respond to the ills and crises of the intertwining of church and state in what we now understand to have been the latter days of European Christendom. That effort took place out of a specific perspective regarding what it meant to be a follower of Jesus. For Anabaptists, that question could only make sense in the context of a disciplined community of like-minded believers. The new sociopolitical order that the Anabaptists envisioned originated in a new imagination about the nature and role of a community of believers. Out of that vision they developed a new mode of engagement with the larger world. That new mode was gradually settled under assumptions about that world and that community of believers that were not alien to Christendom, but moved in directions that the representatives of both Roman Catholic and Protestant Christendom found difficult to accommodate or perhaps even to understand.

I have stressed in this presentation of Anabaptist political thought its multiple origins within a family of groups and the "evolutionary historical development of Anabaptism," because I believe that, for the contemporary situation, these characteristics may be among the greatest strengths of Anabaptism. Rather than standing stridently on a Procrustean dogma, the "complex of 'intramural' conversations that

stands behind the development of an Anabaptist theological and ecclesiological *tradition*" may, to quote Arnold Snyder, require "'a recovery
of Anabaptist conversations,' rather than a 'recovery of *the* Anabaptist
Vision.'"[88] Anabaptist conversations can thereby engage contemporary
concerns, including questions concerning politics. What better way to
remain relevant as faithful interlocutors?

---

88. Snyder, *Anabaptist History and Theology*, 97 (italics in original).

ROBERT BENNE

I appreciate the nuance that Thomas Heilke gives to Anabaptist history, especially its complicated and varied relation to the political sphere. As is the case with most Christian traditions, including the Lutheran, there are a number of different interpretations. Yet he does clearly indicate an Anabaptist consensus that following Jesus directly and literally—especially in his Sermon on the Mount—is the heart of Christian discipleship. Following closely from that conviction is the commitment to an ecclesiology that demands a highly accountable life. And, as the church expresses its "nonresistance, pacifism, and religious freedom," that certainly does not equate to "quietism, self-segregation, or nonparticipation." Such a church does have political implications, as Hauerwas contends when he argues that the church's political witness is to reveal to the world its addiction to coercion and violence. Such a witness is engaged, not passive.

The Anabaptist tradition still ought to instill in us "magisterial Christians" a sense of repentance for the violent suppression that we brought upon them, as well as remind us of how tempting it is for us to compromise and accommodate to the world. The haunting question raised by Anabaptists continues to provoke thought: If such magisterial Christians really did have loyalty to Christ as their first principle, why did they kill each other by the millions in the wars of religion and the two World Wars? A difficult question, indeed.

H. Richard Niebuhr's assessment of the "Christ against culture" perspective continues to hold: It reminds those who hold to other ways of construing Christian life in the world that following Christ will lead to tension and apartness, not a comfortable blending in.

Yet, there are deep problems that persist, the main one being responsibility to the neighbor in a sinful world. If we are realistically to love our neighbors, we need to protect them from evil-doers through the offices of the state. Luther recognized this as he legitimated the office of the sheriff, the soldier, and even the hangman. Further, if the whole biblical record is to be taken into account, it seems that Jesus himself honored such offices. He did not call the centurion to give up his worldly office. He gave a role even to Caesar when he instructed his questioners to give to Caesar what is his. He assaulted the money-changers in the temple. St. Paul certainly understood Christian teaching to mean that the state has a just and godly role in keeping peace and fostering justice. Wolves must be restrained from killing the sheep, even if it involves the use of coercion and deadly force. Honest members of the Anabaptist tradition must admit that they are free-riders on the backs of Christians (and others) who are willing to use such "dubious" methods to protect them and their freedom to exercise their religion.

A closely related problem is the difficulty in making too sharp a distinction between physical coercion and violence and other more subtle means of coercion. During the Vietnam era I once led a demonstration at the Museum of Science and Industry in Chicago against a particularly vile display in which children could pretend to shoot Viet Cong soldiers. This event so upset the director of the museum that he died of a heart attack during the demonstration. We demonstrators never physically touched the poor fellow, but we were certainly implicated in his death.

Likewise, psychological depredations can be far more harmful to children than a strategic paddling. Pressuring someone emotionally can be just as wicked as pushing them physically. Coercive means are woven into our sinful common lives. There is no absolute separation between physical and other kinds of coercion, so those who refuse to engage directly in political life should probably abjure participation in almost any corporate activity.

Finally, the Anabaptist tradition seems to devalue penultimate commitments and loyalties. True enough, the Hauerwases and Yoders of that tradition wisely warn of the danger of elevating the nation state to a godlike level that enables it to permit and require that humans kill each other. Yet they also seem so contemptuous of penultimate loyalties — especially toward the liberal state — that they refuse to make the relative distinctions that are so important in historical existence. From a magisterial Christian point of view, the liberal democratic state is far superior to authoritarian or totalitarian regimes and therefore deserves a measure of honor and loyalty to it. But from an Anabaptist viewpoint, all seem equally corrupt and contemptible, since they simply cannot avoid the use of coercion. This brings us back to a certain avoidance of responsibility to our neighbors, who deserve to live out their lives in the best possible circumstances. Obsessing about physical coercion can lead to irresponsibility.

I certainly admire the faith and courage of Anabaptists who are willing to live an alternative way of life, but it seems that the very existence of that alternative way depends on those who take a more expansive view of responsibility for our earthly existence.

A BLACK CHURCH (PROPHETIC) RESPONSE

Against the backdrop of the present sociocultural scene in the United States, Dr. Heilke's words early in his presentation may prove prophetic:

> Perhaps the Anabaptist movement — with all its flaws — expresses an ever-present possibility of the Christian gospel that is gaining traction as the magisterial churches are becoming gradually "disestablished" and therefore find themselves confronting a world in which their socio-political status looks increasingly similar to that of minority groups like the Anabaptists in what was once Christendom (p. 20).

Anabaptist thought in the spheres of ecclesiology, ethics, and political theory was forged in the context of the distrust and persecution of established ecclesial and magisterial powers, unlike the developmental trajectories of the other traditions represented in this work, except for the Black church. Heilke's treatment was particularly helpful in showing both the complexity involved in the development of Anabaptist identity and the simplicity of some nonnegotiable parameters. The complexities would unfold in the midst of the "two *loci classici*" of either complete withdrawal from the world or else a "millennial revolution" imposing a new civic identity and order.

Much like the other authors in this work, Heilke attempts to describe aspects of the Anabaptist tradition and its engagement with the political realm while avoiding extremes or harmful stereotypes. In the remainder of this response, I will identify some elements in Heilke's work that I believe advanced this project. Then I will raise some general issues and questions for the Anabaptist approach.

The Black church tradition would find many points of general agreement with the section on Anabaptist theological distinctives. First, the point that "Jesus is the central focus" (p. 26) builds principles for life and practice for both individual believers and the believing community. Although Heilke did not express this point directly, it seems to follow that the particulars of Jesus' encounters with spheres of power in the Gospels do much to call for an exemplary life as an alternative strategy of influence instead of reliance upon the possession and use of political power. Second, the emphasis on the "priesthood of all believers" (p. 26) grounds this insistence upon the separation of ecclesiastical matters from the governing state. Finally, and most helpful, is the tendency toward nonviolence that would disallow service in the military or the swearing of allegiance to any earthly political regime. The Sermon on the Mount, as a key part of the life of Jesus, does much to advance this position.

Another helpful section is the treatment on the *Brotherly Union* that emerged from the conference at Schleitheim, Switzerland, in 1527. Heilke, incorporating the work of Gerald Bieseker-Mast, shows that there were internal tensions in the *Brotherly Union* itself. There was a call for separation from the world, but strict separation was difficult to maintain. For example, concerning the use of the "sword," Heilke cites John H. Yoder to illustrate this tension:

> Two orders of preservation and redemption exist together under the same God. In one of them the sword has no place, due to the normativeness of the work of Jesus Christ, whereas in the other the sword has a limited legitimacy, which is tested precisely at the point of its ability to keep itself within limits (p. 31).

The resolution of this tension extends even into the present.

We all have much to learn from the more recent Anabaptist attempts to maintain a distance from direct political engagement, yet nevertheless serve the larger social context. An informative example is Heilke's discussion on the Civilian Public Service (p. 41), its work demonstrating a "peace testimony" to the larger society. The areas of service open to members of the Anabaptist tradition ranged from soil conservation to volunteering for medical experiments (p. 42). Heilke notes that such witness had positive impact for the gospel far beyond the activities themselves, a point shared by many in the Black church who advance the gospel through their prophetic witness and service to others.

The experience of the Black church connects deeply with this movement, whose beginnings were forged under the duress of persecution and martyrdom. The suffering and loss of life were tragic, and Heilke helpfully notes how such duress can hinder theological formulation in multiple ways. At the same time, my response leads me to ask some questions of the Anabaptist tradition.

From a methodological perspective, just what can believers draw from the life of the Lord Jesus in the development of ethics and political philosophy? While we should focus on the life of Christ as a model on many fronts, the unique intentions that he had in ministry while on earth create complex questions about what principles we can and should apply to modern contexts. In addition, consider more specifically the use of violence. The Black church tradition shares an abiding concern for the pursuit of peace, for *shalom*. But many in the tradition believe that the sword can serve a limited purpose, something with which Christians should prayerfully wrestle. Purposes such as defense of family and country, implementation of "justice" in some contexts, and defense of the defenseless may sometimes call for violent response. The history of the United States in various places, in various circumstances, is written in blood. Many Blacks fought and died on this country's battlefields and often gained ground in civil rights as a result of such periods. Some of those who confronted powers lost their lives in pursuit of civil and voting rights and to end practices such as lynching, and not all of this confrontation was nonviolent.

This leads to a final point: The Black church's confrontation with various forms of power was dramatically affected by matters of race and racism. To be sure, each tradition is affected by its broad biblical/theological formulations and their implementation throughout political life. But did race or ethnicity have any significant influence on what happened in particular places, at particular times, under particular circumstances to the Anabaptist tradition and its ongoing development? This is an important question that needs to be raised with all of the traditions represented in this book.

A REFORMED (TRANSFORMATIONIST) RESPONSE

JAMES K.A. SMITH

Historically, the Reformed tradition has not been shy about voicing its critique of Anabaptists. Indeed, one of the historic Reformed confessions singles out the Anabaptists for a particularly strident critique, not with respect to baptism, but precisely with respect to their understanding of civil government. The Belgic Confession is forthright: "We denounce the Anabaptists, other anarchists, and in general all those who want to reject the authorities and civil officers and to subvert justice by introducing common ownership of goods and corrupting the moral order that God has established among human beings."[89]

Fortunately, these stark differences have mellowed, largely because the Reformed tradition has realized its ignorance and misunderstanding in equating Anabaptist reservations with anarchy.[90] More importantly, the Anabaptist "no" to aspects of government and civil society resonates with a strain of the Reformed vision that puts an emphasis on "antithesis," remembering and asserting the distinction between the way things are and the way they are meant to be. In that sense, the Anabaptist tradition represents a "radical" Reformation and has often functioned as a conscience of the Reformed tradition. Richard Mouw has also suggested that this is why debates between Calvinists and Anabaptists have been so intense: It is a kind of "narcissism of minor differences," a sibling rivalry amongst heirs of the Reformation impulse. "Willem Balke's detailed account of John Calvin's many disputes with the Anabaptists," Mouw notes, "provides much evidence that Calvin's own frustrations with the Anabaptists had to do with the fact that the Anabaptists 'out-Calvinisted' the Reformed community"

---

89. The Belgic Confession, Article 36.
90. In 1985, for example, the Synod of the Christian Reformed Church voted to move this passage of the Belgic Confession to a footnote.

on key points of church discipline and the relationship of the church to the world.[91]

So it's not surprising that I resonate with much of Thomas Heilke's view and lament the martyrdom of his Anabaptist forbears. But my task here is to *dis*agree, so let me highlight a couple of points of fundamental divergence.

First, I continue to find Anabaptist principles of political engagement (or *dis*engagement, as the case may be) to be rather simplistic and naïve in their account of political life as an aspect of human culture. Or, to put it differently, it seems to me that the Anabaptist stance vis-à-vis the political falls into the trap of treating political life and institutions as "givens," as a kind of black box that operates apart from our understanding of its emergence or inner workings. We just find ourselves thrown into the world, and there are political powers, authorities, structures, and systems that we have to deal with, and those political systems are taken to be simply synonymous with "the world" of, say, John 17:15 — the world that is under the control of "the evil one."

Behind this assessment of government and politics is a problematic theology of creation that seems to write off swaths of creation as not only fallen, but almost diabolical.[92] There is a kind of all-or-nothing take on government and politics here that is problematic.

In this regard, the Anabaptist account seems to fall back into premodern notions of political life as merely "given," as if government is merely a static "fact of nature." But, of course the political is not merely something that has descended from heaven or existed *de facto* above the fray of human history. Any and every political system and regime is unfolded by human cultural agency over time; the political is historical and contingent and cannot be otherwise. Which also means that the political is open to change, reform, and renewal. It can even, in tiny incremental ways, by the grace of the Spirit and the power of providence, be bent toward kingdom come.

From a Reformed perspective, it looks as if the Anabaptist position

91. Richard Mouw, *He Shines in All That's Fair: Culture and Common Grace* (Grand Rapids: Eerdmans, 2001), 21–22.

92. Conversely, Anabaptists are much *more* confident in the purity of the church than Reformed folk would ever be. Thus, when Heilke identifies "the 'good city' of political philosophy" simply with "the church," Reformed folk will express eschatological caution, emphasizing that "the good city" is one we await (Rev. 21:2).

lacks a biblical theology of creation (even if that must also be a theology of a *fallen* creation) along with a very narrow pneumatology or sense of God's activity outside of the church. Anabaptists thus sequester[93] the political from the scope of Christ's triumphant resurrection from the dead, whereas Paul proclaims all of the things created in and by Christ — including "thrones, or powers or rulers or authorities" — are equally taken up in Christ's *redemptive* accomplishment: He is reconciling *all* things to himself, including the political. In this sense, we seek to follow not only the Jesus of the Gospels but the ascended Christ who now reigns. From a Reformed perspective, it sometimes looks as if Anabaptist political theology (like "red letter" evangelicalism) treats the Gospels as a narrower canon within the canon.

Heilke does not make pacifism a central feature of Anabaptist political theology, but it is an obvious point of tension between Anabaptist and Reformed views. Like the broader catholic Christian tradition, the Reformed tradition affirms a doctrine and practice of just war.[94] This is a point where Anabaptists hold up the model of Jesus in the Gospels as antithetical to such participation in violence; but this is also where their "canon within the canon" shows itself to be problematic. The call to follow Christ, even to *imitate* Christ, is not a call to mimic Christ. The wider canonical injunctions on redeemed image bearers is more complex, especially in light of an eschaton that still awaits, whereas Anabaptist emphases on purity border on a realized eschatology.[95]

While the Reformed position does not simply baptize the status quo, it is characterized by a hope for the *possibility* of political transformation rooted in a theology of creation and culture coupled with a conviction about the creation-wide scope of Christ's redemption — though still tempered by a deep sense of eschatological waiting. This motivates a hopeful but cautious participation in the political sphere with a recognition that the best we can hope for in this meantime is *proximate* justice, neither perfect nor pure.

---

93. In this way, as I'll point out, the Reformed critique of the Anabaptist position is similar to our critique of the Lutheran view.

94. For a recent restatement, see Oliver O'Donovan, *The Just War Revisited* (Cambridge: Cambridge University Press, 2003).

95. On these matters, Oliver O'Donovan's critique of "Jesusology" is particularly germane. See O'Donovan, *The Desire of the Nations: Rediscovering the Roots of Political Theology* (Cambridge: Cambridge University Press, 1999), 120–22.

A CATHOLIC (SYNTHETIC) RESPONSE

J. BRIAN BENESTAD

A cursory study of the Anabaptist tradition might lead one to think that it has nothing in common with the approach to politics of the Catholic Church, which places a heavy emphasis on the transformation of the wider society. That would be a serious mistake. As Professor Thomas Heilke says, "Anabaptist churches provide witness as communities of faith whose members live out the gospel in their individual behavior and in Christian community. In so doing, they build communities of moral excellence that can be understood on Aristotelian/Thomistic grounds, even if they are not explicitly conscious of this philosophical heritage" (p. 36).

Even though Anabaptists regard the church and society as radically distinct, their mode of living in the church positively affects the way they act in their families, schools, neighborhoods, and places of work. The Anabaptist focus on personal ethical behavior and on unity in the community of believers is most compatible with the Catholic emphasis on the importance of the practice of virtue by many individuals for the pursuit of a just social order in any society. Systemic or structural change in society is not enough. Order in the souls of individual citizens is a sine qua non of political and social reform.

Catholics and Anabaptists have a similar attitude toward helping the poor. Both traditions emphasize personal generosity, the reduction of consumption, and the use of their own private agencies to help the poor. Unlike Catholics, the Anabaptists, however, do not call upon the government to undertake political and social reform on either a small or large scale. The example of the Anabaptists is a constant reminder to Catholics not to be content with advocacy for public policy with little or no use of their own resources to help the poor.

Where Catholics and Anabaptists differ sharply is in their attitude toward participation in the life of society and in their posture with respect to the government. Anabaptists embrace pacifism and refuse to serve in the military or "to swear oaths of loyalty to a particular regime" (p. 26). They mistakenly think that the Sermon on the Mount requires Christians to be pacifists. Catholics are willing to use force especially to protect the innocent from being crushed by unjust aggression, although they regard participation in just wars, following St. Augustine, as a lamentable necessity. It is interesting to note that St. Thomas Aquinas discusses the conditions that must be met for a war to be just under the rubric of charity or love. Catholics believe that using lethal force against unjust aggressors can be required by the virtue of charity to protect the innocent from being deprived of their lives, freedom, or property.

Catholic teaching, however, recognizes that some individuals should be exempt from fighting in just wars but with an obligation to serve their county in other ways. The official *Catechism of the Catholic Church* explains: "Public authorities should make equitable provision for those who for reasons of conscience refuse to bear arms; these are nonetheless obliged to serve the human community in some other way" (no. 2311). Thomas Aquinas argues that bishops and priests should not participate in just wars because shedding blood is incompatible with their ministry, especially their duty to say mass, which is a memorial and a making present of the sacrifice of Christ on the cross. Warlike pursuits, he argues further, "hinder the mind very much from the contemplation of divine things, the praise of God, and prayers for the people, which belong to the duties of a cleric" (*Summa theologiae* II-II, qu. 40, art. 2). When clerics do their job well, they are truly serving the human community in an outstanding way. What is unacceptable from a Catholic point of view is to claim exemption from fighting in a just war without performing some other service for the political community.

Catholic teaching also imposes on Catholics the duty of an intelligent, discerning patriotism. President John F. Kennedy captured the Catholic ethic when he famously said, "My fellow Americans, ask not what your country can do for you, ask what you can do for your country." Catholics have an obligation to work for the genuine good of their country, but they don't love their country right or wrong. As mentioned above, I believe that the Anabaptists indeed serve their country by following the example of Jesus in their everyday lives, especially as members of families, productive workers, and good neighbors. Catholics depart from the Anabaptist way in trying to improve the quality of the government and the mores of civil society by direct participation. They draw inspiration from the biblical story about King Solomon's request for a discerning heart (1 Kings 3:9) so that he might govern God's people with wisdom and thereby contribute to their spiritual and material well-being. Wise rule contributes to justice without which "what else is the State but a great band of robbers," as Augustine famously wrote.

Catholics believe it is worth the effort to work for a more just government and just society, but with moderate expectation for success, avoiding utopian projects and premature resignation to injustice. In 2005, in his first encyclical, *God Is Love* (*Deus caritas est*, no. 36), Pope Benedict XVI described the two extremes that have to be avoided:

> When we consider the immensity of others' needs, we can on the one hand, be driven toward an ideology that would aim at doing what God's governance of the world apparently cannot: fully resolving every problem. Or we can be tempted to give in to inertia, since it would seem that in any event nothing can be accomplished.

Those working for reform need not only wisdom, but also patient endurance.

The Catholic writer J.R.R. Tolkien captured the correct attitude toward the reform of society in Gandalf's statement that evil will not be overcome if the Ring of Power is destroyed and Sauron, the evil ruler, is defeated:

> If [the Ring of Power] is destroyed, then [Sauron] will fall and his fall will be so low that none can foresee his arising ever again.... And so a great evil of this world will be removed. Other evils there are that may come; for Sauron is himself but a servant or emissary. Yet it is not our part to master all the tides of the world, but to do what is in us for the succor of those years wherein we are set, uprooting the evil in the fields that we know, so that those who live after may have clean earth to till. What weather they shall have is not ours to rule.[96]

---

96. J.R.R.Tolkien, *The Lord of the Rings*, part 3, *The Return of the King* (New York: Ballantine, 194), 160.

ROBERT BENNE

The Lutheran Reformation began in 1517 with the posting of the 95 Theses on the Castle Church door in Wittenberg by Martin Luther, then a monk of the Augustinian Order. Luther was incensed by the selling of indulgences to release people from purgatory by another monk, John Tetzel. Luther believed the Roman Catholic Church of his time had corrupted the gospel by making the free gift of salvation by grace through Christ into a matter of works. Selling indulgences was a particularly blatant example of such corruption.

But Luther's protest was aimed at something deeper than that distortion. He believed the Catholic Church had compromised the free gift of saving grace through Christ by adding the necessity of works in order to obtain salvation. He ardently taught that salvation (justification) is offered by the pure grace of God through Christ; the repentant sinner is totally receptive. In responding to that grace in faith, however, the Christian's faith becomes active in love. This loving service to the neighbor is exercised in the everyday responsibilities of life. Everyday responsibilities are transformed into vocations for Christians who act out their faith.

Luther had other serious criticisms of late medieval Catholicism. He protested the division of the church into the clergy, who occupied a higher and more serious religious and moral plane, and the laity, who were at a distinctly lower level. On the contrary, Luther thought, *all* Christians have callings (vocations) that are pleasing to God, not merely the clergy.

Further, he was convinced that the Roman Catholic Church had usurped the role of the prince or king by claiming to have coercive power. Luther believed the church rightfully had only the persuasive power of the Word, not of the sword. The secular authorities were responsible for keeping order and justice in society. God reigned in the world through those authorities enforcing his law. He reigned in the church through the gospel, freely given to and accepted by the believer. These two ways were distinct, not separate spatially, and they interacted in the vocation of the Christian.

One of the callings of every Christian is in the realm of citizenship. Luther himself was not bashful in that role. He constantly advised the princes to fulfill their obligation to promote order and justice. (He offered strong advice to them in 1520 in his *To the Christian Nobility of the German Nation*.)

After some followers took his reforming efforts to an extreme by forcefully trying to overthrow secular authority, Luther reacted with fierce anger against them. He called upon the princes to annihilate the rebels and thereafter tended to prefer order over justice from the authorities. This gave the Lutheran Reformation a politically conservative twist.

Luther and his followers had no intention of leaving the Roman Catholic Church; they wanted to reform it. After a number of tragic mishaps, however, Luther was excommunicated in 1521. By necessity, Luther had to rely on the princes and electors among his followers for protection in the next years. That fatefully aligned the Lutheran Reformation with the friendly political authorities of the day. Later the Lutheran churches became state churches—the state protected the churches, provided theological education, helped in the governance of the churches, and collected taxes for their support. This reliance on the state's power and largesse tended to make the churches rather docile before secular authority.

The Lutheran Reformation spread quickly to Central Europe and Scandinavia. The Lutheran churches then established new churches in many lands through their foreign missions. German and Scandinavian immigrants brought Lutheranism to the United States, where it has flourished as one of the largest Protestant traditions. While nearly everyone agrees that Lutheranism has had a marvelous legacy in theology, music, education, and charitable institutions, there is far less consensus on its political legacy.

The Pitfalls: Our Checkered History

Lutheranism has had a bad reputation when it comes to its relation to the public sphere, especially to the state. A good deal of this negative assessment has to do with Ernst Troeltsch's verdict on Lutheranism in his magisterial *The Social Teachings of the Christian Churches*. After a very lengthy analysis of Lutheranism, he makes the following points: "The yielding spirit of its wholly interior spirituality adopted itself to the dominant authority of the day. This passivity involved the habit of falling back on whatever power happens to be dominant at the time." From the very beginning it has, unlike Calvinism and Catholicism, lacked a "capacity to penetrate the political and economic movements of Western nations.... Its tendency is to alleviate but not re-create."[1] Troeltsch thought that Lutheranism was pervasively passive politically.

H. Richard Niebuhr, the great Yale professor, fatefully and fully imbibed Troeltsch's teaching. Although he gets much about Lutheranism right in his account in *Christ and Culture*, he follows Troeltsch in his assessment of Lutheranism's relation to the public square. He sees Lutheranism as essentiality dualist, tempted toward both antinomianism (literally, "against the law" as a guide to the Christian life) in personal ethics and passivity in social and political ethics.[2] Its profound grasp of the wonder and transcendence of God's grace in Christ makes it indifferent to the relative distinctions that are so important in earthly life, especially politics. So it adapts to whatever is, preferring order over the chaos that might accompany constructive change.

Richard Niebuhr's more politically active brother, Reinhold, followed both him and Troeltsch in their assessment. Reinhold concludes,

> By thus transposing an "inner ethic of spontaneous love" into a private one, and making the "outer" or "earthly" ethic authoritative for government, Luther achieves a curiously perverse social morality. He places a perfectionist private ethic in juxtaposition to a realistic, not to say, cynical, official ethic. This has led to an absolute distinction between the "heavenly" or "spiritual" kingdom and the "earthly" one, which destroys the tension between the final

1. Ernst Troeltsch, *The Social Teachings of the Christian Churches* (New York: Harper Torchbooks, 1960), 574–75.

2. H. Richard Niebuhr, *Christ and Culture* (New York: Harper & Row, 1951), 186ff.

demands of God upon the conscience, and all the relative possibilities of realizing the good in history.[3]

Reinhold Niebuhr did later allow that there may be exceptions to this dismal analysis. In a footnote in Volume II of his *Nature and Destiny of Man* he says that this pervasive Lutheran quietism may have a possible exception in the Scandinavian countries with their "impressive development of constitutional democracy." But, he says, he has not found any authoritative analysis of how this development happened in countries where the Lutheran religion was dominant.[4]

As a young, self-consciously Lutheran graduate student at the University of Chicago Divinity School, I decided that I would provide Niebuhr with that authoritative analysis by doing my dissertation on the Scandinavian Lutheran contribution to their democracies and their welfare states. However, the wind was taken out of my sails when I consulted a number of Swedish theologians. It seems that the Lutheran church fought those democratic advancements tooth and nail. Secular socialism was the real source. So I had to find another topic for my dissertation.

In spite of the efforts of American Lutheran scholars such as George Forell and William Lazareth to show that Lutheranism need not be quietistic and dualistic, the Troelstchian/Niebuhrian analysis seemed to stand: Lutheran political ethics is oxymoronic. Moreover, Lutheranism's historical record seemed to bear witness to its bad rap. Luther and his cohorts carried out a Reformation of the church without touching the medieval trappings of an authoritarian and static society. When it was disrupted by the Peasant's Revolt, Luther called for total annihilation of the peasants.

Sadly, during the time of the Civil War in the United States, Lutherans split according to the governments they lived under. Northern and Southern Lutherans didn't unite until 1918. But, even more disturbing, Lutheranism remained quiescent — except for a few heroic souls such as Bonhoeffer — amidst the rise of Nazism in Germany.[5] There are also

3. Reinhold Niebuhr, *The Nature and Destiny of Man: A Christian Interpretation*, *Vol. II* (New York: Charles Scribner's Sons, 1943), 194–95.

4. Ibid., 278.

5. My colleague Paul Hinlicky has published a book on Lutheran theologians' response to the rise of Nazism: *Before Auschwitz: What Christian Theology Must Learn from the Rise of Nazism* (Eugene, OR: Cascade Books, 2013). He points out that several major Lutheran theologians — including Werner Elert and Paul Althaus — were so enthused about Hitler early in the 1930s that they theologically legitimated him as a leader of near-messianic qualities.

the recent cases of Lutheran quietism in the face of authoritarian and unjust governments in Soviet satellite countries, Chile, and South Africa.

Given this record, perhaps we should set aside the whole theological apparatus that has led to such abysmal historical results. The Americanist Lutherans led by Samuel Simon Schmucker did just that amidst the Second Great Awakening of the first half of the nineteenth century.[6] This movement was a robust attempt to build the kingdom of God in America, much like that of the Puritans. The cost for this participation was giving up some Lutheran distinctives, which were deemed not only nonessential, but nonbiblical.

Or, we could set aside the traditional Lutheran reticence about intervening in the public square by joining the liberal Protestant activism that has been so pronounced in America since the 1960s.[7] This has been the option chosen by the Evangelical Lutheran Church in America (ELCA). Here the assumption has been that church officials understand what God is doing in history and therefore can prescribe what public policies will be consistent with God's action and should be supported by the church. They take "Christian" positions on many policies, following what seems to be a straight line from the ethic of the gospel to specific policies that they have discerned. Very often, the agenda dictated by the gospel is almost identical to that of the Democratic Party. (To be fair, straight-line thinking is done by some evangelical and fundamentalist churches that lead to an agenda quite similar to that of the Republican Party, but there seems to be no Lutheran churches among them.)

So, I ask, has our history shown only negative results from our adherence to Lutheran theological ethics? Are our choices traditional Lutheran quietism or Americanist/liberal Protestant activism? Happily, the record indicates better options. Indeed, the condemnation heaped upon

---

6. Schmucker explicitly denied a number of Lutheran distinctives—including the two-kingdoms doctrine—in his headlong commitment to the evangelical effort to "Christianize" the new Republic. Fueled by post-millennial expectations, Schmucker jettisoned the quietism of traditional Lutheranism for an activist involvement in evangelical revivals and voluntary societies. One of the most important voluntary societies was the Christian college. Three classmates—David Bittle, Theopholis Storck, and Ezra Keller—at Schmucker's Gettysburg Lutheran seminary went on to found Roanoke College, Newberry College, and Wittenberg College as instruments of this "Christianization" of America.

7. A foreshadowing of this move toward liberal Protestantism emerged in the Augustana Synod in the teaching and writing of A. D. Mattson, who was a strong devotee of the Social Gospel movement in America. His teaching career at Augustana Seminary from the 1930s to the 1960s influenced many students toward both liberal theology and ethics.

Lutheranism by the Troelstch/Niebuhr analysis has been sharply revised by John Witte, a Reformed scholar trained in both theology and law.

In *Law and Protestantism* Witte argues that early Lutheranism was a species of "constructive Protestantism" that built a Lutheran version of a Christian society. After the volcanic first years of the Reformation, Lutheran theologians had to cooperate with Lutheran secular authorities, especially jurists, to rebuild a new society out of the chaos of the old. Lutheran theologians, employing the two-kingdoms doctrine, worked hand-in-hand with secular agents to reform law, politics, and society. (Fatefully, I might add, the Lutherans gave over to the princes the care and control of the churches, which led in time to passive state churches.)

Witte does a careful analysis of how the reformer Philip Melanchthon worked with great Lutheran jurists to shape a Lutheran society. They all began their work "with a basic understanding of Luther's two-kingdoms framework. While Luther tended to emphasize the distinctions between the two kingdoms, Lutheran jurists tended to emphasize their cooperation."[8] For example, Witte argues that Melanchthon and the jurists tended more than Luther to view the Bible as an essential source of earthly law and to apply the three uses of the law to the governance of the earthly kingdom. In short, they built bridges between the two kingdoms.[9] Witte concludes the book with the bold claim that "a good deal of our modern Western law of marriage, education, and social welfare, for example, still bears the unmistakable marks of Lutheran Reformation theology."[10]

Even though we might delight in Witte's revisionist history—as I emphatically do—we still must seek modern examples of how Lutheran churches might properly relate to the public sphere. After all, it wasn't long before the sixteenth-century Lutheran synthesis of Christ and culture broke down and the Lutheran church necessarily had to seek a new role in a changed society.

It would be foolish to retrieve the Americanist Lutheran approach of Schmucker or adopt the liberal Protestant approach of the ELCA,

---

8. John Witte Jr., *Law and Protestantism: The Legal Teachings of the Lutheran Reformation* (Cambridge; Cambridge University Press, 2002), 168.

9. Witte shows how Melanchthon applied the three uses of the law to criminal law and punishment; the civil use (which governs political and social life) corresponded with deterrence; the theological use (which teaches humans that they are sinners) with retribution; and the educational use (which guides the Christian life) with rehabilitation.

10. Witte, *Law and Protestantism*, 295.

both of which have sloughed off Lutheran distinctives. I would propose, though, that we have two contemporary models that do better.

One emerged in the public witness of the Lutheran Church in America (LCA) from the mid-60s to the mid-80s.[11] A post-war generation of young theologians had gone off to Union Seminary in New York to study with Reinhold Niebuhr. Chastened by the Niebuhrian criticism of Lutheranism but yet maintaining their commitment to Lutheran theological ethics, theologians such as George Forell, William Lazareth, and Richard Niebanck proceeded to guide the formation of a number of important social statements. They employed a more dynamic interpretation of the Lutheran two-kingdoms doctrine with impressive results, including important statements on church and state as well as on nuclear deterrence, which stood against the pacifist-tinged witness of both liberal Protestantism and the US Conference of Catholic Bishops.[12]

The LCA also maintained an office in Washington that carried on a bona fide ministry to political actors. By honoring the lay vocation of politicians as well as the social statements of the church, the office had both pastoral and prophetic dimensions. That office did very little direct advocacy work. No doubt the Church and Society office and the LCA offered too many statements on too many issues, but nevertheless, it provides a positive model for Lutheran witness in the public sphere. That was soon to disappear with the founding of the ELCA and its strong move toward liberal Protestantism.

The other positive example I might mention is that of the Lutheran Church—Missouri Synod. The LCMS is a church based in St. Louis, Missouri, that has maintained a policy of doctrinal strictness that has kept it from merging with any other Lutheran body. In recent years its Commission on Theology and Church Relations has developed excellent reports and opinions on a number of important church and society issues. The reports are directed internally for the edification of pastors and laypeople from a clear Lutheran theological perspective. It has not

---

11. The Lutheran Church in America was constituted by a merger of several ethnic churches in 1962. At the merger it became the largest of the Lutheran churches and was headquartered in Philadelphia. In 1988 it merged into the Evangelical Lutheran Church, which at that time had a baptized membership of 5.2 million. It is now headquartered in Chicago.

12. The rather admirable history of LCA public witness, especially the composition of social statements, is told in *Politics and Policy* by Christa Klein and Christian von Dehsen (Minneapolis: Fortress, 1989). The American Lutheran Church had a similar history, though less developed theologically than the LCA.

engaged in frequent direct advocacy. When it has engaged in public witness, however, it has been strong and forceful, especially on issues of religious freedom and respect for nascent life. With regard to the latter, the LCMS has even organized its own voluntary association—Life Ministries—to engage in pro-life advocacy.

The Possibilities: What Is Enduring in the Lutheran Vision

These positive examples show not only that the Lutheran approach to the public sphere can be done rightly and fruitfully but also that it can make important contributions in the ongoing drama of Christian engagement with the world.[13] In the following I will outline four major Lutheran themes that are of enduring value to the larger Christian witness in the public sphere. However, this "Lutheran attitude" does not lead in a specific ideological direction, if that is taken to mean a rather detailed blueprint for public policy. Rather, the Lutheran vision provides a *framework* for public engagement. It elaborates a set of theological assumptions that stipulate how organized religion and politics ought to be related, not so much for the sake of politics and society but primarily for the sake of the church. What is legally permitted—the direct and aggressive intervention of the church in political affairs—may well not be good for the church and its mission. Undue entanglement in politics can be the ruination of the church.

Further, the Lutheran vision sets a general direction for public policy rather than a specific set of policy injunctions. It tends toward what has been called "Christian realism," though that general tendency can be refracted into a number of different policy directions.[14] There are both liberal and conservative Lutherans who share commitment to this framework.

---

13. In a remarkable article on Lutheranism in America (*First Things*, February 1992), Mark Noll calls for Lutherans to make a badly needed contribution to American thinking and acting with regard to religion and politics. Such a contribution would mitigate the heavily Reformed perspective—now secularized—that dominates American attitudes as it applies personal transformation (sanctification) too easily to the public/political sphere. Alas, Noll says, Lutherans have generally failed in this important task. I wrote my book *The Paradoxical Vision* (Minneapolis: Fortress, 1995) in response to his challenge, in hopes that the Lutheran contribution would be more visible.

14. Christian realism is a school of theological ethics indebted to the thought of Reinhold Niebuhr (1892–1971), who emphasized the persistence of sin in individual and collective life and therefore resisted any sort of Utopian ethics.

The four central themes of the Lutheran vision are (1) a sharp distinction between salvation offered by God in Christ and all human efforts; (2) a focused and austere doctrine of the church that follows from the first theme; (3) the twofold rule of God through Law and Gospel; and (4) a paradoxical view of human nature and history.[15] These four themes also suggest some distinctive ways for the church practically to engage the public order.

Salvation Versus Human Effort

I have stated what is meant to be a distinction as something of a contradiction, but overstatement often has a point. Humans, particularly in the political sphere, are prone to claim redemptive significance for their efforts at social and/or political transformation. The twentieth century has been crammed with those blood-stained attempts. When the God-man Jesus Christ is refused as Savior, the man-god in many different guises is given full sway.

The good news of the gospel is that God saves us through his gift of grace in Christ. He has chosen to reconcile us to him by sending his Son, by breaking through to us from his side, as it were, and not insisting that we climb some ladder of achievement through our own efforts. We *trust* God to save us in Christ; we do not earn our salvation nor even add something to what he has offered. It is sheer gift. We need to do nothing but accept the gift with repentant heart.

This insistence on a strong doctrine of grace puts all human efforts in proper perspective. They deal with penultimate improvements in the human condition, with relative goods and bads, not with salvation. This means that politics is desacralized and relativized. Salvation is through Christ, not through human political schemes, nor through psychological or religious efforts, for that matter. Following from this, we might

---

15. These themes are drawn from my reading of recent interpretations of the Lutheran vision, which is indebted more to Scandinavian and American scholarship on Luther and Lutheranism than to German. These are, in my opinion, more dynamic and open than the German and are more influenced by the strengths of other Christian traditions, especially the Reformed. My main sources are Gustaf Wingren, *Luther on Vocation* (Philadelphia: Muhlenberg, 1957) and *Creation and Law* (London: Oliver and Boyd, 1961); Einar Billing, *Our Calling* (Rock Island, IL: Augustana Book Concern, 1951); Gustaf Aulén, *Church, Law and Society* (New York: Charles Scribner's Sons, 1948); George Forell, *Faith Active in Love* (Minneapolis: Augsburg, 1954); and William Lazareth, *Luther and the Christian Home: An Application of the Social Ethics of the Reformation* (Philadelphia: Muhlenberg, 1960).

appropriately speak of liberation ethics, but never of liberation theology, if that is taken to mean that revolutionary praxis is the same thing as salvation. Such a judgment provides a critical shield against the constant attempts in American Christianity to give redemptive significance to educational, psychological, spiritualist (New Age), and now environmental movements.

One would think that the world has had enough experience of revolutionary change to obviate any claims that political and social "transformation" lead to anything remotely resembling human fulfillment. Ordinary human observation and experience arrive at such a negative verdict. But for religious people to make such claims is even more baffling.

Such sacralizing claims are ruled out by the Lutheran vision. We are obviously not capable of our own salvation. The Lutheran vision, however, aims at cutting off such claims for even more profound reasons than their lack of empirical validity. It does so for the sake of the gospel, for its radicality and universality. The radicality of the gospel insists that salvation is a pure gift; we do not earn it. If we do not recognize that, we dishonor God who gave his Son in the unique and decisive saving act. When we claim a part in the drama of salvation, we at the same time insist that God's action in Christ is not good enough. Something else, presumably our virtuous action, must be added.

Furthermore, the universality of the gospel is compromised if we fail to make a sharp distinction between God's saving act in Christ and all human efforts at improving the world. In any overt or covert claim for human effort as a constitutive part in our own salvation there are always those who are on the right side of the struggle and those on the wrong side. Some are saved and some are damned, not because of their faith or lack of faith in God's work in Christ, but because they either are or are not participants in the group or process that claims to be bringing redemption. Their salvation is dependent on which side of earthly fault lines they find themselves.

The picture is clear; the claims of the man-god always exclude. However, the gospel does not. All humans, regardless of their location among the world's fault lines, are equidistant and equally near the grace of God in Christ.

The New Testament gospel of the suffering God who abjured all worldly power and all worldly group identifications simply rules out those schemes that compromise the radicality and universality of the gospel. The cross of Christ freed the gospel from enmeshment in all human efforts to save the world. No one was with Christ on the cross to die for our sins. Or viewed differently, everyone was with Christ on the cross, but only as passive inhabitants of his righteous and suffering person.

When we are freed from the need to look for salvation in human schemes, our eyes should be clearer to make the very important distinctions among the relatively good and the relatively bad in the realm of human action. Liberated from the worry about our salvation, we can turn non-obsessively to the human task of building a better world, not by prideful claims of transformation, but by determined yet humble attempts to take small steps for the better.[16]

The Purpose of the Church

If the most important event that ever happened in human history is the coming of Christ, then the essential and unique mission of the church from the point of view of the paradoxical vision is its calling by God to proclaim that gospel in word and sacrament. The gospel of Christ is its treasure; the church is the earthen vessel whose sacred obligation is to take the gospel to every nook and cranny of the world. Its calling is to proclaim the gospel and to gather a people around that gospel, forming them through the Spirit into the Body of Christ.

No other institution has that calling; no other institution will promote the gospel if the church fails in its task. So churches must take with utmost seriousness the terrible simplicity of their task. Of course they must be engaged in deeds of charity, and they must be concerned with justice. Of course they must involve themselves in many other activities—financial, administrative, and educational. Of course they must witness in the public sphere. But the church is not primarily a political actor, a social transformer, or an aggressive interest group. If it acts primarily as one of these, it is identified and treated as one more contentious worldly group. What's more, it loses its own integrity, its own reason for being.

---

16. As Luther's famous paradoxical statement in his tract "On the Freedom of a Christian" (1520) describes: "A Christian is perfectly free lord of all, subject to none. A Christian is servant of all, subject to all."

Currently we are witnessing many churches losing confidence and zeal for their essential and unique calling. They no longer believe their gospel message is of utmost importance. They marginalize it in their own activities and institutions. How else can one account for the lack of any real margin of difference between church and secular schools, colleges, hospitals, and homes for the elderly? How else can one account for the disastrous drop in home and foreign missionary activity on the part of so many languishing church bodies?

The Two-fold Rule of God

The Lutheran vision holds that God rules the world in two distinct ways — through the Law and the Gospel. The Law is his instrument to sustain and order the world. God did not abandon the world after the fall. He continues to sustain it through the Law, which refers to all his energies and actions that restrain, guide, and shape the world. Since the Law must deal with human sin, it must have a hard edge to it. Indeed, God often wields the Law of judgment against nations and empires, bringing them to naught. But the Law also builds up human life, working through many agencies to create a more humane and just world.

The Law is summarized in the Ten Commandments and carried by the moral teachings of the church, but it is also discerned by human reason and experience amidst the dynamics of life. The Bible contains many signposts for recognizing the operation of God's Law in the world, but it has no blueprint for the complexities of modern economic, political, or social life. Humans have to work out what God demands anew in every generation. Secular people, since they also have the gift of reason and the benefit of experience, can contribute to this ongoing discernment of the Law, though they may not call it God's Law. Christians are obligated, not only to cooperate with secular people in discerning and doing good works of the Law, but also to imagine and initiate programs that extend human justice.

The Law of God is not salvific. All the efforts that God and humans make in the horizontal realm of the Law may lead to human betterment, but they do not save. Rather, God has chosen a particular route to reconcile humans to himself. That route is Christ. God has reached out to call a disobedient and lost humanity to himself through the cross and the resurrection of Jesus Christ. This is pure gift; in the realm of salvation, humans are completely receptive. Their faith in the saving act of Christ will be acted out in deeds of love, but those deeds of love are the result of faith in God's work in Christ, not a substitute for it.

Christians exist at the juncture of the two ways that God reigns and must live creatively between the horizontal pressures of the Law and the call of the Gospel. However, they must be careful not to confuse these two, that is, to act according to Law when they are in the realm of the Gospel or to act according to the Gospel when they are in the realm of the Law. They are to observe a tentative, though not a final, dualism.

Making the Law into the Gospel

This confusion is a favorite for those, mentioned above, who are tempted to claim salvific effect for human effort. They mistake some ameliorative, but always ambiguous projects for the gospel itself. There are many negative effects of this mistake, the first being a dishonoring of God's will to save through his son, the Christ. But others follow. Human efforts that are invested with salvific import are often dangerous. Reinhold Niebuhr, for example, pointed out the perils of both hard and soft utopianism.[17]

In the "hard" category, the awful legacies of Nazi and Marxist revolutions are a case in point. When humans claim to bring heaven to earth by force, they bring hell instead. A fascinating aspect of hard utopianism is its endorsement by so many respectable intellectuals.[18] One can only make sense of this by reminding oneself that the longing for salvation has not departed from the minds and spirits of even secularized intellectuals; it is merely displaced into utopian schemes whose claims, in retrospect, seem utterly incredible.

---

17. See Niebuhr's discussion of both types of utopianism in *Reinhold Niebuhr on Politics*, ed. Harry R. Davis and Robert C. Good (New York: Charles Scribner's Sons, 1960), 12–36.

18. It remains to be seen whether intellectuals on the left will be called to account for their flirtations with the various Marxist-Leninist regimes and movements of the last fifty years. Intellectuals who showed any affinity with fascist regimes and movements are constantly being exposed for their errors. Philosopher Martin Heidegger's intellectual respectability has been sorely challenged. Even the historian of religion Mircea Eliade, who tried to stay clear of politics for the last thirty years of his life, has been scrutinized for his earlier lapses. But thus far, few intellectuals who sympathized with Marxist-Leninism are being called to account. Indeed, they seem to wear their past enthusiasms as proud, even if faded, garlands of moral authenticity rather than as reminders of their complicity with regimes at least as destructive as the fascist ones we rightfully condemn.

Softer varieties of utopianism abound. The secular world is prone to view an expansion of scientific knowledge as salvific. Or education in a broader sense will save us. Or health and well-being will, or schemes of self-esteem, or new spiritual techniques. The latest version seems to involve ecological concerns. Scientific pursuits, seeking to improve social conditions, and concern for creation are worthwhile endeavors, but such pursuits are not able to reconcile us to God. Yet, depleted religious traditions often grasp at this soft utopianism, and sometimes even at the harder variety, when they lose their confidence in the gospel. Not only does the world mistake the Law for the Gospel; churches themselves do, too.

Making the Gospel into the Law

Reinhold Niebuhr, though he did not put the issue in the concepts I am using, was a formidable opponent of this confusion. He believed that liberal Christianity had taken the radical love of the gospel and turned that "impossible possible" into an ethical norm that could then become a "simple possibility in history."[19] Indeed, his whole career as a public theologian could be understood as a protest against the sentimentality inherent in the liberal tendency to make the Gospel into the Law. From the early *Moral Man and Immoral Society* to the late *Structure of Nations and Empires*, Niebuhr demonstrated the folly of applying the ethic of agape love directly to the struggles for power in the world.[20] Doing so, he argued, led to political irresponsibility. In international affairs it has perennially led to pacifist tendencies, and in domestic affairs it has issued in blindness toward the necessity of countervailing power.

Niebuhr's arguments are essentially Lutheran in character. Although expressed in different language, they are anchored in the Lutheran vision's insight into the dialectical relationship between the radical love of God in Christ and the realistic pursuit of earthly justice, between Gospel and Law. Indeed, I believe Niebuhr to be the greatest practitioner of two-kingdoms thinking in modern religious history. Many of his great contributions to the development of Christian realism

---

19. Reinhold Niebuhr, *An Interpretation of Christian Ethics* (New York: Seabury Press, 1979), 103ff.

20. Reinhold Niebuhr, *Moral Man and Immoral Society* (New York: Charles Scribner's Sons, 1960), and *The Structure of Nations and Empires* (New York: Charles Scribner's Sons, 1959).

are drawn from the Lutheran vision, though he would no doubt resist being claimed for the "Lutheran attitude."

Niebuhr's warnings have gone unheeded in much of American Christianity. The mainline churches rushed headlong toward sentimentalism in foreign policy debates. They demanded "nuclear freezes" even in the midst of Soviet arms buildups. In contemporary politics they believe "soft power" will be the answer to every international conflict. In domestic affairs they commend compassion without accountability.

All this is not to say that Christian love has no relevance to public life. Rather, it operates as both motivation and ideal in the Christian life, which creatively integrates the twofold reign of God. But expressing agape love is no simple matter; it is indirectly related to the norms that govern political and economic life. As Niebuhr has it, agape love judges all lesser efforts, serves as a goad to higher achievement, helps discriminate among options, and is a source for repentance and humility.[21] Further, such love can never be triumphant in history, nor can it be totally defeated. It is instructive to remember that the one person who did live fully out of agape love ended on a cross, crucified by the best and brightest of the time.

The Paradox of Human Nature and History

"Whatever your heart fastens to, that is your god," said Luther. From the paradoxical vision's perspective, humans are irretrievably committed to finding something other than God to which to fasten their hearts. This analysis of inescapable sin, however, is not so simple. We do not fasten to the non-alluring and worthless things of the world. On the contrary, we fasten to the things that really tempt. Highest among our temptations is devotion to ourselves. We are obsessed with ourselves and make ourselves the center of the universe. Our attention to ourselves crowds out everything else except those things we want in order to feed the image of ourselves we have concocted. This obsession may be one of willful assertion or self-pitying negation, but in either case it makes a mockery of the divine command "to love the LORD your God with all your heart and with all your soul and with all your mind" (Matt. 22:37). We love ourselves, or those things that can lend ourselves some semblance of importance and immortality.

---

21. Reinhold Niebuhr, *An Interpretation of Christian Ethics*, 62ff.

Thus, none are good. All human actions are tainted with the effect of our sin, even those performed by Christians. We can never be completely free of the Old Adam in this life. This Augustinian view of human nature extends to human action in society. Human sin is particularly magnified and unrestrained in the life and action of groups. It is especially expressed in collective situations.

Yet, humans are not dirt. Even in their fallen state they possess qualities of their creation in the image of God. There is an essential self that longs for wholeness and completion, though it cannot heal or complete itself. This essential self has capacities for moral reason, for what Luther called "civil righteousness." Humans have capacities for justice.

Moreover, humans never lose their dignity in God's eyes. They are beloved for what God has made them to be, not what they have made of themselves. They are infinitely valuable because they have been given a destiny in their creation and have been redeemed by the work of Christ. They can refuse that destiny and that redemption, but they can never lose the "alien dignity" that their creation and redemption bestows on them.

Humans find themselves in a paradoxical predicament. Created and redeemed by God, they are exalted individuals. They have a capacity for freedom, love, and justice. Yet they use their freedom to fasten to lesser things, creating a hell for themselves, their fellow human beings, and the world around them. They are a paradox of good and evil, manufacturing idols of the good things they are given. And they cannot solve this predicament on their own.

Thus, the paradox of human nature creates the paradox of human history. "History cumulates, rather than solves, the essential problems of human history," wrote Niebuhr.[22] The fulfillment and perfection of history are not ours to grasp; we cannot be gods in history. Indeed, as we have mentioned, great evil is done by those who try to complete history by their own powers.

Rather, it is up to God to bring history to an end (its *finis*) and to fulfill its purpose (its *telos*). God has given us an anticipation of the kingdom in Christ and will bring it to fullness in his own time and by his will. We are in an interim time of struggle between Christ's first coming and the second.

---

22. Reinhold Niebuhr, *The Nature and Destiny of Man, Vol. II*, 2nd ed. (New York: Charles Scribner's Sons, 1949), 318.

Given that scenario, we are freed from trying to manage history according to great schemes. Rather, we must strive for relative gains and wait on God. We must work for reform without cynicism's paralysis or idealism's false hope. Thus, the Lutheran vision leads to a nonutopian view of history that yet is not cynical. It expects neither too much of history nor too little.

The "Lutheran attitude" reflected in these four main themes provides a wholesome nudge to an American Christianity that is all too prone to identify promising human achievements as the salvation of God, to make the church into anything but the proclaimer of the gospel, to apply directly the "gospel ethic" to the power struggles of the world, and to hope for the intractabilities of individual and corporate human sin to be overcome by some sanctified human effort.

Implications for Practical Engagement

Indirect Approaches

Practically considered, the Lutheran vision also moves toward indirect ways of connecting the church to the public world. The second theme particularly calls the church to the task of nourishing and sustaining the callings of lay Christians as they move from the church into the world. If the church is really the church, it will effect an internal "revolution of the heart" among its laity that will indeed affect the world. The church will form the hearts and minds of laity, who will then enter all the complex interstices of the public world that are unreachable by the direct efforts of the church.

Perhaps the most effective public Christian witness of the next century will be done by laypeople who have been formed powerfully in the church and then are able to connect their Christian formation with the learning and activity of their secular callings. Christian senators in legislatures have far more political impact than either church statements or advocacy centers. Christian professors in universities have more effect in shaping the "normal sciences of the day" than the resource materials cranked out by church and society bureaucracies. Christian doctors will have more voice in shaping a humane medicine than theological ethicists in seminaries.

Christian laypersons, however, will also need help and encouragement in connecting their Christian convictions to their public lives. The church must spend far more time in playing another indirect role, that of a mediating institution. It must not only form the hearts and minds of its laity, but also help laity to connect the social teachings of the church with their public lives by providing contexts in which those connections can be self-consciously made. The Lay Academies of Europe were models in this regard, though they seem now to be succumbing to the temptation of the activist American churches: they are more and more letting the society know "where they stand." But if the church is to take seriously its role to mediate its tradition to the challenges of the modern world through the lives of its laity, it will have to give more attention to that task and resist the temptation to pronounce and act on everything in sight.

Moreover, the church must also show more courage and resolution with regard to its related institutions. American Lutherans continued the tradition of their European forebears by creating many charitable institutions. Each Lutheran church had and continues to have many of these sorts of institutions, but the temptation as time goes on is to allow their Christian character to diminish. If the church cannot insist that its vision makes a margin of difference in the life of its schools, colleges, homes, camps, and hospitals, it really has very little business trying to shape and transform the larger public world. The church must begin shaping a "counter society" in its own institutions. Such integrity and courage will be much more persuasive to the broader society than any amount of lecturing.

Direct Approaches

These indirect ways of connecting the church to public life do not preclude more direct ways. There is still room for judicious and authoritative social statements and letters of counsel, and even room for direct action, advocacy, socially responsible investing, and the like. But each of these instances strains the unity and catholicity of the church by precipitating disagreements on issues rarely central to its main task. A wise church will hesitate to engage in direct action.

Christian Care for the Poor: A Case Study

How might the approach outlined above apply to contemporary public policy debates? Consider, for example, ways in which the Lutheran tradition suggests that Christians ought to care for the poor.

Concern for the poor within and outside Israel's covenant community, the requirement to do justice and give alms, the many parables of Jesus concerning care for the poor, his identification with the poor, and the long history of charity in the Christian church (beginning with Paul's gathering of money for the poor of the Jerusalem church, as related in Acts 20:1–5) leave little doubt about the Christian obligation to care for the poor. There are even parables of judgment for those who do not care for the poor: the parable of the Rich Man and Lazarus (Luke 16: 19–31) as well as that of the Last Judgment (Matt. 24:31–46).

In Reformation times, Luther echoed these biblical and historical imperatives: "There is no greater worship or service of God than Christian love which helps and serves the needy."[23] In the "Defense of the Augsburg Confession" in the *Book of Concord*, the authoritative collection of Lutheran confessional documents, we also find strong concern for the poor:

> You ought to see the tears of the poor, and hear the pitiable complaints of many good men, which God undoubtedly considers and regards, to whom one day you will render an account of your stewardship.[24]

Such concern is based theologically on two great convictions: that every human is created in the image of God, and that Jesus died for all sinners. Both convictions bestow on every individual immeasurable worth. This Christian affirmation became so insistent in the Christian West that it became the center of political life, as the political philosopher Glenn Tinder argued in his famous essay "Can We Be Good Without God?" He wrote, "It is hardly too much to say that the idea of the exalted individual is the spiritual center of Western politics."[25]

---

23. Martin Luther, *Luther's Works* (Philadelphia: Fortress Press), 45: 172–73.

24. Article XXVIII (XIV): Of Ecclesial Power, 3.

25. Glenn Tinder, "Can We Be Good Without God?" in *The Atlantic Monthly* (December 1989), 76. Tinder argues that the Christian doctrines of creation and redemption make each individual "exalted," even though "fallen."

By that, Tinder meant that governments have been obligated to treat individuals with care by respecting their rights, to treat them equally before the law, and to include all within the orbit of their justice.

But before these theological convictions gained political relevance, they fueled Christian concern for the poor both within and outside the church. The two central Christian theological convictions issued in action. Faith that they were true became active in love for the poor. That love has certain qualities — qualities that are reflections of the *agape* love of God in Christ for all humans. The love that sets us free in the gospel at the same time calls us to reflect that love in lives of service and care for others. Agape love reaches out to the needy without regard for return; it is other-regarding love. Agape love includes all; it has a universal thrust.

Paradoxically, however, agape love strategically aims at those who need it most — the lost, last, and least. It is steadfast; it is utterly reliable. Further, it aims at restoring the beloved to health and mutuality; it does not aim at keeping the beloved dependent. (All of these qualities of love are taught by our Lord in the parable of the Good Samaritan, Luke 10:25–27.) Agape love is forgiving; it is willing to break the cycle of endless hurt and recrimination in a world of fractured relationships. (This quality is taught powerfully in the parable of the Prodigal Son, Luke 15:11–32.) Finally, agape love appears as sacrificial love in a fallen world that does not reward, but rather punishes it, the crucifixion of Jesus being the prime example.

Yet, this expression of Christian love toward the needy is complicated by the fact that each individual is not only "exalted," but also "fallen." The poor are sinners too.[26] Even in personal relationships, the expression of love for the poor is shaped by prudence. What indeed will be helpful to the needy person? What will restore them to health and independence? Such concerns multiply exponentially when the expression of love in personal relationships is expanded to the expression of justice in social life. Though loving the poor neighbor is sometimes a simple and spontaneous thing, it is often not so. Careful thought must

---

26. It is important to note that those who care for the poor and the poor themselves are likewise sinful human beings. Both are free moral agents and have the capacity for both positive and negative actions. The poor are not simply objects of our care; they are subjects as well and must be treated that way if positive outcomes are to be realized.

be the companion of love if it is not to become an exercise in sentimentality or worse.

Another complicating factor surrounds these questions: Who are the poor, and why are they poor? What income — or lack of income — defines the poor? Are the poor helpless victims of external circumstances they cannot control? Are they poor because they lack crucial capacities that enable them to contribute to the economy? Are they poor because they are improvident or lazy? The answer to each question conditions how we treat them, not only in our personal relations with them, but especially in impersonal, corporate relationships that aim at justice.

In spite of these complications, we Christians are called to love the neighbor, especially the poor. We are to reflect God's agape love for all, both near and far. What, then, are the ways that we express such love?

The most important way we love the poor is to share the gospel with them and to invite them into the life of the church. These actions demonstrate our care for their eternal destinies. In addition, these evangelical approaches convey the love of God and the support of the Christian community to the poor in concrete, earthly ways. As we share and demonstrate the gospel — through the teaching and support of the church — we also offer purpose and hope to lives that are often bereft of such goods. Faith and community support are precious gifts that we are called to offer the poor.

Care for the Poor Through the Laity: The Indirect Role of the Church

Further, when our churches are alive and effective, we form our members in the virtues of love and justice.[27] Those members then express their care for the poor in manifold ways. They volunteer their time in food pantries and kitchens, clothes closets, hospitality networks, home-building organizations, and countless other voluntary associations dedicated to alleviating the plight of the poor. They give their money to innumerable agencies — both large and small — that care for the poor. They organize voluntary associations to address newly discovered needs of the poor. Sometimes they offer poor families within their parishes

---

27. This formation is carried out in manifold ways: in teaching and learning, worship and prayer, and the provision of many opportunities for direct involvement in charitable and justice-seeking practices, both inside and outside the church. While the clergy cannot be involved in all this activity, they are crucial in seeing that it is carried out.

not only support and aid, but also training in the disciplines that enable them to become independent.[28] Some Christians are motivated to organize or participate in advocacy organizations that press for changes in public policy. As citizens they vote for candidates who they think will initiate or support policies on behalf of the poor. Some will even become candidates themselves.

This indirect effect of our church through its laity on behalf of the poor is enormous in both size and impact. Some of it is the product of individual action, but much of it flows through the voluntary associations so characteristic of American life. It is often effective because it grapples with the plight of the poor in concrete and near-at-hand ways. Prudence and love work together. Some of the action aims at legislating policies that not only alleviate the conditions of the poor, but also address the underlying conditions that increase poverty. In this civic exercise Christians of good will and intelligence often agree about the goals of policy but disagree about the means.

The Direct Role of the Church

Although the church's most lasting and pervasive care for the poor is done indirectly through its proclamation of the gospel as well as through the work of the laity and their voluntary associations, there are good reasons for direct efforts by the church as an institution. Challenges of helping the poor often go beyond individual action, so the church throughout history has organized its own charitable institutions — hospitals, homes for the poor and elderly, orphanages, and many other organizations to alleviate poverty.[29] Such institutions continue to be important institutional vehicles for Christian care for the poor. The best of them assuage the poverty of not only the body, but also of the soul.

---

28. One thinks here of the great work of John Wesley's Methodists in the Victorian Era, in which the degraded poor were transformed into good Christians and citizens. See Gertrude Himmelfarb's *Marriage and Morals Among the Victorians* (New York: Alfred A. Knopf, 1986).

29. Luther recommended that each German town develop a common chest that would provide interest-free loans to the poor, who would pledge to repay them. This development went beyond individual charity to an institutional approach. Soon there were scores of "inner mission" institutions in the Lutheran lands. This charitable impulse continued and flourished in America as Lutheran churches founded a profusion of such organizations. American Lutherans had their William Passavant (1821–94), a remarkable founder of charitable institutions, who inspired many others to take up the cause.

Further, churches have felt obliged to offer social statements that call attention to the plight of the poor, analyze the causes of poverty, and call for public policies that address those causes. Such efforts inevitably get into public debates in which the church has no special expertise. Good public policy is notoriously difficult to craft, since it has to be attentive to unintended effects as well as account for proper incentives and disincentives. Such legislation almost always involves compromises and uncertainties. Moreover, the movement from core Christian moral convictions to policy involves a number of steps at which Christians often diverge. There are few, if any, straight lines from that core to specific public policy. Given such complexities, it is best for our church forcefully to call attention to the problems of the poor and insist on public action to alleviate them rather than advocate particular public policies.

However, there are some occasions when the church simply has to cry out a prophetic "no" when public policies actively and plainly oppress or violate the dignity of the poor. In those cases the church must not only object to such policies, but resist them.[30]

Finally, churches have often engaged in the exercise of political power to affect policy on behalf of the poor. They organize advocacy offices in the midst of state and national governments. In these softer forms of exercising power, they exhort their members to apply pressure to their political representatives to promote specific public policies that they consider just-making. In harder forms they use boycotts and divestment strategies. Such efforts should be employed very carefully and infrequently, lest the church damage its universal and transcendent message by involving itself too deeply in coercive and partisan strategies.

In summary, there is little question that we Christians are called to care for the poor. God has commanded such care in his Law and has given us freedom in the Gospel to love the poor neighbor. Our first and most important service to the poor is the sharing of the gospel and the life of the church with them. Further, we are called to care for the poor in many other ways in our personal, associational, and civic lives.

---

30. Our national history has had some horrific instances of mistreatment of the poor that were not—but should have been—protested by the church. Sterilization of the mentally challenged, medical experiments on poor people without their consent, the targeting of poor communities for promoting abortion services, and unjust loan policies foisted on the credit-worthy poor are some examples.

Our church can best motivate us to take up these callings by a vigorous ministry of Word and Sacrament, of worship and teaching, of modeling and practicing.

Such a rich ministry will form in us the virtues of love and justice, which, when expressed in our callings, become the most effective way that we care for the poor. Yet, the church also has an institutional role in direct care and advocacy for the poor, a role that is best carried out by those who are already formed in those virtues.

Conclusion

The perennial themes in the Lutheran vision provide an important construal of the public role of religion. This does not mean it has been complete in either theory or practice. This Lutheran account has been immeasurably enriched by its interaction with the other visions presented in this volume. Perhaps as we continue to interact through history, our convergences might finally overcome our divergences and we can offer a more powerful and unified Christian witness, as well as move toward the unity for which Christ so fervently prayed.

AN ANABAPTIST (SEPARATIONIST) RESPONSE

THOMAS W. HEILKE

It would defy Christian charity to offer a critical response to Professor Benne's introductory pages. He rightly, in my opinion, points to several shortcomings in the "checkered history" of Lutheran engagement with the public and political spheres. It is difficult not to agree that much of this history is the direct consequence of Lutheran (and especially Martin Luther's) political theology. Its nadir was surely the widespread acquiescence and even collusion of the German Lutheran churches with the National Socialist regime, 1933–45. There were also, however, many stories of heroic resistance, including not only the somewhat ambivalent story of Dietrich Bonhoeffer,[31] but others that may accord more nearly with Anabaptist sensibilities.[32]

The recent role of the Lutheran churches in protests and other actions against the now-defunct regime of the German Democratic Republic should likewise not be forgotten. Anabaptist principles of non-resistance notwithstanding, they do point to ways in which Lutherans and Lutheran churches have participated in politics beyond conservative quietism and acquiescence or purely reactionary clerical responses as in Scandinavia. Benne's efforts to rehabilitate Luther's political thought along the lines of Niebuhrian realism, however, raise concerns.

Benne makes several claims with which most Anabaptists would agree in general principle. That the church should be a "counter society" is one. That Christians can and should witness to the political authorities or to the state is another. That church-based institutions such as "schools, colleges, homes, camps, and hospitals" deserve Christian support is a third. Finally, few contemporary Anabaptists would take issue with some version of the Protestant emphasis on justification by faith.

---

31. James Wm. McClendon Jr., *Systematic Theology: Ethics* (Nashville: Abingdon Press, 1986), 187–208, 210.

32. Johannes Schlingensiepen, *Widerstand und verborgene Schuld: Erinnerungen an den Kampf der Bekennenden Kirche in Barmen* (Wuppertal: Jugenddienst-Verlag, 1976).

Here also the differences begin. Various Reformation-era Anabaptist groups expressed this theological position in distinct ways, but rarely in the forensic manner of their Lutheran contemporaries and always with an emphasis on the need to follow "Jesus' nonviolent way amidst savage persecution."[33] Anabaptists understood the living out of one's salvation in fear and trembling to be communal and missional.[34] The political consequence was that whatever a "two kingdoms" theology might mean, it did not imply that Christians participated in inflicting violence and suffering on others. Thus, a doctrine of justification that is not entwined with or rooted in an account of the life of Jesus and its ethical implications is abstract and incomplete.[35]

Christians cannot adhere to the ethical teachings of the Sermon on the Mount and also ignore them, depending on the circumstances. "The lengthy discussions of good works and righteous character, in justification discussions both past and present, hardly mention the kinds of works and character involved. Anabaptists ask: What shape does the justified life take?"[36] Justification, moreover — here, a critique particularly of Protestant accounts — should surely have not merely individual but also "social, perhaps even cosmic, dimensions."[37]

Other immediately obvious differences between Anabaptists and Lutheran understandings may or may not have implications for political thought. The distinction between "laity" and "clergy," although attenuated by Luther's doctrine of the priesthood of all believers, is alien to Anabaptists, as is the attendant notion of "calling," which is inclined to baptize wholesale the secular order. Among these many areas of disagreements, I will focus on one.

Benne argues strongly that the best hope for a Lutheran rehabilitation with regard to political involvement should take its direction from the "Christian realism" of Reinhold Niebuhr. Niebuhr was almost

---

33. Thomas N. Finger, *A Contemporary Anabaptist Theology: Biblical, Historical, Constructive* (Downers Grove, IL: InterVarsity Press, 2004), 122.

34. Ibid., 130–32.

35. Ibid., 137, 142.

36. Ibid., 137. On early Protestant individualism, see my "Friendship in the Civic Order: A Reformation Absence," in John von Heyking and Richard G. Avramenko, eds., *Friendship and Politics: Essays in Political Thought* (Notre Dame: Notre Dame University Press, 2008), 163–93.

37. Finger, *A Contemporary Anabaptist Theology*, 137; cf. McClendon, *Systematic Theology: Ethics*, 62–67.

certainly the theologian most important in the twentieth century for making the case — persuasive even to many Mennonites and other Anabaptists — that nonresistance is the only Christianly consistent form of pacifism, but that it simultaneously renders its proponents socially and especially politically irrelevant.[38]

Niebuhr was ideologically a (chastened) classical liberal whose theology cannot be understood without grasping the genealogy of his movement away from his early liberal pacifism into the classical liberal reasoning of political realism.[39] While Niebuhr rightly and wisely pointed out that the morality of groups tends to create circumstances in which the egotism of individuals in society is not dampened, but collectively amplified, he did not make the further Anabaptist move of asking: How does this insight help us to understand what is church and how to be church? The question did not penetrate his Protestant/American liberal individualism. It is unclear to me how, lacking a strong ecclesiology in the Baptist sense, Benne's project can succeed to become anything more than the "baptized paganism" about which Luther himself had fretted.

Space precludes an elaboration of this argument; I will provide one or two starting points and invite readers to investigate further on their own. In his review of the relationship between church and nation in Western history, Paul Peachey notes a persistent confusion among American theologians, namely,

> the fact *that in the churches of America the Christian ethical imperative has been so fully assimilated to the national ethos that the majority of church people can scarcely distinguish the two and, in time of national crisis, do indeed mistake the "logic" of the latter for the former.*[40]

Niebuhr was among that majority; in his political theology he "understood himself to be making a decisive break with his social gospel forebears,... [but] continued to accept the social gospel's most

---

38. John Howard Yoder, *Christian Attitudes to War, Peace and Revolution: A Companion to Bainton* (Goshen, IN: Goshen Biblical Seminary, 1983), 360. On the error of imputing necessary "withdrawal" to Anabaptist pacifism, see John Howard Yoder, *The Priestly Kingdom: Social Ethics as Gospel* (Notre Dame: University of Notre Dame Press, 1984), 34, 61, 99.

39. See Yoder, *Christian Attitudes to War, Peace and Revolution*, 345, 349, 356.

40. Paul Peachey, "Church and Nation in Western History," in Paul Peachey, ed., *Biblical Realism Confronts the Nation* (Scottdale, PA: Herald Press, 1963), 13 (italics in original).

important theological and social presuppositions." Most importantly, he assumed that the task of Christian ethics was to formulate the means for Christians to serve their societies, particularly American society, "... [and] he never questioned that Christianity has a peculiar relationship to democracy ... [nor that] the subject of Christian ethics was America."[41]

In response to international relations—a dimension of politics about which the chapters in this book have been silent—Niebuhr adopted a more or less classical realist position in which, to my mind, any meaningfully *Christian* contribution essentially disappears. Accordingly, Niebuhr had a profound, but not Christian influence on several major American realist thinkers, and various opposing sides in American foreign policy debates have often claimed his arguments. I know of no *political* or *anthropological* arguments in either *Moral Man and Immoral Society* or *The Nature and Destiny of Man* that cannot be put in the mouth of any number of pagan authors.

The reason for this evaluation appears to be that there are no necessary relationships between Niebuhr's theological and ethical positions.[42] Even on the domestic side, one can wonder if "Niebuhr's views prevailed for no other reason than that they were more in accord with the changing social and religious situation in America" and if, under his tutelage and "in the hope of securing societal good, the task of Christian ethics thus became the attempt to develop social strategies that people of goodwill could adopt even though they differed religiously and morally."[43] This approach is, of course, inadequate from an Anabaptist perspective: while cross-cultural communication is always possible, Christian social ethics emerges from an understanding of the lordship of Christ that is neither morally nor religiously indifferent.

---

41. Stanley Hauerwas, "On Keeping Theological Ethics Theological," in John Berkman and Michael Cartwright, eds., *The Hauerwas Reader* (Durham, NC: Duke University Press, 2001), 59–60.

42. Ibid., 60.

43. Ibid., 61.

A BLACK CHURCH (PROPHETIC) RESPONSE

BRUCE L. FIELDS

Since the Lutheran Reformation began in 1517, the forging of its theology for political engagement has been taking place between two emphases. According to certain observations by Benne, the emphases can be identified through these conflated statements:

> If the most important event that ever happened in human history is the coming of Christ, then the essential and unique mission of the church from the point of view of the paradoxical vision is its calling by God to proclaim that gospel in word and sacrament.... But the church is not primarily a political actor, a social transformer, or an aggressive interest group (p. 69).

Before developing his own view on the Lutheran navigation between these two emphases, Benne also discusses the interpretation of the Lutheran tradition and its relationship with the political sphere as offered by Ernst Troeltsch and H. Richard Niebuhr. Troeltsch, for example, held that Lutheran "interior spirituality" enabled the church to capitulate to the existing dominant authority (p. 61). Niebuhr voiced a similar conclusion, identifying the Lutheran tendency "toward both antinomianism in personal ethics and passivity in social and political ethics" (p. 61). Benne acknowledges a "checkered history" (p. 61) through such examples as the Peasant's Revolt (1524–25) and, in the United States, the split in the Lutheran church during the Civil War (p. 62), but he still seeks to establish certain forms of more activistic involvement in the social, political realm on the part of the Lutheran church.

I want to identify selectively some Lutheran characteristics that enable Benne to make his case before I offer some comments and questions.

Unlike the beginnings of Anabaptist and Black church traditions, the Lutheran church did enjoy some structural protection by the state, which set a tone for particular responses to involvement with government in certain places at certain times. Having noted this, however, Benne focuses on four enduring themes that he sees as contributing to a Lutheran vision of political involvement rather than to concrete injunctions. With these themes the Black church could generally resonate.

First, there must be an insistence on maintaining a distinction between what God does in Christ to facilitate salvation and what human beings can accomplish in the realm of time and space. There is no human capacity for salvation through human effort no matter how noble or beneficial to others.

Second, as alluded to above, the purpose of the church is the proclamation of the gospel. Benne, wisely, reminds those in the church seeking transformation in society that they may run the risk of losing their zeal for the gospel (p. 69). This would certainly short-circuit any authentic hope of transformation of people and societal structures.

Third, there is an insistence that God rules the world in two ways. The Law rules in the world, and the gospel is to rule the church. Though the Law is not salvific, with the good use of reason "and the benefit of experience" (p. 70) it can help strengthen the human community. Christians must continually remind themselves that the nature of the two and the realms where they should be implemented are unique and different. These distinctives must be maintained.

The final enduring theme has its own unique thrust, but also marks a transition to some additional responses. Benne's section on the "Paradox of Human Nature and History" (p. 73) was thoroughly steeped in wisdom. The human tendency is to make ourselves the center of the universe and negate the command to "love the Lord your God with all your heart and all your soul and with all your mind" (Matt. 22:37). I could not express better than he has the paradox of human good and evil:

> They have a capacity for freedom, love, and justice. Yet, they use their freedom to fasten to lesser things, creating a hell for themselves, their fellow human beings, and the world around them. They are a paradox of good and evil, manufacturing idols of the good things they are given. And they cannot solve this predicament on their own (p. 74).

This wisdom is biblically and theologically sound. For example, Paul never denounces creation itself in Romans 1:18ff. The problem is human suppression of true knowledge of God (v. 18). Paul further makes it plain in various sections of Romans that we fallen humans could not save ourselves (e.g., Rom. 5:18–21).

Three small matters remain to address in closing. First, it would have been helpful if Benne had mentioned a specific example of a person or a movement that would entertain the possibility of salvation achieved before God as a result of efforts toward a just transformation of society. For instance, might a sacramental understanding of the poor as derived from the thought of certain liberation theologians be in view? Or is his critique intended to be even more wide-ranging?

Second, it is encouraging that he entertains the possibility of occasions for a prophetic "no" to public policies that inevitably dehumanize people (p. 81). The Black church tradition would say, "Amen!" What is not clear is whether the Lutheran tradition as set forth provides grounds for such a strong response even from a theoretical perspective. Is Benne consistent with the tradition as practiced beyond the example of Martin Luther himself?

Finally, in continuity with my response to the other traditions represented in this work, I raise the question of whether race and ethnicity affected the development, or lack thereof, of the Lutheran tradition over time. I know that in many theological discussions, matters such as race, ethnicity, or class do not enter in. It is refreshing to note Benne's recognition of the impact of the Scandinavian tradition on political engagement. Such discussions, however, are not always given appropriate attention, or at least not every possible racial or ethnic stream gets such a hearing.

A REFORMED (TRANSFORMATIONIST) RESPONSE

JAMES K.A. SMITH

As common heirs of the Reformation impulse, one would expect lots of commonality between the Lutheran and Reformed views. But while there is considerable overlap in matters of soteriology (the doctrine of salvation) and even ecclesiology (matters of the church and worship), it is striking to note how different the political visions of the Reformation could be. The Reformation in Germany and Scandinavia generated different regimes — and different rationales — than those that emerged in Geneva and the "low countries" (the Netherlands, parts of Belgium).

Nonetheless, there is much agreement between Lutheran and Reformed traditions. Both honor and encourage the political vocations of the laity. Both "desacralize" and hence relativize the political, countering any sort of "Pelagian" progressivism (what Benne calls "soft utopianism") that is confident in human effort to bring about the kingdom.[44] Both exhibit a "realism" about human nature and the tragic fallenness of the human condition. This conviction about human depravity tempers expectations and generates policy with eyes wide open.

Any of us who are heirs to multifaceted historical traditions should appreciate Benne's honesty about the mixed inheritance of the Lutheran legacy. In many ways, he's already done the work of a critical respondent in his essay. Nonetheless, in a way that should make a Lutheran happy, let me discharge the responsibility of my station and note points of disagreement — and hence my continued preference for the Reformed view.

---

44. This sort of social Pelagianism is a very live temptation for evangelical activists today. For a helpful and practical antidote, see Tyler Wigg-Stevenson, *The World Is Not Ours to Save: Finding the Freedom to Do Good* (Downers Grove, IL: InterVarsity Press, 2013).

My reservations revolve around the two-kingdoms doctrine or the notion of the "two-fold rule of God."[45] On this account, there is a marked contrast, even antithesis, between Law and Gospel, nature and grace, politics and salvation. Politics and government are instruments of God's rule via the Law; the church and her proclamation of the Gospel is the instrument of God's rule via grace. Grace and gospel are proclaimed via the special revelation of the Word of God; the norms of God's law can be discerned by reason (and which, supposedly, remains universally available to all, despite the fall). The kingdom of God is governed by grace; the kingdom of this world is still governed—and governed by God—but according to the law.[46]

Calvinists have long worried about an undercurrent of antinomianism here—a view that is anti-law (anti-*nomos*), denigrating law *per se* as a remedial reality, a necessary evil. In contrast, the Reformed tradition, while recognizing the salvific limits of the law, also sees the law as itself a gift even for the redeemed, a gracious way that God channels us toward our own good.[47] Rather than seeing law and grace as fundamentally in tension, the Calvinist sees even the law as functioning within the economy of God's grace. This makes a difference for how we approach the juridical realm of politics, and it also changes what we might *hope* for from government and policy.

Perhaps even more pertinently, my suspicions about the two-kingdoms doctrine parallel my concern about the Anabaptist view: Both seem to carve out the political as a realm that is somehow immune

---

45. I think one could note an unwitting parallel between Anabaptists and Lutherans on this point. Anabaptists also work with something of a "two-kingdoms" theology whereby "the world" (including politics and government) is part of the "kingdom of this world," whereas the body of Christ, the church, is the kingdom of God. These are two distinct *and competing* kingdoms, which is why Christians must not implicate themselves in the "worldly" kingdom of politics. Lutherans make the same distinction, but see the "worldly" kingdom of government and politics as *also* under the reign of God (per Romans 13). In this sense, one could say the Reformed view is a *mono*-kingdom view.

46. Thus I'm puzzled as to why Benne, at the end of his essay, thinks "Christian formation" really has any bearing on laypeople's political vocations. I would think Christian formation is informed by the Gospel, whereas their work as agents of government and law is governed by a different order. Indeed, wouldn't it be something of a category mistake, on Lutheran terms, to think *agape* has any relevance to politics? Benne's closing counsel seems inconsistent with his earlier distinction between Law and Gospel.

47. For a parallel discussion, see N.T. Wright's discussion of law in *Justification: God's Plan and Paul's Vision* (Downers Grove, IL: InterVarsity Press, 2009), 246–47.

to grace and shielded from the impact of the gospel.[48] And like the Anabaptist view, the Lutheran view seems to treat the realm of politics and government as a kind of static given, something that is not only *de facto* but even *de jure* void of grace. Government is a Law-realm, not a Gospel-realm, for Lutherans.

In contrast, because of the Reformed understanding of the creation- and culture-wide *scope* of redemption (coupled with an appreciation of how deeply contingent and "made" the political realm is), we can imagine even the governments of this world being reshaped and renewed by the ascended King upon whose shoulders the government will rest (Isa. 9:6). We can imagine even our laws being Gospel-ed precisely because Christ is reconciling *all* things to himself. That is not a recipe for baptizing the status quo; nor is it a guarantee. We realize the limits of any regime change prior to the advent of Christ's coming kingdom, which is why we pray daily, "Thy kingdom come." But in the meantime we can labor in the vineyard of government and politics and policy, working and praying for foretastes that are teasers of justice that rolls down like water, and righteousness like an ever-flowing stream (Amos 5:24).

---

48. There is also a point of *epistemological* difference here. The Lutheran two-kingdoms view depends on a confidence that the norms of good government can be known by "reason," which is allegedly universal and shared by all. In contrast, the Reformed tradition, rooted in a reading of Romans 1:18–31 and other passages, has emphasized the effects of sin on reason itself (what Alvin Plantinga and others describe as the "noetic effects of sin"), thus undermining any confidence in universal epistemic insight into God's norms for creation. For a relevant discussion, see Alvin Plantinga, "The Reformed Objection to Natural Theology," *Proceedings of the American Catholic Philosophical Association* 54 (1980): 49–63.

J. BRIAN BENESTAD

The essential mission of the church, Robert Benne argues, is to answer God's call to proclaim the gospel of Jesus Christ in word and sacrament so that all people may attain eternal salvation. It follows, then, that the church "is not primarily a political actor, a social transformer, or an aggressive interest group" (p. 69). If the church focuses on its essential mission, Benne believes that "the most effective public Christian witness of the next century will be done by laypeople who have been formed powerfully in the church and then are able to connect their Christian formation with the learning and activity of their secular callings" (p. 75). Otherwise stated, when the church successfully focuses primarily on its salvific mission in all its institutions, then its members, highly educated and formed in the faith, have the greatest chance of shaping and transforming the public square by living every aspect of their lives as serious Christians.

In addition to the giving of alms by individual church members, the church itself as an institution offers valuable help to the poor by establishing hospitals, homes for the elderly and the poor, and other similar organizations. Lutheran churches also think it is their duty to issue statements on matters pertaining to the life of the poor, including a call for specific public policies. Benne's judgment is that the Lutheran church should be hesitant to endorse specific policies about which reasonable Lutherans can disagree. He emphasizes that the church has no specific expertise in crafting specific public policies to address complex political issues. Given this fact, "it is best for our church forcefully to call attention to the problems of the poor and insist on public action to alleviate them rather than to advocate particular public policies" (p. 81).

There is one exception to this wise recommendation. Sometimes the church must issue a "prophetic 'no'" followed by appropriate action to oppose policies that oppress or demean the poor such as "unjust loan policies foisted on the credit-worthy poor" and "the targeting of poor communities for promoting abortion services" (p. 81, n30).

Finally, Benne argues that Lutheran churches should be very wary about exercising political power on behalf of various causes. Such action, he argues, should be careful and infrequent, "lest the church damage its universal and transcendent message by involving itself too deeply in coercive and partisan strategies" (p. 81). As one might expect, Benne concludes, "Our church can best motivate us to take up these callings by a vigorous ministry of Word and Sacrament, of worship and teaching, of modeling and practicing" (p. 82).

The best understanding of Catholic social teaching requires the Catholic Church to exercise the same kind of restraint and the same level of involvement recommended by Benne. However, there are mistaken interpretations of Catholic social teaching that promote heavy engagement of the institutional church in crafting debatable public policies to help the poor and do other things as well. When this kind of action becomes the priority, the poor are less well served as are other causes—and the credibility of the church is diminished as well!

The differences between the Lutheran and Catholic visions of religion in the political order begin to emerge by reflecting on the four central themes of the Lutheran vision: (1) "a sharp distinction between salvation offered by God in Christ and all human efforts" to live in accordance with God's will (p. 67); (2) following from the first theme, the focus of the church on the gospel of salvation rather than political reform; (3) "the twofold rule of God through Law and Gospel"; and (4) the paradox that good and bad are ever-present in human nature and history.

The first two themes, properly interpreted, protect Lutherans from seeking salvation through political action rather than through Jesus Christ, or from ascribing redemptive significance to such things as environmental movements, or from turning the church into a humanitarian institution rather than the messenger of salvation. These are laudable goals shared by the Catholic Church.

A Catholic approach, however, would not draw such a sharp distinction between the gift of salvation and human effort. Man's free will accepts the gift of salvation by cultivating the desire to receive what God is offering in Jesus Christ and by responding in deed. This cultivation of desire to receive God's gift and subsequent action in the world would necessarily promote some transformation in the culture. A Catholic approach would, furthermore, not so sharply distinguish the church's mission to bring the gospel message from its work to make known its social teaching.

When he was still a cardinal, Joseph Ratzinger (Pope Benedict XVI) wrote the following in a church document: "The church's social teaching is born of the encounter of the gospel message and of its demands (summarized in the supreme commandment of love of God and neighbor in justice) with the problems emanating from the life of society."[49] In one of his encyclicals Pope John Paul II wrote, "The teaching and spreading of her social doctrine are part of the church's evangelizing mission."[50]

Additional differences emerge in the interpretation of the third theme. Benne says that the Lutheran vision draws a sharp line between God's rule through the Gospel and through the Law. Between the two, Christians "are to observe a tentative, though not a final, dualism" (p. 71). Catholic teaching applauds the Lutheran effort to prevent Christians from making the Law into the Gospel by embracing hard and soft utopianism such as, respectively, Marxism and the elevation of ecological concerns far above what is reasonable. Catholics also agree with Benne's concern about the tendency to make the Gospel into Law. Otherwise stated, many wrongly try to forge a political and legal ethic on the basis of the Sermon on the Mount.

But Catholic teaching would never speak of a dualism between the Gospel and the Law. The realm of the Law needs to be touched by the Gospel so as to facilitate its acceptance. A French Jesuit theologian explains,

> The repercussions of political and social conditions in the lives of individuals can, in fact, render easier or more difficult the birth and development of religious life in humanity. It is therefore the duty of the Christian to create in this world conditions favorable to Christian life.[51]

---

49. Congregation for the Doctrine of the Faith, *Instruction on Christian Freedom and Liberation* (March 22, 1986), no. 72.

50. *Sollicitudo rei socialis (On Social Concern)*, no. 41.

51. Yves de Montcheuil, S.J., *Problèmes de Vie Spirituelle* (Paris: Éditions de L'Epi, 1961), 199.

Believing this to be true, Pope John Paul II often asked visiting bishops, "What have you done to change the culture?"

Another reason not to sharply separate the realms of Gospel and Law is to facilitate the cooperation between faith and reason for the sake of the public good. Pope Benedict XVI spoke about this in England's Westminster Hall on September 17, 2010. While reason theoretically has the ability to discern the relevant ethical principles for the governance of the temporal realm, it can go astray under the influence of culture or various ideologies. It was, after all, the "misuse of reason" that led to the slave trade and to the totalitarian regimes of the twentieth century.

As a remedy for the weakness of reason, Pope Benedict suggests that religion can help "purify" reason, making it a more fit instrument of ethical discernment. Here and in other contexts Pope Benedict makes the point that faith can correct the aberrations of reason, and reason can likewise help faith overcome its errors. "This is why I would suggest that the world of reason and the world of faith ... need one another and should not be afraid to enter into a profound and ongoing dialogue, for the good of our civilization."

Every civilization needs reason and faith working together for the sake of the common good.

THE BLACK CHURCH (PROPHETIC) VIEW

BRUCE L. FIELDS

Introduction

The Black church, like the church in general, always exists in the tension between the "already and the not yet." Because of the heritage of slavery, Jim Crow, and the pervasive impact of racism, the Black church has uniquely manifested this tension in the United States. The "already and the not yet" concerns the understanding that God has broken into human history in a unique way through Jesus Christ, bringing the offer of forgiveness of sin and a transformed existence.

Transformation "already" extends to social, cultural, political, and economic structures, so such convictions about the nature of "transformation" affect a church's self-understanding and subsequent ministry involvements. Concurrently, the "not yet" signifies elements of the kingdom that are still to be actualized beyond the realm of current space and time. This perspective may motivate some believers and churches to adopt a more passive stance toward structural transformation, focusing their hope in the totality of justice in the hereafter. Different people and different congregations in the historical Black church have manifested a leaning toward one emphasis or the other. Some have attempted a commitment to a balance.

Such a balance can be accomplished within the prophetic role of the Black church: speaking truth to those in power and speaking truth to God's people, the people in the Black church itself. In light of the "already and the not yet," messages of comfort, confrontation, correction, and confirmation must be preached. God is a God of *comfort*, especially for the oppressed, but his holiness calls for *confronting* evil wherever it is found, instituting *correction* even for his own people. Yet God also *confirms* his advocacy of those who seek him (Ps. 115:11). As a part of God's people, the Black church hears and proclaims each of these messages. All this proceeds, however, with the understanding that the "ideal," or the "perfect," will not be achieved in the realm of time and space.

The Black church has been a place of *comfort* for its people. They are reminded of the Lord's power to sustain people in life and transform other needed areas of life, bringing much-needed comfort. I can remember the times when as a child I would see my pastor and other church leaders doing seemingly menial work during the week, but on Sunday my pastor was "Reverend" George Brown, and the other leaders were addressed as "Deacon" Taylor or "Deacon" Mayo. Leadership in the Black church could *confront* evil on the structural level, whether it be for unfair housing practices or children in police custody being manipulated by detectives to incriminate themselves further. This practice, too, was a childhood memory, not so much for myself, but for family members and friends.

Correction was another perpetual ministry applied to the people in the church. There are attitudes and behaviors that are right or wrong, regardless, and these were the product of biblical chapter and verse. Confronting practices such as drunkenness, dishonesty in business practices, gossip, fornication, and adultery enjoyed regular appearances in sermons. The church was, nevertheless, the place of *confirmation*. God has his ways of blessing faithfulness. One of the most powerful messages I heard from my pastor-grandfather was, "Work hard in the classroom, work hard on the athletic field, and God will make a way for you." I have found his words to be confirmed.

Historical Development and Central Principles

The Black church was forged in a particular historical and sociocultural context that has profoundly shaped the tradition. To understand the Black church and its relation to politics, we must consider its development in the midst of suffering and oppression and the theological distinctives that emerged as a result.

Historical Background

The history of Blacks in America began much as it continued in the centuries that followed: as a story of oppression and perseverance. The first people of African descent were brought to Virginia in 1619 as indentured servants. As Lerone Bennett Jr. explains, the roots of slavery can be traced to the time when white "paupers, ne'er-do-wells, religious dissenters, waifs, prisoners and prostitutes"[1] were sent to the colonies as indentured servants. But the traders soon moved their focus away from Europe, as the emerging African slave trade offered greater commercial benefits:

> [Africans] were inexpensive: the same money that would buy an Irish or English servant for seven years would buy an African for life. They were visible: they could run, but they could not blend into the white crowd. Above all else, they were unprotected. And the supply, unlike the supply of Irishmen and Englishmen, seemed inexhaustible.[2]

As Bennett further documents, the movement toward laws of perpetual enslavement of people of African descent quickly developed in the North American colonies. Virginia and Maryland enacted laws during the 1660s forbidding intermarriage between Caucasians and Blacks while also setting the status of Black enslavement for life. "Under the new dispensation, which was adopted with minor modifications by other colonies, children born of African women were ruled bond or free, according to the status of the mother."[3]

Bennett observes a rationale for such practice that would prove to be of an insidious nature, namely, "religion."[4] The slaves were simply labeled as "heathen," offering justification for their need for "salvation" and humanization. To be "human" was to think and behave like the enslavers and the people who comprised their sociocultural settings. To convince slaveholders of the possibility of such humanization could be a hard sell, as Albert J. Raboteau records:

---

1. Lerone Bennett Jr., *Before the Mayflower: A History of Black America* (New York: Penguin, 1984), 35.
2. Ibid., 45.
3. Ibid. The history, of course, is much more complicated than presented here, but Bennett implies the pull of commerce as a factor in the emerging policy of Black enslavement.
4. Ibid., 46.

Repeatedly the clergy had to remind their charges that black people were equal to whites in the sight of God. Francis Le Jau, missionary to Goose Creek, South Carolina, reported in 1709 that "Many Masters can't be persuaded that Negroes and Indians are otherwise than Beasts, and use them like such," but "I endeavor to let them know better things."[5]

In its very founding, the United States institutionalized a subhuman view of African-Americans. The Constitution declared them three-fifths of a person and upheld their slave status. Not only is the history of Black people in the United States founded on slavery, but even after the Emancipation Proclamation and the end of the Civil War, structural practices perpetuated racism. Segregating practices under "Jim Crow" laws denied Blacks access to education, jobs, and public establishments, disenfranchised Blacks from voting, and denied them access to investment capital and land. James H. Cone would further comment on the period after Reconstruction and the removal of federal troops in the South (1877):

> Assured of no federal interference, southern whites were now free to take back the South, to redeem it from what they called "Negro domination," through mob violence — excluding blacks from politics, arresting them for vagrancy, forcing them to work as sharecroppers who never got out of debt, and creating a rigid segregated society in which being black was a badge of shame with no meaningful future. A black person could be lynched for any perceived insult to whites.[6]

To complicate matters, white churches were often complicit in this denigration.

It is beyond the scope of this writing to mention every realm of the historical relationship between Black people and the present dominant race in the United States. Suffice it to say, there was a struggle to gain basic rights of citizenship despite Constitutional amendments after the Civil War. Voting rights, for example, had to be solidified; equality in

---

5. Albert J. Raboteau, *Slave Religion: The "Invisible Institution" in the Antebellum South* (New York: Oxford University Press, 1978), 100–101.

6. James H. Cone, *The Cross and the Lynching Tree* (Maryknoll, NY: Orbis, 2013), 5–6.

education and job opportunities were issues as well. Laws had to be passed and implemented to support basic civil rights. A matter much more difficult to confront was a pervasive perspective among many whites that Blacks were simply "less than." They were considered incapable of thinking and performing in things like business, science, and education at the level of white people. Such perspectives have been, and still are, difficult to root out.

The Rise of the Black Church

The widespread and deeply rooted mistreatment of Blacks required a unified response, and the "religious" justification of slavery demanded counterclaims rooted in true religion. As Henry Highland Garnet, a nineteenth-century minister and abolitionist, extolled:

> No oppressed people have ever secured their Liberty without resistance. What kind of resistance you had better make you must decide by the circumstances that surround you, and according to the suggestion of expediency. Brethren, adieu! Trust in the living God. Labor for the peace of the human race, and remember that you are three millions.[7]

Garnet's statement unites some important themes in the attempt to address with any validity and meaning the relationship between the Black church and politics. The Black church was forged, not only in historical Christian confession, but also in resistance revealed in multiple forms. The "circumstances that surround you" at the time of Garnet's speech were slavery and all its political ramifications.

From that time, the political climate of the nation has had an inextricable effect on the mission and message of the Black church. Faith in God and faith in the Lord Jesus sustained believers in the midst of the maddening inconsistencies of what Frederick Douglass, a vociferous abolitionist, would label as "slaveholding religion."[8] Douglass

7. "An Address to the Slaves of the United States of America" (August 16, 1843), in *Great Speeches by African Americans*, ed. James Daley (Mineola, NY: Dover), Kindle Edition (Locations 198 out of 2888).

8. Frederick Douglass, "Slaveholding Religion and the Christianity of Christ," in Milton C. Sernett, *African American Religious History: A Documentary Witness* (Durham, NC: Duke University Press, 1999), 106.

affirmed that "I love the pure, peaceable, and impartial Christianity of Christ: I therefore hate the corrupt, slaveholding, women-whipping, cradle-plundering, partial and hypocritical Christianity of this land."[9]

Garnet affirms that ultimate concern must be maintained for all humankind, that none suffer unjustly. He also draws a clear line that contrasts the "hypocritical Christianity" that perpetuated slavery with the "Christianity of Christ" that fought against it. The Black church today maintains this emphasis on a robust faith that fights against injustice.

In light of this central concern over injustice, the Black church in the United States was founded on the gospel and on protest. I will briefly survey beginnings from two denominations that dominated in terms of numbers of conversions among slaves and freed Blacks from the Great Awakening onward—namely, the Methodists and the Baptists.[10]

C. Eric Lincoln and Lawrence Mamiya observe that Black Baptist churches arose primarily in the South, whereas the Methodists emerged in the North.[11] Slaves, overall, were not seeking major political upheaval. They were seeking a place to process the reality of a plantation system that defined their worth and role within the construct of slavery. At various times and in various places in the South, Blacks were not allowed to found a church that was not affiliated with a white denomination.

During the antebellum period, however, Blacks began to protest against these practices, and some independent Black Baptist organizations began to appear.[12] Lincoln and Mamiya identify some concurrent developments that contribute to the rise, not only of the Black Baptist churches, but also of Black Methodist churches:

---

9. Ibid.

10. Raboteau, *Slave Religion*, 132. Other denominations certainly had ministry among the slaves and freed Blacks, and even the Quakers campaigned vehemently against slavery (p. 111), but the Methodists and the Baptists still dominated in terms of conversions and follow-up instruction.

11. C. Eric Lincoln and Lawrence H. Mamiya, *The Black Church in the African American Experience* (Durham, NC: Duke University Press, 1996), 20.

12. Ibid. Raboteau contributes a reminder that other denominations were successfully ministering in the South among slaves: "The revival itself became a means of church extension for Presbyterians and, particularly, for Methodists and Baptists. The mobility of the Methodist circuit rider and the local autonomy of the Baptist preacher were suited to the needs and conditions of the rural South" (*Slave Religion*, 132).

Partly as a result of heightened race consciousness, partly in reaction to the discrimination of southern white Baptists and the paternalism of northern white Baptists, the independent church movement initiated among black Baptists in the antebellum period intensified during the Reconstruction and its aftermath.[13]

Separation from parent denominations did not immediately result in questionable doctrinal developments. One could raise the question of whether a ground of slavery itself was at minimum a heresy of biblical anthropology in the church.

Lincoln and Mamiya are also helpful in tracing the development of protest giving rise to Black churches among the Methodists. It is important to remember that,

> Unlike most sectarian movements, the initial impetus for black spiritual and ecclesiastical independence was not grounded in religious doctrine or polity, but in the offensiveness of racial segregation in the churches and alarming inconsistencies between the teachings and the expressions of faith. It was readily apparent that the white church had become a principal instrument of the political and social policies undergirding slavery and the attendant degradation of the human spirit.[14]

I can only mention one such event, but it would prove to be climactic. The African Methodist Episcopal Church (AME) was begun in 1787 when Richard Allen, Absalom Jones, and other Black church members walked out of St. George's Methodist Episcopal Church in Philadelphia when they were pulled up from their prayer on a balcony that they helped to finance for renovations. They were told they could not pray in that place. The resulting pathway to an independent Black church denomination was arduous, but Allen and his cohorts prevailed.[15] These events did much to inspire the founding of other Black churches in this denomination and in others.

---

13. Ibid., 27.

14. Lincoln and Mamiya, *The Black Church in the African American Experience*, 47.

15. See my *Introducing Black Theology: Three Crucial Questions for the Evangelical Church* (Grand Rapids: Baker, 2001), 17. For a helpful treatment of ecclesiological developments in the Pentecostal wing of the church, see Cheryl J. Sanders, *Saints in Exile: The Holiness-Pentecostal Experience in African American Religion and Culture* (New York: Oxford University Press, 1996).

Theological Confession and Historical Experience

The nature of the Black church is a matter for much debate. I will not give immediate attention at this juncture to the question of whether the Black church may still be considered alive,[16] although the meaning and significance of that question will be engaged below. For the moment, however, consider a number of factors that come to bear on authentic constructions of what the Black church is.

A first factor is the foundational matter of biblical and theological tradition. The church as the community of the redeemed through faith alone in Jesus Christ has been long confessed. This provokes reflections on the meaning of the Cross, the motivation and power for living before God, the hope of glory as an orienting factor in the life of the church, as well as in the role of suffering. Related to these matters is the question of what confession should be guarded and maintained, versus what can be modified or even discarded while still being the church.

Second, the potential impact of theological communities and denominations must be considered. There are Black churches among Methodist, Baptist, and Pentecostal denominations. Many Blacks worship in predominantly Caucasian churches in various Protestant denominations, and many Blacks worship in Roman Catholic churches. This reality reverberates in a unique way when thinking about the nature of the Black church, not only because of the impact of the Protestant Reformation, but also because of the impact of Methodists and Baptists stretching back to the days of enslavement.

The Black church is therefore not defined solely in terms of a particular denomination or denominations. This is not to suggest that denominational identity is irrelevant, but rather that for the Black church, doctrine, liturgy, and ministry emphases alert us to similarities and dissimilarities. Even so, there are some common characteristics that distinguish the Black church in the United States.

Confession is not the only factor that contributes to a people's self-awareness, self-identity, and network of values, hopes, and dreams. The Black church has been forged against the backdrop of remembering and processing sorrow and pain, which was accentuated by the hypocrisy

---

16. See Eddie Glaude, PhD, "The Black Church Is Dead." www.huffingtonpost.com/eddie-glaude-jr-phd/the-black-church-is-dead_b_473815.html

of a nation that claimed religious freedom, battled Great Britain for self-governance, and claimed to be "Christian." It could not, however, embrace fellow image-bearers of God and release from bondage people of African descent whom they would also meet at the foot of the cross of Christ. Confession may drive much of the Black church's perspective on politics, but so does this historical, experiential dimension.

Raphael G. Warnock formulates a definition that helpfully summarizes some unique characteristics of the Black church, proposing an emphasis that transcends denominational lines:

> Thus, when I refer to the black church, I speak of the varied ecclesial groupings of Christians of African descent, inside and outside black and white denominations, imbued with the memory of a suffering Jesus and informed by the legacy of slavery and segregation in America. While this historical phenomenon has its deep roots in the independent black church movement, the tragedy and depth of racism ensures the relevance of such a designation for black congregations and caucuses of various configurations who, consciously and unconsciously, live within the conflicting intersectionality of being black and Christian in America.[17]

Being of African descent is not a doctrinal matter, but it is critical for what contributes to the nature of the Black church. That identity was constructed not only on traditional confession, but also on the "legacy of slavery and segregation in America." Warnock argues for developmental stages in the mission and ministry of the church against the backdrop of historical events and people exemplified by the rise of the independent Black church movement.[18]

This concept of the development of the Black church recalls the impact of racism in the past and its persistent effects in the present. Though the ideal would be the eradication of racism from the souls,

---

17. Raphael G. Warnock, *The Divided Mind of the Black Church: Theology, Piety, and Public Witness* (New York: New York University Press, 2014), 9. Warnock is well aware that other pastor/scholars and sociologists argue for a different thrust in relationship to Christian tradition as well as social impact, or lack thereof.

18. Warnock introduces these developmental stages on pages 8–12. This type of independent activity on the part of Black church leadership is part of the reason why Warnock would insist that liberation would include liberation of the soul from the domination of sin, but it would also encompass liberation from sin manifested in human sociopolitical structures.

behaviors, and social constructs of believers, the sociocultural realities of race in the United States continue and often help to perpetuate various forms of racism. In light of these unfortunate realities, members in the Black church must remain socio-politically vigilant, confronting the evil of racism and offering correctives that point toward justice and respect for human dignity.

Political Theological Distinctives

The immediate conjunction of the Black church and politics has both theological grounds and practical realities. The theological grounds are focused in the areas of the centrality of Scripture, God and creation, human spirituality that gives evidence of African roots, and eschatological hope. In more recent times, particularly after the Civil Rights Movement of the 1960s, the substance of these theological categories has undergone some changes (among some churches) in light of practical realities highlighting the legitimate role of "experience" in the church's thought.

View of Scripture

The view of Scripture as the Word of God is well established in Black church tradition. If there are differences of opinion regarding the nature of Scripture and its role in the Black church, the differences focus more on hermeneutics, the interpretation and application of Scripture. Thabiti M. Anyabwile argues that even during the days of slavery, slaves "did not disparage the sacred Scriptures. The Bible was almost universally held in high regard. Southern African Christians accepted that the Bible was indeed the word of God...."[19] Slaves depended on divine revelation emerging in "visions, voices and signs."[20]

In the totality of his work, Anyabwile maintains that until Blacks were allowed into more liberal theological institutions, a view of Scripture as the Word of God was the dominant understanding in the Black church. From my own Baptist background, there was never any

---

19. Thabiti M. Anyabwile, *The Decline of African American Theology: From Biblical Faith to Cultural Captivity* (Downers Grove, IL: InterVarsity Press, 2007), 36. Though I do not agree with all of Dr. Anyabwile's conclusions in his book, I do believe that he represents well the dominant view of Scripture in the Black church.

20. Ibid., 33.

thought expressed that the Bible was anything other than the Word of God. Scholars such as Cain Hope Felder and Vincent Wimbush question the credibility of "uncritical" readings and interpretations of the Scriptures, but all this hermeneutical complexity demands attention far beyond the scope of this present work.[21]

The historical background of the Black church's approach to Scripture is important to mention, however. One key factor is that

> [n]ot only were reading and writing forbidden among slaves as a rule, but there was an attempt to discourage a common language by intermixing persons of different African tribes. Thus, blacks had their own Tower of Babel experience forced upon them.[22]

Literacy rates at the time of emancipation were very low. This forced slaves to develop listening and memory and in a way enabled them to undermine traditional and forced interpretations.[23] The distinctively oral, and thus aural, African-American encounter with Scripture continues to be recognized as a hallmark of the Black church today. The hermeneutics of African-American preaching are also seen as overlapping with but then transcending the early church's traditional Christ-centered categories while also pushing beyond merely modern, critical approaches.[24]

The crucial point here is that the Black church encounters the Bible as God's Word addressing them in the midst of their complex, perplexing political experience, and that shapes their distinctive culture of hearing and remembering it.

---

21. See Cain Hope Felder, *Troubling Biblical Waters: Race, Class and Family* (Maryknoll, NY: Orbis, 1990). In his "Reading 5" in his book *The Bible and African Americans: A Brief History* (Minneapolis: Fortress, 2003), Vincent Wimbush is particularly critical of a fundamentalist shift in the reading and application of the Bible:

"... the Protestant-defined Bible is considered the deracialized, depoliticized, and universal guide to truth and salvation.... Insofar as the Protestant canon is not questioned, and insofar as the foundation or presupposition for the reading of the canon is claimed to be something other than African American historical experience as remembered and understood by African Americans, it entails a severe and even disturbing rejection of African American existence" (Kindle Version, Loc 607 of 880).

22. Thomas Hoyt Jr., "Interpreting Biblical Scholarship," in Cain Hope Felder, ed., *Stony the Road We Trod: African American Biblical Interpretation* (Minneapolis: Fortress, 1991), 27.

23. Renita J. Weems writes, "According to the historian Leon Litwack, at the time of their emancipation, around 5 percent of the emancipated population could read" (*Been in the Storm So Long: The Aftermath of Slavery* [New York: Random House, 1979], 111). See Renita J. Weems, "Reading *Her Way* through the Struggle: African American Women and the Bible," in Felder, *Stony the Road We Trod*, 60–61n5.

24. David T. Shannon, "An Ante-Bellum Sermon," in Felder, *Stony the Road We Trod*, 102.

God and Creation: Holistic Life

God is the God revealed in Scripture, yet he also works in "mysterious ways."[25] Creation not only demonstrates his creative power, but also unveils a theatre to behold his power at work in every way. From the witness of Scripture and of human events over time, Black people discern that God is a God of justice who cares about the oppressed, but he also calls for individuals and communities to do what is right. For them there is no inherent separation between the "sacred" and the "secular." All aspects of life are experienced holistically, including the political sphere.

Spirituality and Community

J. Deotis Roberts observes that human beings are social, "gregarious."[26] They desire community and a sense of belonging. This inherent need and desire for community inevitably leads to the formulation of principles governing the behavior of the members of a group. To have community is to have the political, the forging of principles and laws arising from said community to accomplish the common good, assuming that in a given setting there is consensus on what constitutes the "good." Christians traditionally locate these fundamental human characteristics within the image of God. The need for community and the capacity for morality are aspects of even fallen image bearers.[27]

Accordingly, Peter J. Paris argues for particular characteristics of spirituality among people of African descent. All elements of life are integrated, profoundly interrelated. Beginning with an African concept of spirituality, he argues for parallels with this concept among African Americans.[28]

---

25. I do not know how many times I heard this expression from the older people of Beautiful Plain Baptist Church as I was growing up. It was meant to be consistent with biblical truth, but it was also a response to day-to-day trauma, such as sudden death from heart attacks, strokes, and complications from diabetes. Even young people could get involved with alcohol and eventually die from complications. Death and misfortune would visit at times, but the church clung to the belief that God was still at work and he had his reasons for what unfolded, good or bad.

26. J. Deotis Roberts, *The Prophethood of Black Believers: An African American Political Theology for Ministry* (Louisville, KY: Westminster/John Knox, 1994), 104.

27. Louis Berkhof, *Systematic Theology* (Grand Rapids: Eerdmans, 1986), 204.

28. "The 'spirituality' of a people refers to the animating and integrative power that constitutes the principal frame of meaning for individual and collective experiences. Metaphorically, the spirituality of a people is synonymous with the soul of a people: the integrating center of their power and meaning. In contrast with that of some peoples, however, African spirituality

There are two parallel elements that have enormous repercussions for moral and political matters.

First, human beings should be considered in terms of both individuality and sociality, being part of a community. Paris identifies this corporate dimension as a "community of belonging."[29] Individuals are essentially humanized, morally formed as persons, in family and in community. This is one of the reasons that there is often a demand for individuals to think and to act in ways that facilitate the community's well-being.[30] The individual is valued, but this value is concurrently affected by the impact of the individual, positive or negative, upon the family, tribe, or community. Under communal and traditional tutelage, the African and the African American both view life more holistically.

The other parallel element concerns the significance of moral underpinnings embraced within the community. Morality is not merely cognitive recognition; it is behavior, applicable to both the private and the public. Paris teases out the moral connection between this private/public insistence on morality and the institution of slavery:

> Consequently, [African Americans] have never been able to conceive of societal structures or their leaders as morally neutral in the exercise of their duties. Nor have they been able to view their resistance to racism in anything other than moral terms. As a racially despised minority in the so-called new world, they always knew that their survival both as individuals and as a group depended on their capacity to deal constructively with the immorality of racism.[31]

Morality exercised at the public level puts the members of a community on a potential collision course if standards are not mutually embraced and executed consistently. Such inconsistency feeds fear, hostility, and distrust if not acknowledged and remedied in a manner that authenticates the true repentance of the abusers of power.

---

is never disembodied but always integrally connected with the dynamic movement of life" (Peter J. Paris, *The Spirituality of African Peoples: The Search for a Common Moral Discourse* [Minneapolis: Fortress, 1995], 22). Though Paris does not mention God specifically in this quote, he does recognize the existence of a supreme being in many African religious traditions, with hierarchies of authority (p. 42).

29. Ibid., 117.
30. Ibid., 126.
31. Ibid., 117.

Eschatology: Longing for the New Creation

Eschatology, reflection on final events, has a place in the Black church's assessment of political involvement. Admittedly, theological tradition related to "last things" can have great impact on any church's engagement in the sociopolitical realm, or the lack thereof. For example, a particular brand of premillennialism — the view that Jesus will return bodily and rule on earth for a thousand years before the execution of final judgment (an interpretation of Revelation 20:1–6) — could demotivate a church community from political involvement. From this perspective, the political realm is viewed as largely evil or at least hopeless until Christ's return. By contrast, the Black church typically puts eschatological hope to political work. Thus, James Cone, regarded as one of the initial formulators of Black Theology, argues for a struggle to change present conditions of injustice:

> No eschatological perspective is sufficient which does not challenge the present order. If contemplation about the future distorts the present reality of injustice and reconciles the oppressed to unjust treatment committed against them, then it is unchristian and thus has nothing whatsoever to do with him who came to liberate us.[32]

Cone's conviction is affected by his understanding of the ministry and message of Jesus Christ. Eschatology arouses hope because it encompasses a vision of what God has done, is doing, and will do, namely, further his kingdom while ensuring justice. Black Theology is characterized by an activistic call to participate in God's program, to work for justice in laws and policies in continuity with God's activities.

Having a more dominant view of God's kingdom actualized beyond the realm of time, Pentecostals have historically been nonengaging in the political sphere.[33] Dr. Anthea Butler notes that the same historical reality holds true for Black Pentecostals, though this lack of involvement has changed since the Civil Rights Movement.[34] She concludes

---

32. James H. Cone, *A Black Theology of Liberation* (New York: J. B. Lippincott Company, 1970), 241.

33. Gina Meeks makes this observation in "Pentecostals in Politics: A Silent Minority," *Charisma News* (November 11, 2011). http://www.charismanews.com/politics/32308-pentecostals-in-politics-a-silent-minority (accessed 10/16/2014).

34. Anthea Butler, "Pentecostals, Politics and the Black Church," *Penn Current* (December 2, 2010). http://www.upenn.edu/pennnews/current/node/3465 (accessed 10/16/2014).

that though the Black church nowadays does not seek to accomplish its sociocultural and sociopolitical objectives in the same way, with the same sense of unity as exemplified during the Civil Rights era, there is a general consensus among many Black churches that the church should still be involved in local communities.[35] This is not to conclude that matters of racism and social justice are no longer unifying causes; rather, it suggests a certain fragmentation in the Black church, including Pentecostals, on objectives and methodology for confronting injustice.

Just as there are often departments of Practical Theology in many seminaries, practical theology drives political involvement in the Black church. Theological foundations and the practical realities of life emerge together as necessary considerations for the particular contexts in which believers and congregations live and minister. Proponents of Black church life and ministry readily acknowledge that life with all its intricacies is experienced in the now. Awareness of theological and historical effects informs present situations in any Black church. The realities of life, or "experience," naturally incorporate community or inter-community relationships affecting the individual members of said communities. Communal interaction, in both churchly and political realms, naturally relates to laws and public policies. The practicalities of life in the Black church make political engagement constant and critical.

Positive and Negative Roles of Government

Is government, a coordinator of the political, simply a providential provision for fallen humanity or an integral part of God's creation? Should it be considered a "postlapsarian"[36] development, intended to restrain the evil in human hearts that inevitably orients behavior toward acts of greed, malice, and murder? While not all in the Black church see the existence and function of government in this way, most tend toward a positive view of government. As Eric Gregory observes,

> Followers of this tradition typically hold that political institutions are not so much a remedial "order of providence" but an aspect of

---

35. Ibid.
36. Eric Gregory, "Politics," in *The Oxford Handbook of Evangelical Theology*, ed. Gerald R. McDermott (New York: Oxford University Press, 2013), 397.

God's creation with their own normative integrity to pursue the public common good and establish justice.[37]

Two sample considerations establish a primal form of government before the fall: the doctrine of the Trinity, and God's relationship with Adam and Eve (Gen. 2:15–17).

A type of order, government, is revealed in the life of the Triune God. Without extensive biblical examples, we can still observe a cooperative dimension among the members of the Godhead. The Son is "sent" (John 17:18; Gal. 4:4) to do the Father's will (Heb. 10:7). The Spirit is also "sent" (John 14:26; in conjunction with the Son, John 15:26) to fulfill roles in the overarching plan of salvation (John 16:6–8, 14; Eph. 1:13–14). These observations are not intended to justify any particular form of government. They simply demonstrate an order in the Godhead, suggesting cooperative responsibilities before "the foundation of the world" (Eph. 1:3–10). While the Triune God's fellowship is unique, human image-bearers are social by analogy.

Whatever the nature of Genesis 2:14–15, in terms of it being considered an "Edenic Covenant" or a "Covenant of Works," at least it establishes beginning principles governing the relationship between God and the first human couple. Some form of cooperation had to be implemented among them to fulfill the command of Genesis 1:28. Relational underpinnings would unfold to give expression to the exhortation of Genesis 2:24. My point is that some forms of government were manifested before the fall. Thus, after the fall, the political realm became distorted like many other good elements of creation. But government itself is a good element of creation.

Beyond this theological affirmation, we can emphasize secondly that the role of the government of the United States in the history and tradition of the Black church is a complex and perplexing phenomenon. Much of the complexity stems from the specific structure of government with its local, state, and federal levels. In any form of government, unless there is a powerful, singular voice or a network of unified voices, a univocal decision and implementation of a designated decision are difficult to generate. The United States, being a land of immigrants, adds another layer of complexity that can thwart commonality. Such

---

37. Ibid., 396.

historical and contemporary complexities contribute to a perplexing assessment of the role of government in the Black community and the Black church.

Historical Experiences with Government

The complex and perplexing interplay between the Black church and governing institution begins very early in the life of the nation. Often laws and public policies have enshrined and perpetuated injustice; at other times government has been the engine of positive change. To illustrate this complexity and perplexity, in line with the Black church's emphasis on experience, we can turn to W.E.B DuBois's monumental work, *The Souls of Black Folk*.[38] After this, I will mention some products of governmental actions that many even in the Black church would suggest were positive initiatives.

DuBois lauded some extraordinary ways that the Bureau of Refugees, Freedmen, and Abandoned Lands (commonly called the Freedmen's Bureau) provided for former slaves after the Civil War, particularly in the areas of education and the possibility of land ownership. The Bureau was entrusted in some areas with the provision of food and shelter, but other aims drew DuBois's primary attention. The Bureau provided elementary education, not only for Black children, but also for all classes of people in the South. DuBois also mentioned that during the period of the Bureau's existence, a number of Black colleges were founded, including Fisk, Atlanta, Howard, and Hampton. Education was critical for the flourishing of the newly freed slaves, not only in helping meet immediate needs, but also for building a future.

Yet DuBois also expressed criticisms of the Bureau because of inadequate attention to some needed areas. First, he was concerned that it gave no attention to reconciliation between former slave holders or advocates of slavery and the newly freed slaves. This silence gave the churches an opportunity to minister effectively, but the churches, particularly in the South, simply baptized the sociocultural norms of their memberships when it came to race relationships. DuBois's second concern was the paternalistic attitude possessed by some "helpers"

---

38. W.E.B. DuBois, "Of the Dawn of Freedom," in *The Souls of Black Folk* (New York: Penguin, 1989), 13–35.

toward the former slaves. This attitude undermined the confidence and vision needed to motivate these former captives to implement all that was available to them for building new lives. Finally, because of various pressures in the matrix of the federal government, the Bureau failed to make more land available to the Freedmen for ownership and communal development.[39] Land ownership would have facilitated important possibilities, such as crop development and the prospects of an economic livelihood, social standing in the community in general, and valuable possessions to pass on to posterity.

The law stated:

> The commissioner, under the direction of the President, shall have authority to set apart, for the use of loyal refugees and freedmen, such tracts of land within the insurrectionary states as shall have been abandoned, or to which the United States shall have acquired title by confiscation or sale, or otherwise, and to every male citizen, whether refugee or freedman, as aforesaid, there shall be assigned not more than forty acres of such land....[40]

Further statements of the law established rental relationships with the Bureau for three years with the aim of the eventual procurement of the land by the holder. One can only imagine what might have happened if the provisions of this law had been implemented in greater numbers— what changes it would have brought over time in many communities. However, the lack of consistent application, whether intended or not, kept the freed men and women in a position of greater dependence on governmental decisions and provisions. Progress on many levels was achieved, but the ownership and development of land would have enhanced a sense of dignity and contribution to communal well-being for everyone. Blacks and Caucasians would have had a greater chance over time to meet as equal contributors to the sociocultural setting.

Instead, governmental actions paved the way for entrenched discrimination. Supreme Court decisions such as *Plessy v. Ferguson* (1896)

---

39. Ibid., 31.
40. Sec. 4 of Chap. XC.—*An Act to establish a Bureau for the Relief of Freedmen and Refugees.* US, *Statutes at Large, Treaties, and Proclamations of the United States of America*, Vol. 13 (Boston, 1866), 507–9. The matter of the availability of forty acres was often associated with the provision of a mule.

permitted segregation in "separate but equal" facilities that were anything but equal. Acts of violence against Blacks escalated, local law enforcement often turned a blind eye, and the fight began for anti-lynching laws and other legal protections. There were many contentious engagements between the Black community and the various levels of American government. Throughout it all, the Black church remained an important presence and influence. Progress in establishing equal rights for Blacks did advance, but it did so with painful slowness up to and after passage of the Civil Rights Act of 1964 and the Voting Rights Act of 1965.

Although federal legislation did not resolve all matters of discrimination, these Acts did address major issues such as voting rights, public accommodations, desegregation of public facilities and education, and equal opportunities for employment.[41] Many significant people and events, including those shaped by Christian faith, contributed to the emergence of this monumental legislation. Even this pathway, however, bears witness to the checkered history of the Black church's interplay with governmental structures.

The 13th, 14th, and 15th Amendments to the Constitution had set a framework to establish civil rights for freed slaves, at least at the federal government level.[42] But little in these amendments defined the needed parameters of implementation and enforcement, thus enabling states and localities to formulate laws and policies that blunted their impact. After 1900, the federal government stopped actively enforcing civil rights violations against Blacks. There was a resurgence of interest in civil rights after 1945, and Congress did try to make some changes to enhance the lives of Blacks, passing civil rights-oriented bills in 1957 and 1960. But the need remained for comprehensive legislation to protect more effectively the rights of citizenship for Black people.

The Supreme Court decision of *Brown v. Board of Education of Topeka, Kansas* (1954, which essentially outlawed segregated facilities for Black and Caucasian children), the March on Washington in 1963, and other sociocultural developments helped create a more favorable environment for Congress to enact legislation and garner presidential

---

41. *Major Features of the Civil Rights Act of 1964* (Public Law 88–352). www.congresslink.org/print_basics_histmats_civilrights64text.htm (accessed 10/20/2014). Most of the following material will come from this source.

42. These are also known as the Civil War amendments, or the Reconstruction amendments.

support. Furthermore, public sentiment was powerfully affected by two interrelated developments: the expansion of mass media and the role of the Black church, in particular through the Southern Christian Leadership Council. The video and audio capacities of television delivered coverage of places and events much more quickly to living rooms around the country. Americans watched the demonstrations, police activities, and violence against peaceful protestors, arousing more sympathy for the Black struggle for civil rights.

This increased awareness in turn eventually put more pressure on legislators to vote for the Civil Rights Act. Demonstrators often met at Black churches before the marches. The singing and the inspiring messages of leaders such as Rev. Dr. Martin Luther King Jr. helped arouse courage in the marchers because there was much to fear in many of the Southern cities.[43]

The pervasive presence of the Black church not only inspired hope and courage, but also enabled the church to provide an aura of credibility to the movement. This did much to allay fears in some people that the Civil Rights Movement was merely the product of thuggery or communists. Yet even the Civil Rights Movement leaves behind a mixed, or at least disputed, legacy. No political engagement has been an unambiguous success at combatting the racism and injustice that are so deeply entrenched in American society.

Thus, Black people and the Black church have mixed views of the proper role of government: at times governmental actions have promoted injustice, at other times government has achieved positive ends. In the contemporary scene, precise opinions on the proper role of government remain diverse and divisive. Suffice it here to suggest that the differing views of the nature and mission of the Black church held by particular evaluators greatly affect their evaluations.

Christian Participation in Government and Politics

One should not be surprised by the fact that in the Black church there is no official, doctrinal position on the question of individual Christian involvement with government and politics. The history and tradition

---

43. For a helpful summary of events during this march, see "Martin Luther King, Jr. and the Global Freedom Struggle." www.mlk-kpp01.standford.edu/index.php/encyclopedia/enc_birmingham_campaign.

of Black people in the United States, however, inevitably compel some awareness of the political realm, although degrees of awareness and activity vary among members in a given Black church. Unfortunately, a matter such as incarceration of a family member or young friend can put even a young child on a collision course with such intimate knowledge of the laws governing his or her life.

Against this backdrop, J. Deotis Roberts argues that involvement in politics is virtually an obligation on the part of Black believers.[44] Such involvement will not be the same for everyone, but the Black church's role in the Black community, particularly since the Civil Rights era, has been one of preaching the gospel while concurrently maintaining awareness of political interworkings affecting the community. Roberts also insists that the Black church has long been a place of political information and mobilization, and this should be maintained.

Political engagement, however, can cause major repercussions for the believer or the church that chooses to be aware and is willing to inform and mobilize people for political action. Roberts identifies three ways political gatekeepers might regard such churches. First, they may be seen as enemies of the political realm because they continually express views on matters some politicians would rather not address. Second, such churches may be labeled as confused. There are always some churches that tend toward the view that faith and politics are mutually exclusive, teaching that faith and its expressions in life are above the mundane and distorted world of laws and policies. Yet other churches are very politically engaged, so much so that they are criticized for being too caught up in the temporal realm. Finally, such churches may be dismissed by some as irrelevant because they cannot generate "real answers" to "real problems."[45] Roberts, of course, disagrees on all fronts, yet he acknowledges that to be a church committed to Christian faith, and thus to justice in all areas of life, takes a great deal of courage and commitment. Yet it is essential in light of the alternative.

Roberts would go so far as to argue that leadership in the Black church should be exposed to courses on political issues in their seminary

44. Roberts, *The Prophethood of Black Believers*, 106. Roberts is incorporating the argument of Donald E. Messer (*Christian Ethics and Political Action* [Valley Forge, PA: Judson Press, 1984], chap. 1) that in a real world, Christians cannot afford to withdraw from the political realm. Withdrawal simply enables potentially unscrupulous people to dominate the process.

45. Ibid., 108.

curriculum. He argues thus, because "Blacks are often less effective as they move from church politics to electoral politics, from personalities to issues."[46] He further suggests that the Black church would have greater effectiveness in informing and mobilizing the community if leadership in churches had something similar to "think tanks" made up of pastor/scholars and others with diverse spheres of knowledge who could inform discussion and strategize about best ways to address areas of concern. Examples of such areas include electoral politics, criminal justice, and waste disposal.

Given the complex history of Blacks and government, members in the Black church simply need to know more about the realities of the political world. Knowledge of people, like city officials, and the inter-workings of power are essential when attempting to address needs of the larger community. Matters of criminal justice are absolutely critical. Issues related to the interplay of race, money, and power emerged from early days in the life of the nation, and they have injected much into the structure of the legal system in pervasively unjust ways. Such imbalances in the administration of laws need to be identified and rooted out.

Roberts also encourages awareness of environmental justice. For example, churches in many urban settings can ask questions such as, Why is it that many landfills and waste processing centers are often built in or near Black communities?[47] Increased awareness of issues in these areas would not ensure total success, but it would lead more clearly to effective resistance or even paths of progress.

Again, the Black church's involvement in political interrelationships has resulted in some blessings and some disappointment. Historical and contemporary scrutiny will affirm government's ambiguous contributions, for this interaction has not always resulted in justice. The benefit of any aid given by the government, even when needed and requested, must be determined by the standard of greater genuine freedom for people in the community. Does such aid enable people to work eventually for their needs, so they have more reason to regard themselves and others with dignity? Will such aid result in eventuating into various initiatives in terms of business, education, the arts, or informed

---

46. Ibid., 110.
47. Ibid. See pages 109–14, where there is much more detail.

participation in the political process? Any help, even that which is facilitated by well-meaning people, cannot be long regarded as positive if it keeps others in a state of dependence.

Through it all, Roberts affirms a position of continual evaluation and criticism:

> The church affirms loyalty to a higher standard and source of value, the kingdom of God. Its source of life and action is the ethic of love. It therefore stands in judgment upon all human situations, whether individual or collective, including its own life. It is only when the church is self-critical that it brings the proper credentials to political thought and action.[48]

Such critical correction and confrontation arise best when the Black church also hears God's comfort and confirmation in the gospel.

Case Study on Poverty

How, then, might the Black church's hearing and proclamation of the gospel address an issue such as domestic poverty? In an interview held during the 2012 Presidential campaign, journalist Tavis Smiley and seminary professor Dr. Cornel West spoke of their recent journey through eleven states studying poverty.[49] Their tour and the resultant book were titled *The Rich and the Rest of Us: A Poverty Manifesto*.[50] They mentioned many adverse conditions facing the poor of all races. They considered it a crime against justice that the top 1 percent of the population controlled 42 percent of the nation's wealth. They also spoke of the "demonization" of the poor on the part of some who blame "the victims," often taking the form of attributing poverty to laziness or bad character.

Smiley and West were quick to point out that because of economic conditions, particularly since the recession of 2008, many who had been a part of the middle class were moved to the brink of poverty through no fault of their own. They attributed this principle of "through no fault

---

48. Ibid., 105.

49. The interviewers were Amy Goodman and Juan Gonzalez. www.youtube.com/watch?v=2tKxK9ZCDAY (accessed 10/27/2014).

50. Tavis Smiley and Cornel West, *The Rich and the Rest of Us: A Poverty Manifesto* (New York: SmileyBooks, 2012).

of their own" to many already in the "slavery" of poverty. Smiley and West decried the lack of attention from the White House, the lack of a national plan to end poverty, and corporate greed as factors contributing to this nonsensical situation.

Many other statistics and studies of poverty highlight the particular plight of the Black community and point to possible solutions. The national unemployment rate is currently 7.6 percent, while the unemployment rate for Blacks is 13.7 percent.[51] An estimated 38 percent of Black children live in poverty.[52] Everyone who has studied the matter agrees that poverty is a problem in the United States, and the problem is accentuated for Black people. There is also much agreement on the need for life-sustaining employment. Nuances and differences in opinion begin to emerge, however, in the analyses of what causes poverty and what steps are most likely to alleviate it. Some attribute poverty to the structural legacy of racism and greed for power and money. Others understand the problem primarily as a lack of job opportunities and quality education. Voices are truly mixed in the Black church.

Many would agree that the solution involves some coordinated network of agencies. The Black church often advocates for cooperative efforts combining government and other social institutions, including the church. Michael Holzman, for example, argues that quality education is a critical starting point, though he would also argue that coordinated efforts with government are also critical. Education is still the hope of progress even as it was after emancipation and Reconstruction. On this point, Holzman echoes the conviction of W.E.B. DuBois, writing a century before:

> Had it not been for the Negro school and college, the Negro would, to all intents and purposes, have been driven back to slavery. His economic foothold in land and capital was too slight in ten years of turmoil to effect any defense or stability.... But already, through establishing public schools and private colleges, and by organizing the Negro church, the Negro had acquired enough leadership and knowledge to thwart the worst designs of the new slave drivers.

---

51. Arthur Delaney, "Black Unemployment," *Huffington Post* (July 22, 2013). http://www.huffingtonpost.com/2013/07/22/black-unemployment_n_3624725.html.

52. Smiley and West, *The Rich and the Rest of Us.*

They avoided the mistake of trying to meet force by force. They bent to the storm of beating, lynching and murder, and kept their souls in spite of public and private insult of every description; they built an inner culture which the world recognizes in spite of the fact that it is still half-strangled and inarticulate.[53]

Yet, Holzman argues, it is difficult to offer a quality education to Black children in many urban cities for a number of reasons. First, there is often a lack of needed funding for facilities and quality teachers. Second, many households lack sufficient familial support to provide accountability and proper motivation for achievement. Holzman specifically focuses on the lack of fathers present. This leads to a third consideration: a high incarceration rate among young Black men, due in part to harsh drug laws.

Holzman forcefully argues the need for networks of cooperation to break the cycle of poverty. Laws and law enforcement should be reexamined. For example, as a law is being written, and when it is enforced, is there consideration of the fact that convicted felons often have great difficulty finding decent jobs? A decent job is an important step in breaking the cycle of poverty. On the matter of education, are the gatekeepers of educational opportunity, such as admissions officers at prestigious colleges and universities, aware of and accounting for the conditions that affect school performance in many urban settings? Individual drive is indeed essential for successful completion of degrees, but the environment from which candidates come is also a critical consideration.

Traditionally, the Black community has had to depend on government intervention to meet the needs of individuals in the church and in the surrounding neighborhoods because of the pervasiveness of poverty. This is not to suggest that churches are not making significant efforts to provide food, housing, and financial assistance to individual families. Rather, government programs often prove critical because the needs are simply too great. At the same time, however, dimensions of poverty remain where only the church can effectively minister. Spiritual

53. "The Way of the Black Poverty Cycle," in *The Washington Post* (May 31, 2013). http://www.washingtonpost.com/blogs/answersheet/wp/2013/05/31/the-way-out-of-the-black-poverty-cycle. This quote comes from DuBois's work, *Black Reconstruction in America, 1860–1880* (New York: The Free Press, 1998), 667.

dimensions contribute to the problem, and here the church can perform an essential service.

In any given setting, the goal should be that of *shalom*, "signifying peace, completeness, wholeness, harmony, fulfillment, unimpaired relationships, and fulfillment of one's undertaking."[54] Poverty is then a "diminished capacity for life" that is in turn the product of fallacious human decisions and actions.[55] The church can do much to redirect desires and actions in the normal processes of teaching, preaching, and discipleship.

First, the church can serve in its *corrective* role, reiterating that wealth is not necessarily a sign of divine pleasure, nor is poverty necessarily a sign of divine disapproval. Situations are governed by God's perspective, and we are not always privy to his rationale for what may be.[56] Moreover, standards of "fairness" and "justice" in a given sociocultural and political environment may not be one and the same as God's.

Second, the church can be a source of *comfort*. Situations of great need may move some to seek God's face more diligently. Situations of poverty also provide opportunity not only for analysis of why specific conditions exist, but for *confirming* supernatural generosity as in the case of the churches of Macedonia: "for in a severe test of affliction, their abundance of joy and their extreme poverty have overflowed in a wealth of generosity on their part" (2 Cor. 8:2 ESV; see vv. 1–7).

Finally, the Black church can serve an important role *confronting* injustice and assaults on human dignity. Those who exercise authority are responsible to work under the auspices of moral law; they are not free simply to do what is advantageous to themselves, select persons, or parties.[57] The Black church has always strived to achieve justice because conditions in life and the teaching of Scripture demand the effort. The church has all the more reason to hold government officials to account, for their decisions affect access to basic rights of citizenship, and — even more poignantly — the experience of human dignity. The Black church and the government must cooperate in a multilayered network

---

54. Craig M. Gay, "Poverty," in *The Oxford Handbook of Christianity and Economics*, ed. Paul Oslington (New York: Oxford University Press, 2014), 624.

55. Ibid., 622.

56. Ibid.

57. Ibid., 630.

to achieve justice and alleviate the sufferings from poverty. As Craig Gay reminds us,

> Justice must, therefore, be completed by mercy. Both are necessary for *shalom*. Providing the norm for institutional behavior, justice renders unto each his or her due, while mercy compensates for the impersonality of institutions and for the accidents of birth and circumstances.[58]

The Black church can be a powerful instrument to help achieve such justice and mercy.

Conclusion

The legacy of the Black church and politics is one of complexity and perplexity. While the prophetic voice of speaking justice to power has been continual over centuries, the political sphere by nature has not responded with consistency. The presence of Black people in the halls of power is absolutely critical, as their voice serves as a constant reminder of the potential degeneracy of human government. The triumph over the lasting contamination of racism must be completed by a Holy Spirit-empowered love ascending through churches to embrace one another regardless of race and ethnicity. It arouses some hope to entertain this possibility, but the full scope of fallen human constructs must also be considered.

The questions for the Black church, and any church that names the Lord Jesus as Savior, must be: On what is your hope ultimately built? To have the hope of the "good," what must be done? The political realm is needed, but mere formulation of law does not ensure the health of a people. A government is only as just as the justice that resides in the hearts and minds of its people. For this reason, the church's message of comfort for the oppressed, confrontation of the oppressors, correction for God's own people, and confirmation of God's advocacy for his oppressed people remains essential.

The message of the Black church is not so much a unified systematic or political theology as it is a tradition of practices—reading Scripture orally, communally, and concretely; informing, mobilizing,

---

58. Ibid., 629.

and organizing communal networks; offering hope to its people and resisting oppression, affirming the dignity of all. Thus, the Black church, reflecting on the atrocities inflicted upon it in the past by even religious people, must ultimately be a light to illuminate what can be accomplished for the benefit of individuals, communities, the nation, and all of God's world.

AN ANABAPTIST (SEPARATIONIST) RESPONSE

THOMAS W. HEILKE

It should not be surprising to find a number of close affinities in substance if not in style between Anabaptists and the Black church. An oppressed minority? Check. Traditionally excluded from the halls of power? Check. A somewhat amorphous grouping of churches and movements? Check. Nevertheless, one might reasonably object that whatever stories of oppression various Anabaptist groups can tell, their European origins and mostly white skins have, since at least the end of World War II, afforded them all the privileges and opportunities of the majority in societies such as Canada and the United States, and of the elite minorities in countries such as Mexico and Paraguay. Mostly true. On the other hand, the "typical" Anabaptist, at least among Mennonites, is no longer of European extraction: Kinshasa, the capital city of the Democratic Republic of the Congo, has one of the largest urban concentrations of Mennonite Anabaptists in the world.

Christians worldwide, moreover, have suffered extensive persecution in the twentieth century in gross numbers not equaled at any time in their 2,000-year history.[59] But when looking specifically at the United States, it is indeed the Black church that confronts the most obstacles and challenges, and these are deeply inconsistent with the story America wants to tell about itself. These conditions exist primarily not because of religious belief, but because of race, and they have often been erected and stubbornly maintained by people claiming to be followers of Jesus. Accordingly, I will ask forbearance of my Black brothers and sisters, recognizing that I cannot claim any kind of solidarity with them unless expressly invited. I will, however, point to areas of agreement and, from an Anabaptist perspective, suggest a point or two of caution.

---

59. Paul Marshall with Lela Gilbert, *Their Blood Cries Out: The Worldwide Tragedy of Modern Christians Who Are Dying for Their Faith* (Dallas: Word Publishing, 1997).

It is difficult in general terms to pin down much agreement or dis-agreement concerning engagement with the political realm, since, as Professor Fields points out, the Black church is relatively amorphous, separated into many denominations and hence many perspectives on what politics means and what it means for African Americans to par-ticipate in politics in the US context.

As I write these paragraphs, the news is filled with the latest episode of violence directed against African-American Christians: the shooting of ten of them, killing nine, during a Bible study meeting in the historic Emanuel African Methodist Episcopal Church in Charleston, South Carolina. The accused murderer is reported to have claimed online that he hoped to ignite a race war, and comments the suspect reportedly made during the Bible study as he was preparing to shoot provide addi-tional evidence that the crime was racially motivated.

Public discussion revolves around whether the accused should be tried under federal hate crime legislation or as a terrorist; few talk of religious persecution. The shooting, however, took place in a church building, yet another in a long chain of violent acts against African-American churches. This incident occurred in a church building because the Christians there were doing what Christians do: meeting in a relatively defenseless place open to others to join them, which the shooter did for nearly an hour before committing his crime. Such approachability may have made the Bible study meeting a target of con-venience in lieu of other, less accessible venues for a mass shooting.[60] Yet it is seemingly especially because these Christians were in church that the man could do what he did.

Whether or not exploiting a vulnerability is a form of opportunistic persecution, it is certainly the case that the community of the Emanuel AME Church has delivered a remarkable witness in the aftermath. The response of those directly affected by the actions has been one of extraordinary charity, forgiving the accused shooter, declining revenge,

---

60. See, e.g., "One of the friends who briefly hid Roof's gun away from him said, 'I don't think the church was his primary target because he told us he was going for the school. But I think he couldn't get into the school because of the security ... so I think he just settled for the church'" (Mitch Weiss and Michael Biesecker, Associated Press, June 20, 2015); "Man accused of church killings spoke of attacking college" (*St. Louis Post-Dispatch*, retrieved June 20, 2015); Charlotte Krol, "Dylann Roof's friend: Charleston church 'wasn't primary target,'" *The Telegraph*, retrieved June 20, 2015.

and reaching out to his family. Despite the exclusion and persecution they and their ancestors have suffered, these Christians are bearing witness to their faith in a profound way, reducing to tears a reporter covering the story. The response of this Christian community is closely parallel to the response of the Anabaptist Old Order Amish community in the wake of the 2006 West Nickel Mines School shooting, in which ten school girls were shot and five died.

It is hard to demur from a claim that the work of the church includes "comfort, correction, and confirmation." That may not be the sum of its work, but given especially the minority, excluded, and frequently denigrated status of its members, such a community-building and individual-building mission seems an incontrovertible part of what a church following Jesus would do.

I would especially point to Black church eschatology as an interesting meeting point for that church and the Anabaptist tradition. The point did not receive emphasis in my account, but Anabaptist nonresistant pacifism cannot be understood as a coherent and moral stance apart from a specific Christian eschatology. Indeed, one could argue for the *immorality* of Anabaptist nonresistant pacifism apart from such an eschatological account.[61] Black church eschatology, on the other hand, seems in Fields's view to lead to a strong activism "to work for justice in laws and policies in continuity with God's activities," but the bent of such activism clearly depends in part on which one of the many strands of the Black church is making the call. The only Anabaptist caution here would be a reminder not to confuse church and society in the midst of that activism, thereby introducing some version of a thinned-out Niebuhrian ecclesiology. Fields takes critical note of this possibility.

Fields makes no assumptions about holding power when speaking truth to political authorities, but seems comfortable with the prospect of having African-American Christians hold it. He offers no final doctrine of politics, which I do not see as a deficiency, since such doctrines in the American context are ever inclined to become apologies for

---

61. See Stanley Hauerwas, "On Being a Church Capable of Addressing a World at War: A Pacifist Response to the United Methodist Bishops' Pastoral *In Defense of Creation*," in *The Hauerwas Reader* (Durham, NC: Duke University Press, 2001), 426–58; also John Howard Yoder, *Nevertheless: The Varieties of Religious Pacifism* (Scottdale, PA: Herald Press, 1971); and "Peace without Eschatology?" in Michael G. Cartwright, ed., *The Royal Priesthood* (Grand Rapids: Eerdmans, 1994), 143–67.

American-style democracy, especially in its international dimensions, just as they were inclined in earlier eras to become apologies for the best possible version of the regime prevalent or generally most approved at the time.[62]

The Black church has undoubtedly taught us, especially through the Civil Rights Movement, a principle that Anabaptists would affirm: If the ruling authorities make moral claims regarding their rule, then use their language to call them to account. That is an integral part of the Christian witness to the state. Two of the greatest examples of such witness continue to be the "I Have a Dream" address and the "Letter from Birmingham Jail" of the Baptist minister Dr. Martin Luther King Jr.

---

62. Consider, for example, Thomas Aquinas's "On Princely Government" and especially its arguments by cosmological analogy.

ROBERT BENNE

It is difficult to respond to Bruce Fields's account of the Black church's relation to political life. African-Americans have a history of oppression unlike that of any other racial or ethnic group in America, and it is perilous for white people to comment. Yet, this is my task, so I will offer a few points of comparison with the Lutheran tradition.

Any thoughtful person must have high respect for a church that has persisted and flourished under the conditions of slavery, persecution, and racism. Christians here and around the world appreciate the religious vitality and depth of the Black church. Think, for example, of the great spirituals that were written to bring comfort during a time of great oppression and how they symbolize the tradition's vitality. We know the Christian spirituality that exudes from such music is born of profound faith in the midst of suffering. The music demonstrates that the faith and hope of this great tradition is built upon Christ, the solid rock.

The historical injustices toward African-Americans provide a jarring example of one of the central themes of the Lutheran vision that I outlined, the paradox of human nature and history. Human sin runs deep, and, as I noted in my essay, it is particularly magnified and unrestrained in the actions of groups. For far too long, many white Americans were oblivious to the call to love their neighbor and instead upheld structures and systems that diminished the life chances of African-Americans. What was the result? The perpetuation of sinful institutions like chattel slavery, Jim Crow laws, racism, and discrimination. Lutherans are well aware of the ways sin can be expressed in collective inattention and actions, just as we are well aware of our desperate need for the gift of grace in Christ.

Most Christians understand why vast majorities of African-American Christians vote for Democrats in local, state, and national elections. Democrats have by and large been for the expansion of the welfare state, which has provided a safety net for millions of Black brothers and sisters. Furthermore, liberals have been in the front ranks of those attacking continuing racism and searching for strategies of Black empowerment.

But when it comes to the institutional church, the story becomes one of "complexity and perplexity," as Fields well documents. The Black church provides a full spectrum, from apolitical Pentecostalism to the partisan activism of churches pastored by the likes of Al Sharpton. Those churches that tend toward the Sharpton pole often invite political figures seeking election to campaign from their pulpits, something matched among some white churches of the Religious Right. Both instances run counter to the principles of the Lutheran tradition, which strongly resists such fusing of religion and politics.

Given the breadth of the Black church tradition, Fields notes that the tradition doesn't have an official position on Christian participation in government, but states that "the history and tradition of Black people in the United States, however, inevitably compel some awareness of the political realm" (p. 116). He then speaks favorably of J. Deotis Roberts and his contention that "involvement in politics is virtually an obligation on the part of Black believers" (p. 117). Fields makes a compelling case for why the Black church encourages political participation and shows ways that its prophetic voice has been essential.

Although Fields offers words of caution about this enterprise, the Lutheran tradition would speak even more forcefully about its potential dangers. Awareness of politics is beneficial, and may indeed be necessary for African-Americans in the face of ongoing injustice. But Lutherans warn against excessive entanglement of religion and politics to protect the transcendent character of the Gospel. While the Gospel may lead to political initiatives, it is not itself a political initiative. It would be better from a Lutheran perspective to carry the prophetic impulse through strong individual leaders (Martin Luther King Jr.) and voluntary associations (the NAACP, the Urban League, and others) than to do so directly through the churches. Their reason-for-being is political, while the church's is not.

As a cultural institution *par excellence*, the Black church has an indispensable role in addressing the social and spiritual needs of the

Black community. While its more directly political role is important, its spiritual and cultural roles are even more so. Like the churches of John Wesley's movement in Victorian times, the Black church can become an even more important source of moral information for its members in a time in which the Christian way of life is threatened by the moral and spiritual chaos of these turbulent times.

JAMES K.A. SMITH

Unlike the other views in this book (Anabaptist, Lutheran, Reformed, Catholic), the Black church view is not so much defined by confessional distinctives as it is by the distinctive (and heartbreaking) experience of our African-American sisters and brothers in Christ. In other words, the distinguishing characteristic of a Black church political theology is contextual, engendering an attunement to prophetic concerns for justice that were forged by an experience of astonishing, ongoing injustice.[63]

The expression of oppression, marginalization, and disenfranchisement has made the Black church attentive readers of Scripture, sensitive to the widows, orphans, and strangers who can be so easily missed by those of us who read from positions of comfort, power, and privilege. But it also means, I think, that this prophetic witness can—and should be—incorporated into the other views. While one likely does have to choose between the Anabaptist or Reformed views and make a choice between the Lutheran or Catholic stance, it seems as if the prophetic witness of the Black church can—and ought to—character any of the other views. It might be the only view that is *not* mutually exclusive to the others.

And yet, admittedly, it has often been professing Christians from these other traditions who are responsible for the injustices suffered by the Black church. So while theoretically, from an "academic" standpoint, these views are not mutually exclusive, clearly "on the ground" experience proves otherwise. So I could imagine the Black church would

---

63. In this sense, we find important parallels between Black theology and indigenous theological voices (and, in Central and Latin America, liberation theology). On indigenous theology, see Richard Twiss, *Rescuing the Gospel from the Cowboys: A Native American Expression of the Jesus Way* (Downers Grove, IL: InterVarsity Press, 2015). For a positive Reformed interaction with liberation theology, see Nicholas Wolterstorff, *Until Justice and Peace Embrace* (Grand Rapids: Eerdmans, 1983), 42–68.

be suspicious of their view being "co-opted" and merely absorbed into the other views. That is understandable. Yet it seems that a prophetic witness is precisely a call to the people of God to become otherwise. So one can hope.

It's very difficult for me to find points of disagreement with the Black church view. To the contrary, it seems that the only proper Reformed response would be confession, lament, and affirmation.

The fundamental agreement stems from the significant overlap between the Black church emphasis on "holism" and the Reformed tradition's emphasis on the same. When Fields notes that "for [the Black church] there is no inherent separation between the 'sacred' and the 'secular,'" that sounds like a page from the Reformed hymnbook.[64] We also share the Black church's deep eschatological longing[65] that, in turn, generates a "call to participate in God's program, to work for justice in laws and policies in continuity with God's activities" (p. 110). Again, this could have been uttered by Abraham Kuyper. As a result, we also share a "positive view of government."

In short, it seems to me that the Black church view could be equally described as "transformationist."[66] Indeed, one could read the Civil Rights Movement in the twentieth century as a transformationist project: Bearing witness from the specificity of the gospel's injunction to *love*, informed by the specifically Christological exemplar of nonviolence, and fostered by the practices of the Christian church, the Civil Rights Movement in its animating impetus was an endeavor that refused to imagine that society was impervious to the rule of Christ, but instead imagined it could become "a beloved community." As Charles Marsh comments in his remarkable history of the Civil Rights Movement, "the beloved community" they sought should "finally be described as a gift of the kingdom of God introduced into history by

---

64. Indeed, I was encouraged by Fields's citation of Reformed theologian Louis Berkhof in this context.

65. Though admittedly, in practice, the middle-class comfort of white Reformed folk no doubt lulls us into a comfort level with the present order that blunts this eschatological orientation. There is a gap, one might say, between "official" Reformed doctrine and "functional" Reformed practice.

66. Of course, these overlapping sensibilities make Reformed racism and oppression all the more reprehensible. For a Black Reformed response in the context of South African apartheid, see the Belhar Confession: http://www.crcna.org/welcome/beliefs/ecumenical-faith-declaration/confession-belhar.

the church, and thus it exists within the provenance of Christ's mystery in the world."[67] It was in the church, nourished by the Word made flesh, their imaginations fueled by the gospel, that they learned to long for a better country (Heb. 11:16), but also imagined that *this* country could look more like it.

67. Charles Marsh, *The Beloved Community: How Faith Shapes Social Justice from the Civil Rights Movement to Today* (New York: Basic Books, 2005), 207.

A CATHOLIC (SYNTHETIC) RESPONSE

J. BRIAN BENESTAD

This is the context in which many Black churches were founded: A situation of grave injustice brought about by the official acceptance of slavery since the very founding of the nation in 1787 and then by widespread support for Jim Crow laws after the Civil War.

Not surprisingly, Professor Bruce Fields says that "the Black church in the United States was founded on the gospel and on protest" (p. 102). The Black church inculcated faith in the "Christianity of Christ" that opposed slavery and segregation after emancipation. It gave Black Christians a place to worship God, free from "the offensiveness of racial segregation in the churches" (p. 103), and free from those white churches that "had become a principal instrument of the political and social policies undergirding slavery and the attendant degradation of the human spirit" (p. 103). The Black church provided a place of refuge for oppressed Blacks both during the time of legalized slavery and during the period of segregation and other forms of racism after the Civil War until the present day. Besides offering comfort, the Black church confronted the evil of racism and continues performing that service to this very moment.

The mission of the Black church to promote respect for the dignity of Black people—and others as well—necessarily led to dealings with the government, either protesting unjust laws or cooperating with the government's efforts to overcome racism. The Civil Rights Act of 1964 and the Voting Rights Act of 1965 were results of these efforts. The passage of these acts was greatly facilitated by the support of many Christians, black and white, conservative and liberal. The Supreme Court's landmark decision *Brown v. Board of Education* (1954) and the 1963 March on Washington helped pave the way for the passage of these historic acts.

Because government has the capability of overcoming injustices, Fields concludes that "involvement in politics is virtually an obligation on the part of Black believers" (p. 117). He also believes that the Black church "has long been a place of political information and mobilization, and this should be maintained" (p. 117). Black political activity is not limited to race issues but extends to other matters, such as the environment and poverty. In fact, Fields concludes, "Thus the Black church, reflecting on the atrocities inflicted upon it in the past even by religious people, must ultimately be a light to illuminate what can be accomplished for the benefit of individuals, communities, the nation, and all of God's world" (p. 124). Consistent with its Christian identity, the Black church must be concerned about the good of all on the face of the earth. Black expectations of governments, however, are moderate because the Black church keeps in mind that a "government is only as just as the justice that resides in the hearts and minds of its people" (p. 123).

Finally, Fields's discussion of poverty brings up the neuralgic issue of why Black children have difficulty receiving a quality education in their neighborhoods: inadequate educational facilities, not enough quality teachers, lack of "sufficient familial support to provide accountability and proper motivation for achievement," and the absence of fathers in families (p. 121).

In a dialogue with the Black church, the Catholic Church would find many points of agreement: the emphasis on promoting faith in Jesus Christ, homilies focused on building faith and explaining Christian morality, belief in the Bible as the Word of God, the church as a place of refuge for the oppressed, forgiveness of enemies, the duty of the government to protect the oppressed, moderate expectations of government, the conviction that just government depends on holiness and justice in individual citizens, and the duty of churches to work for the good of all.

In any good dialogue the Catholic church would also explore with its interlocutors the possibility of preparing young people for a lifelong commitment in marriage and would address the difficulty of dealing with the absence of fathers in so many Black families. The serious problem of divorce in the Catholic Church would necessarily enter into the dialogue on family life. Another fruitful subject of dialogue would cover the problem of the culture evangelizing the church and not vice versa. The Catholic Church could explore with the Black church ways to teach the faith and hold on to it in a dechristianized culture. Still another subject of dialogue should be the difference between political statements on injustice on which all Christians should agree and statements about which there could be reasonable disagreement among committed Christians.

The United States owes so much to Black Americans for having imposed on them slavery, segregation, Jim Crow laws, and racism. Meaningful dialogue that begins with our shared values is an important starting point for learning from each other's traditions and working together to overcome past injustice.

THE REFORMED (TRANSFORMATIONIST) VIEW

JAMES K.A. SMITH

While the Protestant Reformation is rightly considered a religious movement and a doctrinal revolution within the Western church, it was also essentially and immediately a political movement. For religious reasons, the Reformers challenged the received arrangements between the Emperor and the Pope, bishops and princes, the church and (what passed for) "the state."

One could already see this in a somewhat haphazard, ad hoc manner in Martin Luther's protests; but as Michael Walzer notes in his classic study, *The Revolution of the Saints*, it was particularly the Reformed stream flowing out of John Calvin's Geneva that engendered a more radical shift in how Christians came to understand the nature of politics and "the political" per se. "It was the Calvinists," he points out, "who first switched the emphasis of political thought from the prince to the saint (or the band of saints) and then constructed a theoretical justification for independent political action."[1]

This stream of Reformed thought generated distinct political experiments in Geneva and the Netherlands as well as the Huguenots' France, the Presbyterians' Scotland, and the Puritans' New England. The Reformation was not merely a soteriological manifesto that happened to impact politics; rather, the Reformers' understanding of the gospel and Scripture included a distinct — and, they believed, biblical — understanding of "the political" as part of its DNA.

---

1. Michael Walzer, *The Revolution of the Saints: A Study in the Origins of Radical Politics* (Cambridge, MA: Harvard University Press, 1965), 2.

Given the breadth and variety of movements, figures, and traditions spawned by the Protestant Reformation, I hesitate to describe "the" Reformed view on the church and politics. My goal, instead, is to outline *a* Reformed view of the relationship between church and politics. This model grows out of the magisterial Reformation, with a specific focus on a stream flowing out of John Calvin's Geneva that "got in the water," so to speak, in the Netherlands and nourished the thought of the theologian and statesman Abraham Kuyper.[2] This "Kuyperian" stream of the Reformed tradition, while coming from a little tribe, has had a disproportionate impact on Christian discussions of faith and politics because it has shaped the work of influential scholars such as Herman Dooyeweerd, Nicholas Wolterstorff, Richard Mouw, and Jonathan Chaplin. Furthermore, Kuyperian sensibilities influenced activists such as Chuck Colson and James Skillen, elected officials such as Paul Henry, and the work of public policy think tanks such as Cardus and the Center for Public Justice.[3] In what follows I try to encapsulate the theological and theoretical distinctives of this specific Reformed tradition as it bears on questions at the intersection of faith and politics, church and state.

A. Historical Development and Theological Undergirding

A Reformed understanding of the relationship between the church and politics is bound up with a wider constellation of convictions about the nature of creation, culture, and the common good. So before we consider specific views about government, citizenship, and political participation, I want to contextualize those specifics within the wider web of a Reformed social vision. We can summarize this in five key themes.

---

2. For an engaging, illuminating biography of Kuyper, situating him in the history of late 19th-century Europe, see James Bratt, *Abraham Kuyper: Modern Calvinist, Christian Democrat* (Grand Rapids: Eerdmans, 2013).

3. The work of Dooyeweerd, Wolterstorff, Mouw, and Chaplin will be engaged below. For more information about the Center for Public Justice, visit http://www.cpjustice.org; to learn more about Cardus, see http://cardus.ca. To see Chuck Colson's debts to Kuyper, see Colson and Nancy Pearcey, *How Now Shall We Live?* (Wheaton, IL: Tyndale, 1999). For more on the late US Congressman Paul B. Henry, see *Serving the Claims of Justice: The Thoughts of Paul B. Henry*, ed. Douglas L. Koopman (Grand Rapids: The Paul B. Henry Institute for the Study of Christianity and Politics, 2001).

1. The Sanctification of Ordinary Life

There are many different ways to tell the story of the Protestant Reformation. A favorite angle centers on the heroic tale of Martin Luther, an Augustinian monk newly convicted by his discovery of the apostle Paul's forensic gospel, furiously hammering his 95 Theses to the church door in Wittenberg, Germany. A different angle is emphasized by scholars as diverse as Michael Walzer, Nicholas Wolterstorff, and most recently, the Canadian philosopher Charles Taylor. This angle on the story sees the Reformation not only as a narrowly theological debate about personal salvation, but more broadly as a Christian reform movement concerned with the shape of social life.

As Taylor tells the story, the Protestant Reformation was one of several "reform" movements in the late Middle Ages and early modern period that all railed against the distorted social arrangements of medieval Christendom. In particular, the Reformation called into question the "two-tiered" or "multi-speed" religion that had emerged, with "renunciative vocations" on the top tier (monks, nuns, priests) and everybody else mired in domestic ("secular") life, consigned to the lower level, as second-class spiritual citizens. The "religious" worshiped, while everyone else just worked.[4]

In this climate, the really revolutionary impact of the Reformation issued more from Geneva than Wittenberg. Calling into question this two-tiered, sacred/secular arrangement, Reformers such as John Calvin and his heirs refused such distinctions. *All* of life is to be lived *coram Deo*, they would say—that is, before the face of God. *All* vocations can be holy, for *all* of our cultural labors can be expressions of tending God's world. There is no "secular" because there is not a square inch of creation that is not the Lord's.

The result is what Taylor calls "the sanctification of ordinary life." This hallowing of earthly, "worldly" life includes our social, economic, and political lives. This is rooted in a distinct theology of creation, not so much as an account of "origins" as a theological account of the *status* of material, embodied, earthly life. Economic exchange and political

---

4. See Charles Taylor, *Sources of the Self: The Making of the Modern Identity* (Cambridge, MA: Harvard University Press, 1989), 211–33, and idem, *A Secular Age* (Cambridge, MA: Belknap Press, 2007), 61–89. For further discussion, see James K.A. Smith, *How (Not) To Be Secular: Reading Charles Taylor* (Grand Rapids: Eerdmans, 2014), 26–46.

organization are features of a "very good" creation (Gen. 1:31), since creation itself includes the task of cultivating the social, economic, and political potential of creation.

That is the task and mission of "culture"—the cultivation of the inherent possibilities latent in creation, tending them according to God's norms so that creation can expand toward what God desires. Indeed, that is what it means to bear God's image (Gen. 1:27): we bear God's image to his world *by* taking up the cultural mandate of Genesis 1:28–30. Creation is not called into existence ready-made with schools, art museums, and parliaments. Rather, creation is called into existence, and humanity is blessed by the Creator and charged with the mission of unfurling the possibilities of these cultural goods. Thus Kuyper, while taking up concrete questions about poverty and government, situates this within a wider theology of culture that emphasizes "human art acts on every part of nature, not to destroy it or simply to impose another structure alongside it, but to unlock the power that lies hidden within it."[5]

2. Faithful Revolutions: Politics and/as Human Culture

Both historically and theoretically, the previous point has a significant implication: "the political" does not fall from heaven ready-made, nor is government constructed and instituted by God in the garden. Government and the political institutions that shape our lives are not "divine" in the sense of being handed down from God like the descent of the New Jerusalem (Rev. 21:1–2). Like all of the cultural institutions and practices that shape and direct our lives (e.g., language, education, business), government and political life are products of *our* creation. The political is made from the bottom up, not received top-down. But as with the cultural mandate more generally, our making is a response to God's call and is thus responsible *to* God. We are called to order our political life *well*, in accordance with what God desires for his creation. While the political is made by us, it is normed by God.

We so take this for granted today that we might not feel the revolutionary impact of this insight. In the early modern era, it was precisely this account of political life as a human product that pushed back on various mythologies of divine sanction that veritably identified the status quo

---

5. Abraham Kuyper, *The Problem of Poverty*, ed. James W. Skillen (Grand Rapids: Baker, 1991), 30.

with divine order and underwrote the authority of kings and princes with the imprimatur of the Creator himself. Nicholas Wolterstorff observes,

> In the sixteenth century, a profoundly different vision and practice came forth from the "reformed" church in Switzerland and the upper Rhine valley. The structure of the social world was held up to judgment, was pronounced guilty, and was sentenced to be reformed.[6]

In many ways, "all of us in the modern world are inheritors" of this "new way of inserting oneself into the social order that came into the lights there in central Europe three and a half centuries ago."[7] In other words, modern liberal democracy is, in some sense, the heir of this Reformed vision.[8] Wolterstorff, echoing Walzer, summarizes the upshot this way:

> The saints are responsible for the structure of the social world in which they find themselves. That structure is not simply part of the order of nature; to the contrary, it is the result of human decision, and by concerted effort it can be altered. Indeed, it *should* be altered, for it is a fallen structure, in need of reform. The responsibility of the saints to struggle for the reform of the social order in which they find themselves is one facet of the discipleship to which their Lord Jesus Christ has called them. It is not an addition to their religion; it is there among the very motions of Christian spirituality.[9]

The way things *are* is not necessarily an indicator of the way things ought to be. There is no inherent virtue in, or divine sanction behind, the status quo. The organization of societal structures needs to be evaluated in light of the Creator's call for justice—which might require that we sometimes reform, even overthrow, the status quo.[10]

---

6. Nicholas Wolterstorff, *Until Justice and Peace Embrace* (Grand Rapids: Eerdmans, 1983), 3.

7. Ibid.

8. This argument is further developed, conceptually, in Nicholas Wolterstorff, *Justice: Rights and Wrongs* (Princeton, NJ: Princeton University Press, 2008). For a more historical consideration, see John Witte, *The Reformation of Rights: Law, Religion, and Human Rights in Early Modern Calvinism* (Cambridge: Cambridge University Press, 2007).

9. Wolterstorff, *Until Justice and Peace Embrace*, 3.

10. This is the point at which the Reformed model departs from the Lutheran emphasis on "natural" orders and maintaining one's "station" in life. As Wolterstorff puts it, while there are "world-formative" elements of Lutheranism, "the focus of its formative efforts was mainly on ecclesiastical structures and on individual 'inwardness.' The stance of Lutherans toward the structures of the social world was as much acquiescence as was that of the medieval" (ibid., 10).

3. The Structural/Systemic Nature of Sin

Just because culture and its institutions are products of human making doesn't mean we are free to make them however we want. To the contrary, such institutions are judged as needing reform only to the extent that they fail to meet divine norms and expectations—because they fail to realize the Creator's standards for justice. The Reformers' emphasis on the contingent nature of political arrangements was bound up with the recognition that, all too often, things are *not* the way they're supposed to be.[11]

In other words, the Reformers emphasized the all-too-human nature of government and political institutions precisely in order to point out the ways that they are disordered and harmful, infected by sin. Governments need to be reformed, perhaps even overthrown, precisely because they fail to conduct themselves according to God's order for social, communal, and political life. Later thinkers in the Reformed tradition would articulate this in terms of "creation order"—by which they meant the norms and standards relevant for each sphere or sector of human culture as established by the Creator. That is, the norms for creational flourishing are established by the Creator, not made up by creatures. These norms are the standard for judging whether our cultural products are "good" or "just."[12] When the recognition of disordered social life is bound together with the previous point regarding human responsibility for making and maintaining cultural institutions, then any *dis*order is a call to *re*order. The revolutionary cry, "Things have got to change!" follows from the evaluation, "This is not the way it's supposed to be!"

However, because the Reformed tradition has a robust appreciation for the way institutions shape and foster our lives, they are equally attentive to the negative impact of bad institutions. While the Reformers' emphasis on "total depravity" is often noted with respect to personal

---

11. See Cornelius Plantinga, *Not the Way It's Supposed to Be: A Breviary of Sin* (Grand Rapids: Eerdmans, 2006).

12. For a succinct discussion of "norms" as "God's laws for culture and society," see Albert Wolters, *Creation Regained: Biblical Basics for a Reformational Worldview* (Grand Rapids: Eerdmans, 1985), 14–18. The seminal discussion is found in Herman Dooyeweerd, *A New Critique of Theoretical Thought*, Vol. 3 (Lewiston, NY: Edwin Mellen Press, 1997). For commentary, see Jonathan Chaplin, *Herman Dooyeweerd: Christian Philosopher of State and Civil Society* (Notre Dame, IN: University of Notre Dame Press, 2011), 62–70 and 86–95.

salvation, the Reformed tradition equally emphasizes the way in which sin weaves itself into systems and structures *beyond* individual choices and decisions. In other words, sin is not just attributable to individual agents and actors; there is also a sense in which systems and structures and policies can be disordered—that sin can take on a life of its own in structures that transcend individual choices.

Because "social structures are not something natural," but instead "the result of human decision," "they can be altered by us. Indeed, they *must* be altered, for they are fallen, corrupt. The structures *themselves* are corrupt and in need of reform, not only the persons who exist within these structures."[13] In order to right the wrongs of racism or oppression, it is not enough to convert the racists or fan the compassion of the oppressor; we will need to reform the systems and structures that advantage whites, for example, or slaveholders. The solution to political injustices is not individual conversion but systemic reform. Good policy won't save anyone, but neither will revival sweep away systems of unjust privilege.

4. Thy Kingdom Come: Eschatology and Cultural Life

Calvinism, we have noted, unleashes a distinct impulse to reshape society. Indeed, according to Charles Taylor, "Calvinism is marked out by a militant activism, a drive to reorganize the church and the world."[14] Taylor rightly notes that some observers are puzzled by this: Why would a stream of Christianity that so emphasizes the sovereignty of God and divine predestination give rise to a bottom-up desire to *change* things? Instead of "revolutionary activism," wouldn't one expect Calvinism to "produce only a fatalistic quietism"?[15]

Taylor points out an important distinction: Such activism would be paradoxical "if activism were meant to *bring about* the salvation of those whose lives were thus reordered. But that would be an absurd and blasphemous aim." Indeed, the goal of Calvinist social reform is not soteriological, nor is it undertaken as some kind of pre-evangelistic

---

13. Wolterstorff, *Until Justice and Peace Embrace*, 9. Wolterstorff goes on to note how this resonates with the insights and emphases of liberation theology (ibid., 44–52).

14. Taylor, *Sources of the Self*, 227. Taylor notes that this is Calvin's "striking difference from Lutheranism."

15. Ibid., 228.

prelude to cultivate openness to the gospel. Social and political reform is pursued as an end in itself in service to the Lord of every square inch of creation. Such reform is not a pursuit of salvation, but rather an *outcome* of regeneration:

> While humans can do nothing to bring about reconciliation, the reconciled person feels the imperative need to repair the disorder of things, to put them right again in God's plan. His desire and effort in this direction are only the fruit of God's reconciling action in him; they flow from his regeneration.[16]

Thus Taylor, following Walzer, sees "horror at disorder" as one of the distinguishing features of Calvinist and Puritan social visions:

> To the Calvinist, it seemed self-evident that the properly regenerate person would above all be appalled at the offense done to God in a sinful, disordered world, and that therefore one of his foremost aims would be to put this right, to clean up the human mess or at least to mitigate the tremendous continuing insult done to God.[17]

In later Reformed thinkers, this concern for disorder is not only a matter of what offends God but also what hurts our neighbor. In other words, righting wrongs and reordering disordered laws and policies would be a way of loving our neighbor since the vulnerable and marginalized — the widow, the orphan, and the stranger — suffer not just at the hands of unjust individual actors but also because of disordered laws and institutions. The more society is ordered toward *shalom*, the more we would foster the flourishing of all. Disorder harms the common good; reform pursues the common good.

This Reformed impulse to reorder and reform could easily give license to a draconian, almost fascist agenda: *We* are the reordered, regenerate elect; *we* know what God wants for society; therefore, *we* will impose it. And there have been some troublesome proposals and experiments in this regard that claim to have a Reformed pedigree: one might point to South African apartheid as a particularly egregious example, or the "reconstructionist" theocracy of R. J.

---

16. Ibid.
17. Ibid.

Rushdoony.[18] But most instances of such mistaken imposition have usually forgotten another key aspect of the Reformed vision: a robust eschatology that cultivates a healthy sense of our living in the "not yet."

First, the eschaton functions as a normative vision for contemporary cultural labor. Biblical descriptions of the coming kingdom (such as Isa. 11:6–8 or Rev. 21:1–21) are clues and signals to what a flourishing creation looks like. Culture-making is not a nostalgic project of recovering a lost Eden because even that "very good" Eden called for history to unpack its potential. Instead, it is the New Jerusalem that pictures, in broad strokes, what God desires for his creation.[19] It is in that coming city, not the memory of a lost Garden, that we see the way it's supposed to be. Nicholas Wolterstorff has perhaps best captured this Reformed sensibility in his discussion of *shalom*, the Hebrew word (often translated as "peace") that captures the fullness and wholeness of creation put to rights: "Shalom is the human being dwelling at peace in all his or her relationships: with God, with self, with fellows, with nature."[20]

Second, this eschatological orientation also serves as a kind of Augustinian check-and-balance on any pretension that *we* are going to institute "the kingdom." It is this eschatology that curtails any utopian activism. As Kuyper admonished the First Christian Social Congress in 1891, "Even if we pursue this path of justice to its very end, the goal that God has in view will never be reached by means of legal measures designed to improve social conditions. Rules alone will not cure our sick society."[21]

---

18. For a critical discussion of the South African case, see Alan Boesak, *Black and Reformed: Apartheid, Liberation, and the Calvinist Tradition* (Maryknoll, NY: Orbis, 1984). For a relevant critique of reconstructionism, see Richard John Neuhaus's insightful essay, "Why Wait for the Kingdom? The Theonomist Temptation," *First Things* (May 1990).

19. See Richard Mouw, *When the Kings Come Marching In: Isaiah and the New Jerusalem*, Rev. ed. (Grand Rapids: Eerdmans, 2002).

20. Wolterstorff, *Until Justice and Peace Embrace*, 69. Wolterstorff notes that if *shalom* is the biblical vision of creation in its fullness, then *shalom* was already future *in the Garden*. In this sense, creation calls for our cultural labor in order to help creation reach its potential (=*shalom*). However, we now inhabit a creation wracked with sin and fractured relationships, so the pursuit of *shalom* is not just a call to "develop" creation, but also to right wrongs, contest injustice, and counter the effects of sin. "An implication of this," Wolterstorff concludes, "is that our work will always have the two dimensions of a struggle for justice and the pursuit of increased mastery of the world so as to enrich human life. Both together are necessary if *shalom* is to be brought nearer. Development and liberation must go hand in hand. Ours is both a cultural mandate and a liberation mandate—the mandate to master the world for the benefit of mankind, but also the mandate 'to loose the chains of injustice …' [Is. 58:6–7]" (ibid., 72).

21. Kuyper, *The Problem of Poverty*, 72–73. Kuyper goes on to emphasize that consideration of "eternity" is integral to "the social question."

Third, the eschatological pictures of Scripture signal what Richard Mouw calls "the promise of political sanctification," glimpsed when we see "the kings come marching in" to the New Jerusalem as pictured in Isaiah 60. Our political labor that accords with *shalom* will be taken up in the transformed City of God:

> "In many ways the promise of political sanctification is a mysterious, and even a baffling, notion. But it is also true that in many ways it is a very encouraging promise for us in the present age. For one thing, we can act politically in the full assurance that our political deeds will count toward the day of reckoning that will occur in the transformed City. This vision of the political future is not one which should inspire us to be politically passive."[22]

5. Diversity and Development in Creation

Finally, a Reformed theology of culture recognizes and values certain sorts of pluralism as an essential feature of a "very good" creation. The picture of creation in Genesis 1–2 is one of a plethora of "kinds," a diversity of creatures who stage an expanding play in the theater of God's glory. The "good" is not synonymous with unity or uniformity. A flourishing creation reflects a rich diversity celebrated (and desired) by the Creator.[23]

Rooted in a creational theology that recognizes and even celebrates plurality, a Reformed social vision affirms a plurality of social realities as inherent to—and called for—by a good creation itself. As Herman Bavinck summarizes, Scripture teaches

> That the distinction of soul and body, of man and woman, of parents and children, of authority and obedience, of inequality in gifts and powers, in talents and goods, in calling and task; the duty to work and the privilege of rest, and thus the change of day and night, of work days and Sabbath; the earthly calling and man's heavenly destination—all these are *founded in creation*, called into being by God's will. Therefore they have to be acknowledged and

---

22. Mouw, *When the Kings Come Marching In*, 37.

23. For further discussion of the good of creational diversity, see Richard J. Mouw and Sander Griffioen, *Pluralisms and Horizons: An Essay in Christian Public Philosophy* (Grand Rapids: Eerdmans, 1993), 125–29.

honored as unchangeable ordinances. The intent of grace, which entered immediately after the fall, always and everywhere has been to maintain and restore these original relationships.[24]

Bavinck's peer and collaborator, Abraham Kuyper, would capture the same vision in his notion of "sphere sovereignty" — that there are multiple modes of social relationship (the family, the corporation, the church, the school) that each have their own calling, integrity, and norms *apart from the state*. Each is a mode of human collaboration "after their own kind," like the diversity of God's creation in Genesis 1. Indeed, Kuyper emphasizes that these unique spheres are called forth by the Creator:

> In this independent character [of these social spheres] a special *higher authority* is of necessity involved and this highest author-ity we intentionally call: *sovereignty in the individual social spheres*, in order that it may be sharply and decidedly expressed that these different developments of social life have *nothing above themselves but God*, and that the State cannot intrude here, and has nothing to command in their domain.[25]

Human social life is not meant to be governed by one overarching organization; instead, creation itself calls for diverse modes and levels of social organization. Each of these is subject to the Lordship of the Creator known in Christ, and each has norms that are unique to its calling. In other words, the array of social institutions are all subject to God's sovereignty while also sovereign "within their sphere." Richard Mouw and Sander Griffioen helpfully describe this as "associational pluralism" — that is, a healthy society includes and fosters a plurality of human associations.[26]

This recognition of an original, creational diversity of social relation-ships and institutions is complemented by an emphasis on history and the

---

24. Herman Bavinck, "Christian Principles and Social Relationships," in *Essays on Religion, Science, and Society*, ed. John Bolt (Grand Rapids: Baker Academic, 2008), 141, emphasis added.

25. Kuyper, "Calvinism and Politics," his third Stone Lecture at Princeton Theological Seminary, 1898, published as *Calvinism* (Grand Rapids: Eerdmans, 1943), 91, emphases original.

26. Mouw and Griffioen, *Pluralisms and Horizons*, 16–18 and 117–19. They rightly note that this "Reformed" theme overlaps in important ways with Catholic Social Teaching on "subsidiarity."

need for—and good of—*development*. Each of these original relations and institutions calls for unpacking and development, and over time they will take on different expressions and configurations as a result. As we already noted, creation isn't called into existence ready-made with art museums and parliaments: these are artifacts and institutions that are elucidated from creational potential *over time*. Thus Bavinck continues:

> Each of the various walks of life—family, society, the state, occupation, business, agriculture, industry, commerce, science, art, and so forth—has a certain measure of independence, which it owes to the will of God as it manifests itself in its own nature. *In time*, by God's providence, they develop and are changed in accordance with their nature. The authority of the government over its subjects, of the husband over his wife, of the father over his children, of the master over his servants—this authority is considerably different today from what it was in the days of Paul. The gospel fully honors this development....[27]

This theme of development and the differentiation of spheres of social life was especially explored by Herman Dooyeweerd, a philosophical heir of Bavinck and Kuyper. As Jonathan Chaplin summarizes, "For Dooyeweerd, cultural development is a normative calling in which humans disclose the entire realm of 'normative meaning' in creation."[28] Reformed engagement with social and political life takes seriously the developments of history, both affirming time as the horizon within which creational seeds germinate and grow, and also recognizing that cultural development can be *dis*ordered.

B. The Role of Government and Christian Participation in Politics

A Reformed understanding of politics and government grows out of this broader "theology of culture" that I have summarized. Let's now consider the specific implications of this for a Reformed understanding of politics, government, and Christian participation in the state.

---

27. Ibid., 143. This emphasis on "development" is not synonymous with confidence in "progress," although it is sometimes misunderstood (and misapplied) in that way.

28. Chaplin, *Herman Dooyeweerd*, 79. Chapter 5 of *Herman Dooyeweerd* is devoted to explaining why "Dooyeweerd's conception of cultural development and history has at its heart the notion of the 'process of disclosure'" (71).

1. Government Is Part of the Good Order of Creation

While there is debate about this even within the broader Reformed tradition,[29] the vision I am laying out sees politics and the institutions of political life as an essential and integral part of creation itself. As James Skillen summarizes it,

> Although there is no mention in Genesis 1 of legislatures, courts, and governors of political communities, neither does the passage mention universities, farms, art galleries, publishing firms, and large-scale industries. All such organizations and institutions have come into existence as human generations have emerged and built creatively on the achievements of past generations. Inherent in God's command to govern and develop creation is the task of public governance that will differentiate from other kinds of human responsibility in the course of social and cultural development over many generations.[30]

Now, we might more carefully distinguish the good (i.e., creational) nature of government from the more specific *expression* of government that is "the state." Dooyeweerd argues that the state is the product of good, legitimate differentiation in time as humanity organized itself in networks beyond kin.[31] As Skillen summarizes it, "administrative justice ... would exist even without sin."[32] Thus politics, government, and "the state" in particular are all understood to be aspects of a good but fallen creation.

This conviction propels believers into government and politics. If government and the state are creational goods, then these are legitimate,

---

29. For example, Kuyper himself grants that "the impulse to form states arises from man's social nature, which was expressed already by Aristotle, when he called man a *zoon politikon* [a political animal]." However, Kuyper believes that had not sin intervened, humanity would have remained governed directly by the sovereign Lord, the creator, and would have functioned as a worldwide family or tribe. "[W]ithout sin," Kuyper suggests, there would have been neither magistrate nor state-order.... Neither bar of justice nor police, nor army, nor navy, is conceivable in a world without sin; and thus every rule and ordinance and law would drop away." For Kuyper, while government is a creational good, "[e]very State formation ... is therefore always something unnatural" (Kuyper, "Calvinism and Politics," 79–80).

30. James W. Skillen, *The Good of Politics: A Biblical, Historical, and Contemporary Introduction* (Grand Rapids: Baker Academic, 2014), 23.

31. See Chaplin, *Herman Dooyeweerd*, 156–61.

32. Skillen, *The Good of Politics*, 119.

even necessary, vocations for creatures created in God's image and re-created in Christ. Thus the Reformed tradition has produced a number of statesmen and politicians whose Reformed convictions have propelled them into government agencies and as elected officials, including Kuyper, who was for a time Prime Minister of the Netherlands; his collaborator Herman Bavinck, who was a member of the Dutch Senate; and former US Congressmen Paul Henry and Vern Ehlers.

2. Both Church and Government Should Be Limited to Their "Sphere"

Even while the Reformed tradition encourages participation in government and politics and sees opportunity to foster *shalom* through legislation and policy, it also repeatedly cautions against idolizing government or falling into the trap of thinking government is the *only* way to pursue *shalom*. This stems in part from the Reformed tradition's eschatological orientation, which runs counter to any kind of political utopianism.[33]

Following Augustine, the Reformed tradition cultivates a kind of holy ambivalence about politics — engaged but not *over*expecting. Politics is the art of the possible, not the mechanism by which we impose "kingdom come." So we should not overestimate what can be accomplished in politics or by government.[34] At times, this means "faithful" Christian labor in government and "faithful" Christian political participation might settle for compromises.[35]

But the Reformed tradition's limited expectations of government grow more systematically out of the principle of sphere sovereignty. Positively, government and politics are viewed within the wider web of cultural "spheres," which also (and often *more* so) contribute to flourishing and the welfare of the commonweal. Thus the Reformed

---

33. For Kuyper, Bavinck, Groen van Prinsterer, and their heirs, the French Revolution stands as *the* version of idolatrous politics. Indeed, their political party in the Netherlands was called the "Antirevolutionary Party," defining itself by this opposition to the French Revolution, which stood as the embodiment of both anti-social individualism and unbelieving, "immanentist" utopianism. For a discussion, see Kuyper, *The Problem of Poverty*, 43–57.

34. Furthermore, society is always more than culture. Or, as it is sometimes said, politics is downstream from culture. In this sense, James Davison Hunter's argument in *To Change the World*—that evangelicals have overestimated how much cultural change is accomplished by political action—expresses a Reformed sensibility (see *To Change the World* [New York: Oxford University Press, 2010]).

35. For further discussion of this point, see James K.A. Smith, "Faithful Compromise," *Comment* (Spring 2014): 2–4, and Ray Pennings, "The Devil's Advocate: Perfection Waits for Another World," *Comment* (Spring 2013): 110–15.

tradition emphasizes societal and institutional pluralism for the common good. The state shouldn't do the work of the family and become an ersatz parent, just as the family shouldn't do the work of the state and become a vigilante police force. The common good is served when this variety of human modes of organization are all carrying out their God-ordained task in creation. The health of civil society *beyond* the state is crucial for a society that reflects *shalom*. In this sense, the Reformed tradition emphasizes a limited role for government, not because of a libertarian emphasis on individuals (let alone any kind of Ayn Rand-ian ideology) but rather because of an appreciation for so many other modes of human community that have a role to play in fostering human flourishing.[36]

As we have already seen, Kuyper emphasizes that each of the spheres of human society answer directly to the sovereignty of God. The state and education and commerce all ultimately answer to God and are called to find expressions that submit themselves to the Creator's norms for creation. But precisely because they answer *directly* to God, in this respect it is not the responsibility of the *church* to oversee the other spheres, nor should the state police the responsibilities of the other spheres. Thus Kuyper was opposed to all "Constantinian" arrangements, even though he also emphasized that the state is answerable to God's authority (and thus rejected any notion of the public as a "secular" sphere). "A free Church in a free State" was the motto of the weekly newspaper Kuyper edited. Opposing government intervention in affairs of religion — and hence opposing the very notion of a "national church" — Kuyper would equally require the state to make room for the integrity of the church and would expect religiously motivated discourse to be permitted in public discourse.[37] Thus when he came to the United

---

36. There is a fundamentally communitarian picture of politics and society in play here. Thus politics is not the sum of individual actions, nor is political activity limited to individual acts (like voting). All of these spheres find expression and embodiment in institutions. Thus Reformed political activity tends to reflect a concern with reforming systems, policies, and institutions. For more on this point, see Jonathan Chaplin, "Loving Faithful Institutions: Building Blocks of a Just Global Society," *Comment* (Fall 2011): 12–19, and James K.A. Smith, "We Believe in Institutions," *Comment* (Fall 2013): 2–4.

37. See, for example, Nicholas Wolterstorff's critique of Richard Rorty on this point in "An Engagement with Rorty," *Journal of Religious Ethics* 31 (2003): 129–39. For a (concessionary) response, see Richard Rorty, "Religion in the Public Square: A Reconsideration," *Journal of Religious Ethics* 31 (2003): 141–49.

States in 1898, Kuyper was not just flattering his American listeners when he praised their Constitution "concerning the liberty of worship and the *coordination* of Church and State."[38]

The error of medieval Christendom, for Kuyper, was that the church was considered a "total," comprehensive social institution. To use later language, there was a failure of "differentiation," a failure to distinguish between distinct spheres. Relevant here is Kuyper's distinction between the church as "institute" and the church as "organism."[39] On the one hand, Kuyper *agrees* with advocates of a "state church": "[W]e and they agree that Christ's church and its means of grace cover a broader field than that of special grace alone" (189). In other words, they both agree that the church — as the body of Christ — is called to have an impact beyond merely "spiritual" matters. The body of Christ is to be the agent by which the "significance" of Christ for "nature" is made manifest. "We both acknowledge that the church does two things: (1) it works *directly* for the well-being of the elect, lures them to conversion, comforts, edifies, unites, and sanctifies them; but (2) it works *indirectly* for the well-being of the whole of civil society, constraining it to civic virtue" (189–90). So the church is called to have a "leavening" effect on society, impacting all the spheres of human cultural production.

However, Kuyper disagrees with the national church advocates "in how to reach that good goal." The disagreement, in other words, is about strategy. The national church party thinks that the way to have this impact is to "include civil society in the church" (190). Kuyper, by contrast, emphasizes that the church *as institute* should be a "city on a hill amid civil society" (190) *from which* the church as organism infiltrates and leavens civil society. As he later put it,

> This institute does not cover everything that is Christian. Though
> the lamp of the Christian religion only burns within that institute's
> walls, its light shines out through its windows to areas far beyond,

---

38. Kuyper, "Calvinism and Politics," 99, emphasis added. (Note that Kuyper doesn't read this as the "separation" of church and state.) Kuyper would also criticize his own Reformed tradition on the continent, including Calvin and the framers of the Belgic Confession, for too often forgetting these principles and seeking to enlist government "in the matter of religion." For further discussion, see John Bolt, *A Free Church, A Holy Nation: Abraham Kuyper's American Public Theology* (Grand Rapids: Eerdmans, 2001).

39. Abraham Kuyper, "Church and Culture," from *Common Grace* in *Abraham Kuyper: A Centennial Reader*, ed. J. Bratt (Eerdmans, 1998), 187–201.

illumining all the sectors and associations that appear across the wide range of human life and activity.[40]

Thus he suggests that we picture these as concentric circles, with the church as institute—administering the sacraments, exercising discipline, forming disciples—and nourishing a vibrant core of believers who, as an organism, infiltrate and leaven civil society (194–95).[41] While he certainly emphasizes that "the institute does not cover everything that is Christian" (194), he goes on to note, recalling the concentric circle metaphor: "Aside from this first circle of the institute *and in necessary connection with it*, we thus recognize another circle whose circumference is determined by the length of the ray that shines out *from the church institute* over the life of people and nation" (195, emphases added).[42]

As institutions, the church and the state have different jurisdictions. But Christians formed in and by the church as institute are then sent (*missio*) *as* the church as organism to take up a variety of vocations—including some in government and politics—seeking to bend the kingdoms of this world closer to the kingdom of the beloved Son and the *shalom* God desires for his creation. As spheres, the church *as institute* is distinct from the state, but the church *as organism* is called to be faithfully present[43]— and a reforming influence—in *every* sphere, including the state.

3. Principled Pluralism and Christian Influence "in the Meantime"

As noted above, the Reformed perspective has a healthy sense of both the vagaries and contingencies of history, as well as an appreciation for the ubiquity of sin this side of the eschaton. As such, the Reformed tradition not only affirms institutional or "associational" pluralism, but also recognizes (and somewhat laments) the reality of what Mouw and Griffioen call "directional" pluralism (or what James Skillen calls "confessional pluralism"[44])—that not all citizens agree on "the good" or the ultimate

---

40. Ibid., 194.

41. Kuyper, in a mode of Protestant flourish, actually claims that the church as organism *precedes* the church as institute—and could even "manifest itself" where the church as institute has ceased to function (195).

42. So it is the worship of the church as institute that *forms* those who will be the rays of light in civil society. This integral role for the church as institute has not always been appreciated by Kuyperians.

43. The notion of "faithful presence" is developed in Hunter, *To Change the World*.

44. Skillen, *The Good of Politics*, 125.

ends of the state. As such, we shouldn't be surprised by deep disagreements in our political life together. Nor should Christians active in politics seek to make their faith the law of the land. Instead, for theological reasons, Christians should cultivate a commitment to "principled pluralism."

What do we mean by "principled" pluralism? Skillen summarizes two aspects of this. First, it means that one of the key responsibilities of government is to recognize, make room for, and protect the integrity of the other "spheres" of human social organization beyond the state. He notes, "Most of human social life is *not* political in character; most of our institutions and organized activities are neither departments of government nor created by the political community." For the sake of the common good, then, government has a "responsibility to recognize and protect each person and each legitimate human vocation, institution, and organization."[45] In many ways, following through on this principle will mean curtailing the sprawl of the so-called "welfare state" — not in the name of an anti-government libertarianism, but rather in the name of "associational pluralism."

Second, the state that operates according to principled pluralism will uphold "confessional pluralism": "Political communities should treat all citizens — all members of the political community — on an equal civic basis without giving special privilege or negative discrimination to any of them because of their religious commitments."[46] Thus the Reformed tradition champions religious liberty for *all* religious traditions, not just the free exercise of Christian faith. Perhaps even more significant in a contemporary context, this Reformed perspective values the religious freedom *of institutions and organizations*, not just individuals. Therefore, Reformed organizations such as Cardus and the Institutional Religious Freedom Alliance champion policy and advocate for legislation that make room for collectives, not just individuals, to be animated and directed by religious faith. Not only should I be free to worship "privately" on Sundays, but our business or art museum or Christian university should also have the freedom to be organized around specifically Christian principles.[47]

45. Ibid., 124.
46. Ibid., 125.
47. See Stanley Carlson-Thies, "Religious Freedom: The Cornerstone of Strong Social Architecture," *Comment* (May 31, 2013): http://www.cardus.ca/comment/article/3974/religious-freedom-the-cornerstone-of-strong-social-architecture-part-one/.

However, though the Reformed tradition advocates for pluralism, we would simultaneously emphasize that Christians both should, and should be *able* to, speak and participate in the public/political sphere *as Christians* and to speak not only in terms of generic "natural" laws or principles but from the specificity of the gospel's claims.[48] In other words, Christian political witness does not just appeal to the lowest common denominator of "general" or "natural" revelation; it includes publicly testifying to what we know via "special" revelation. Thus one will constantly hear Calvin, Kuyper, and Bavinck make appeals to the insights of God's Word *for* government and political community.[49] In Oliver O'Donovan's phrase, this is an *evangelical* political theology, appealing not just to Law but Gospel.[50]

In this sense, Kuyper's histories of Western political thought and the evolution of its institutions — in which Calvinism, not surprisingly, plays an outsized role — accords with O'Donovan's point regarding the specifically *Christological* impact upon Western politics: "Like the surface of a planet pocked with craters by the bombardment it receives from space, the governments of the passing age show the impact of Christ's dawning glory."[51]

4. Common Grace: The Spirit Works Outside the Church, Too

Because of the Reformed tradition's affirmation of "common grace" — a restraining operation of God's grace[52] outside the "special," salvific grace extended to the elect[53] — we are not surprised to find passionate

48. See Robert Audi and Nicholas Wolterstorff, *Religion in the Public Square: The Place of Religious Convictions in Political Debate* (Lexington, KY: Rowman & Littlefield, 1996).

49. This doesn't preclude being attentive to the fact that non-Christian citizens obviously don't accept Scripture as an authority in political discourse. But appeals to Scripture need not be merely deontological — appealing to "laws." Appeals to Scripture can also attest to enduring aspects of human nature, which then inform good policy. Christians can appeal to "what we know as Christians" (per Plantinga, "Advice to Christian Philosophers") without that becoming a "God-said-it-that-settles-it" kind of conversation-stopping appeal.

50. Oliver O'Donovan, *The Desire of the Nations: Rediscovering the Roots of Political Theology* (Cambridge: Cambridge University Press, 1996), 81. Compare Mouw, *Political Evangelism* (Grand Rapids: Eerdmans, 1973).

51. O'Donovan, *Desire of the Nations*, 212.

52. Vincent Bacote supplements and expands Kuyper's notion of common grace with a pneumatology in *The Spirit in Public Theology: Appropriating the Legacy of Abraham Kuyper* (Grand Rapids: Baker Academic, 2005), 117–48.

53. See Richard Mouw's comprehensive discussion in *He Shines in All That's Fair: Culture and Common Grace* (Grand Rapids: Eerdmans, 2002).

advocates for justice and wise stewards of the common good outside the body of Christ. This gives license to a strategic, selective, ad-hoc collaboration with "co-belligerents." Faithful, "Christian" political action need not always be focused on religious issues; it includes political labor on a range of issues with a view to seeking *shalom*. But as such, we might find that non-Christians and believers of other religious traditions significantly overlap in our concerns about "this-worldly" flourishing. Thus Christians concerned about creation care legislation may find themselves collaborating with naturalistic environmentalists.

Indeed, sometimes Christians should be humbled to see non-Christians more passionate about injustice than we are.[54] And especially in an increasingly secularized, naturalistic society, it should not be surprising that Christians will find common cause with Jews, Muslims, and Mormons on many issues of "penultimate" concern, even if we have ultimate differences. So faithful Christian political participation does not require any sort of "purity."

Furthermore, law and policy can be channels *of* such common grace. In other words, one of the ways the Lord of creation can send rain on the just and the unjust is through laws and policies that systemically reflect something of what God desires for creation and human flourishing. Thus Christians can be motivated to contribute legislatively as an expression of "kingdom" work, human culture-making oriented toward *shalom*.

C. A Case Study: "The Problem of Poverty"

So what difference does this make for how Reformed Christians approach political issues? As a case study of what all this looks like "on the ground" and in the trenches of political life, we might consider a concrete historical example with contemporary relevance: Abraham Kuyper's wrestling with the problem of poverty.[55] In 1891, Kuyper gave the opening address to the First Christian Social Congress, focused on "the social question," which was really the question of poverty and

---

54. Kuyper pointed out that Christians had been put to shame by the socialists when it came to being passionate about the injustice of poverty: "[A]t the late date of this Congress," he said, "we find ourselves fighting a rearguard action. The socialists themselves, and not only our Christian leaders, expose our failure to act" ("Problem of Poverty," 26–27).

55. Compare also Abraham Kuyper, *Guidance for Christian Engagement in Government* [English translation of *Our Program*], trans. and ed. Harry VanDyke (Grand Rapids: Christian's Library Press, 2013).

inequality in late-nineteenth-century industrialized Europe. The "social question" was the question posed in the worlds of novelists Victor Hugo and Charles Dickens: Why in our era of technological and industrial progress does it seem that poverty is increasing as the chasm between rich and poor widens? The "social question," it turns out, is perennial.

So how does Kuyper, as a Christian statesman, address the question? What are the outlines of a distinctly Christian response? And how might his counsel be constructive for today? Let's note several features of his approach.

First, Kuyper's diagnosis is systemic and "architectonic": he doesn't think the problem is individual sloth or moral failure (though he's also not averse to saying these can be factors). Nor does he think poverty is to be expected and accepted this side of the eschaton. (He specifically criticizes those who flippantly cite "the poor you will always have with you" as an excuse not to change the status quo.) Rather, he decries the "rule of money" and the ways that the "plutocracy" have overtaken the reins of government in order to turn it into an engine for their own gain:

> The ineradicable inequality between men produced a world in which the stronger devours the weaker, much as if we lived in an animal society rather than in a human society. The stronger, almost without exception, have always known how to bend every custom and magisterial ordinance so that the profit is theirs and the loss belongs to the weaker. Men did not literally eat each other like cannibals, but the more powerful exploited the weaker by means of a weapon against which there was no defense. And whenever the magistrate came forward as a servant of God to protect the weak, the more powerful class of society soon knew how to exercise such an overpowering influence that the government, which should have protected the weak, became an instrument against them.[56]

This could be understood as a violation of sphere sovereignty: the interests and ends of the market have, in such cases, taken over the ends of the state.[57] But this, Kuyper emphasizes, is often the result of human cultural development that has been distorted by both error and sin:

---

56. Kuyper, *Problem of Poverty*, 33.

57. For a contemporary articulation of this concern, see Gideon Strauss, "Market Economy? Yes! Market Society? No!," *Comment* (August 1, 2005): http://www.cardus.ca/comment/article/359/market-economy-yes-market-society-no/.

Error insofar as there was ignorance about the essence of man and his social attributions, as well as about the laws[58] that govern human association and the production, distribution, and use of material goods. *Sin* insofar as greed and lust for power (expressed either through force or through vicious custom and unjust law) disturbed or checked the healthy growth of human society.[59]

Because government is of *our* making, and because our making is distorted by error and sin, legislation and law can actually become a source of the problem: "Out of these false principles, *systems* were built that varnished over injustice and stamped as normal that which actually stood opposed to the requirements for life."[60] The problem of poverty is, in a significant sense, a failure of statecraft: "The art of statecraft," Kuyper explains, "intervenes so that out of society a community may develop, and that the community, both in itself and in its relation to the material world, may be ennobled."[61] The legislation and statecraft that *produced* such poverty failed to do this. Thus, facing the problem of poverty will require *reforming* government and reordering law in accord with "the requirements of life" signaled in the Creator's vision of *shalom*.

Second, Kuyper criticizes solutions and responses that are rooted in either poor political theory or misunderstandings of human nature. His primary target is the "utopianism" he sees growing out of the animating impetus of the French Revolution: "This is the pivot point on which the whole social question turns. The French Revolution, like present-day liberalism, was anti-social, and the social need that now disturbs Europe is the evil fruit of the individualism enthroned by the French Revolution."[62] By prioritizing the individual, it destroyed an "organic" conception of society and replaced it with atomistic competition; and by cutting us off from "the horizon of eternal life," the "theory, the system, inevitably resulted in a kneeling before Mammon."[63]

This is why Kuyper's prescriptions will frustrate both "right" and "left," so to speak. On the one hand, Kuyper spends a lot of energy

---

58. By these "laws" Kuyper means creational *norms* woven into the grain of creation itself.
59. Kuyper, *Problem of Poverty*, 31.
60. Ibid., 31–32, emphasis added.
61. Ibid., 30.
62. Kuyper, *Problem of Poverty*, 88n1.
63. Ibid., 45.

criticizing "utopian" (what we might call "progressivist") visions and policies that, because of their anti-social assumptions, only foment the problem. "By wrenching loose everything that held life together in human dignity, it was inevitable that a profound *social need* would be born."[64] Why call the arsonist as your fireman? Instead, we need "an architectonic critique of human society, which leads to the desire for a different arrangement of the social order."[65] Indeed, "[w]e fall short in our duty as Christian citizens if we shirk the serious task of reconstructing whatever is manifestly in conflict with the ordinance of God."[66]

But Kuyper opposes all "revolutionary" strategies: "Our implication is not that the structure must be wholly destroyed and an entirely new order set up in place of the old society. Rather, the right of history always remains valid, and there is no possibility of complete demolition.... On the other hand, one may not say that everything is finished if one only puts a few dabs of paint and replaces a shingle here and there."[67] While Kuyper is a reformist[68] rather than a revolutionary, he believes that genuine reform is more than putting Band-Aids on a fundamentally disordered status quo. Kuyper sees government as the steward of a national *community*; indeed, one might describe his model as "communitarian."

This is why Kuyper, while critical of progressivist "statism" (attributing a messiah-like role to government) is also critical of those who might suggest the solution to poverty is simply private charity. Granted, charity is not unimportant: "Never forget," Kuyper admonishes, "that all state relief for the poor is a blot on the honor of your Savior."[69] But he then immediately qualifies: "It is perfectly true that if no help is forthcoming from elsewhere, the state must help. We may let no one starve from hunger as long as bread lies molding in so many cupboards.

64. Ibid., 44.

65. Ibid., 51.

66. Ibid., 72. And as will become important when engaging the Lutheran view (I anticipate), note that Kuyper says the "principles" according to which we should be reconstructing a disordered society are known by special revelation: "The principles by which we are obliged to text the existing situation and existing juridical relationships lie clearly expressed in the Word of God" (72).

67. Ibid., 90n9.

68. "... the course of our historic development may be altered only through gradual change and in a lawful way" (66).

69. Ibid., 78.

And when the state intervenes, it must do so quickly and sufficiently."[70] Kuyper sees a legitimate role for the state in protecting the vulnerable.

Finally, we see a dynamic relationship between the church and politics in Kuyper's program. Because politics is downstream from culture (that is, because law and policy often *reflect* social attitudes as much as they affect them), we can have a political impact by shaping the wider ethos of a culture. This is precisely what the church—in tandem as institute and organism—is called to do. Thus Kuyper portrays Jesus as something of a "community organizer":

> The overthrow of the idol Mammon and the refocusing of life's purpose from earth to heaven would, alone, have revolutionized popular consciousness. But Jesus did not stop there. He also *organized*. He set apart and sent out his church among the nations to influence society.[71]

If inequality and poverty are generated, to some extent, by the greed and disordered desires of the wealthy and those who legislate policy, then shaping and re-forming those desires is not irrelevant to the macro problem of poverty, even if such a focus is not adequate to fully address the problem. The church is not the state, but the church bears witness to the state and sends saints from its formative space to be a leavening organism in the political realm, hoping (against hope) to bend the kingdom of this world toward the kingdom of our God.

---

70. Ibid., 94n10.
71. Ibid., 40. The three ways are through the ministry of the Word, the ministry of charity, and the "equality of brotherhood" that flows from the fact that *all* are equally welcome at the Lord's table (40–41).

THOMAS W. HEILKE

Professor Smith's chapter illustrates clearly the distinction Roland Bainton identifies between Luther and Calvin concerning human possibilities: "The drive of Calvinism stems from optimism as to God despite pessimism as to man." While a Reformed Christian might have at least as "gloomy" a view of human sinfulness as either a Lutheran or an Anabaptist, Calvin trades the Lutheran "Your sins are forgiven" for "If God be for us, who can be against us?"[72]

In this view of God, at least in regard to politics, Calvin stands in significant contrast to the other major Protestant reformers and, indeed, to nearly all other strands of the Christian tradition. Calvin's God "is able to perform that which he has promised [and] has a plan for mankind to be achieved within the historical process." Calvin, in Bainton's estimation,

> renewed the role of St. Augustine who terminated the early Christian expectation of the speedy coming of the Lord and envisaged successive acts in the historical drama in which the Church came well-nigh to be equated with the kingdom of God.

In contrast to Augustine, "Calvin substituted for the great and imminent day of the Lord the dream of the Holy Commonwealth in the terrestrial sphere."[73] What this option means is well described in what Charles Taylor says about Reformed orientations toward the social and political realms.

Smith is too fine a scholar merely to echo Calvin's sensibilities. As he suggests, and as we should be more frequently reminded concerning all great traditions, the Reformed tradition does not end with its originator. It seems impossible to me that one could discard the basic

---

72. Roland H. Bainton, *The Reformation of the Sixteenth Century* (Boston: Beacon Press, 1952), 113–14.
73. Ibid., 114–15.

political theology that Bainton describes and still meaningfully call oneself a Reformed Christian, but I take seriously Smith's caution that he intends not to present *the* Reformed view, but to "outline *a* Reformed view of the relationship between church and politics." It is a view that begins in Calvin's Geneva and is nurtured in the Netherlands, with one of its intellectual zeniths being the work of Abraham Kuyper.

The result of Calvin's optimism is that, in places, Smith's Reformed depiction of the human nature of politics rings nearly Aristotelian, and I find myself applauding a great deal of what he says. The statement that "government and political life are products of *our* creation" does not reject Augustine's two kingdom political theology, but with a rightly placed confidence, it certainly attenuates any near-Manichean interpretation of that theology.

In contrast to such views, this confident theology sees Christians not merely as pilgrims passing through this world, but as full participants in the political order, so that they must take responsibility for it. Thus, as Nicholas Wolterstorff says so ably, "The structure of the social world was held up to judgment, was pronounced guilty, and was sentenced to be reformed." Christians must "struggle for the reform" of that order as a part of their discipleship, because they "are responsible for the structure of the social world in which they find themselves." Much of Smith's chapter is a description of what sorts of political involvements this responsibility entails.

We see immediately why the Anabaptist and Reformed chapters of this book are placed at some distance from one another: the nub of the historic political-theological differences between Anabaptist and Reformed Christians is located in this very point. The Anabaptist contrast may be summarized thus:

> The alternative to all this is the biblical demand that holiness is the separateness of a called *people* and the distinctiveness of their social existence. The need is not, as some current popularizers would suggest, for most Christians to get out of the church and into the world. They have been in the world all the time. The trouble is that they have been *of* the world, too. The need is for what they do in the world to be different because they are Christian; to be a reflection not merely of their restored self-confidence nor of their power to

set the course of society but of the social novelty of the covenant of grace. Instead of doing, each in his or her own station or office, whatever a reasonable person would do in the same place according to the order of creation; the need is for what they do there to be judged and renewed by the difference it makes that Christ, and not mammon or mars, is their Lord.[74]

The problem, in other words, is to let the church be the church and Christians be Christians first and foremost—not as a separate "sphere," but as a separate kingdom, involving themselves socially or politically wherever they may be on the basis of a firm understanding of who they are apart from any given society, rather than assuming a symbiosis between the two. In the final paragraph of his chapter, Smith is nearly speaking the language an Anabaptist would affirm.

A few of their differences can be indicated in a series of questions that Anabaptists ask of all magisterial political theologies. They are intended not as rhetorical put-downs, but as opening questions for some of the issues that need to be explored together. In the chapters collected here, we can already find partial answers that show points of agreement and disagreement and the beginnings of conversation.

1. Is the relationship of church to political authority and society one of identity? If not, what is it, and what—especially—is the church? For Anabaptists, it is "'the creation of a distinct community with its own deviant set of values and its coherent way of incarnating them.' The church's business is first of all to be that 'deviant' community, that is, to be the church."[75] In comparison and contrast to the other historical traditions, what sense can this claim make in a magisterial Christian context? In a "post-Christian" one? In a secular liberal democracy?

2. Are Christians really responsible for the direction of political history? If so, how do they know what that direction should be, and what available means of persuasion, coercion, and violence

---

74. John Howard Yoder, "A People in the World," in Michael G. Cartwright, ed., *The Royal Priesthood* (Grand Rapids: Eerdmans, 1994), 80–81.

75. James Wm. McClendon Jr., *Systematic Theology: Ethics* (Nashville: Abingdon Press, 1986), 74. He is citing John Howard Yoder, *The Original Revolution: Essays on Christian Pacifism* (Scottdale, PA: Herald Press, 2003), 28.

may they use to make history come out right? What does it mean under such circumstances to say that Jesus is Lord? Is that form of lordship displayed in the life of Jesus itself?

3. How do we know the content of the natural law or of the norms of the Creator? What accounts for the politically significant ways their contents have changed with regard to, say, the relative merits of democratic versus aristocratic versus monarchical systems of government, or in regard to forms of economic life, or on the question of persecuting dissenters and heretics? What is the relationship of this content and its historical changes to the life example of Jesus?

4. Walter Kaufmann has argued that "organized Christianity could be defined as the ever renewed effort to get around [the Sermon on the Mount] without repudiating Jesus."[76] Is he right? In personal as well as social ethics, what does it mean to say that Jesus is Lord and to look to New Testament (not natural law or order of creation) standards? Does this different ethic truly require also "the possibility of a different doctrine of humanity, of Christology, or of nature, of sin or grace or law?"[77] Do we require a specific kind of eschatology that is not utopian in order to make the ethics of the Sermon on the Mount credible for the contemporary world? Does this kind of nonutopian eschatology remain infeasible to or for anyone but Anabaptist Christians, even in a global circumstance in which the vast majority of Christianity is disestablished? Why?

---

76. Walter Kaufmann, *The Faith of a Heretic* (New York: Doubleday, 1963), 231, also 233, 235, 242.

77. John Howard Yoder, *The Priestly Kingdom: Social Ethics as Gospel* (South Bend: Notre Dame University Press, 1984), 108.

A LUTHERAN (PARADOXICAL) RESPONSE

ROBERT BENNE

There is so much to agree with in the alluring picture of the Reformed vision of the relation of the church and political life that is outlined by James K.A. Smith. Its notion of vocation in which the Christian participates critically in the political order is very persuasive, in wholesome contrast to classic Lutheran notions in which the Christian more or less does what the world demands in his or her calling, but does it willingly and joyfully. Persuasive also is the notion that the world is meant to be changed in accordance with God's will, not accepted as an order that has been established almost mythically since the creation. I particularly like the Reformed conviction that the church as an institution should indirectly affect the political world, not directly through any exercise of ecclesiastical power, much as I have argued in my chapter.

Indeed, I believe that Lutherans in America have learned much from this Reformed tradition. They have been prompted to overcome a tendency toward quietism and uncritical acceptance of the world's ways. They have become far more active in political life than they were before they rubbed shoulders with the dominant Reformed tradition in America.

But, alas, such activism also reveals a temptation in the Reformed tradition: Its overconfidence in its knowledge of God's will in education and politics, paradoxically leading it to integrate too readily with the reigning secular claims and ideologies of the day.

Before I get to examples of this temptation, let me note that Smith does not deal in any detail with the "biblical norms" that are to reorder worldly knowledge and politics, though he does refer to scholarly discussions of those norms in a footnote. Although Lutheranism classically employs a third use of the law (that which guides the Christian life), Calvinism tended to construe the law in a more detailed and comprehensive manner. (A church history professor of mine once illustrated this by noting that in Calvin's Geneva, beer halls were required to have an open Bible featured in the main drinking room to encourage pious conversation; in Luther's Wittenberg, beer halls were used merely to drink beer.) This gave Calvinism organizing and transformative capacities that Lutheranism didn't possess.[78]

This issue of biblical norms is crucial. If they are too detailed and inflexible, they become legalistic and have theocratic tendencies. Puritan politics tended in that direction. If the biblical norms are too general and abstract, all sorts of unconscious or hidden norms from "the world" are incorporated into the transformative vision. So, for example, if the Reformed vision has a strong preference for change and transformation, as Smith avers, it is likely to opt for secular ideologies that are "progressive" or even revolutionary in orientation. It is tempted to smuggle such schemes into its vision less critically than it should.

In Christian higher education, the Reformed vision has been exemplary in insisting that faith (the Christian theological vision) and learning (the claims coming from secular fields) must be related. But it has opted for "faith and learning integration," which is a bit too confident, either in claiming there is such a thing as "Christian economics," on the one hand, or too uncritical in its absorption of secular norms and adoption of them as Christian, on the other. As a Lutheran involved deeply in faith-learning dialogue, I prefer a more dialectical approach that assumes there will be lots of loose ends, convergences, and divergences in such a dialogue. Integration is a hope for the eschaton.

A similar problem arises in political life. A strong orientation toward "transformation" tempts the Reformed to adopt secular schemes that seem to promise vigorous movement toward the kingdom of God. Although I would hesitate to charge the classical Reformed vision — such as that positively outlined by Smith — with identifying progressive or revolutionary movements with the kingdom of God, the more desiccated versions of the Reformed vision in mainline Protestantism make

---

78. Oddly enough, a scholar out of the Reformed tradition, John Witte Jr., has argued in *Law and Protestantism* that early Lutheranism had just as much transformative energy as Calvinism. It brought forth lasting reforms in many spheres of life that still reverberate. (See *Law and Protestantism: The Legal Teachings of the Lutheran Reformation* [Cambridge: Cambridge University Press, 2002].) This revisionist view of Lutheranism suggests that Lutheran theologians and magistrates worked cooperatively for reform, much like the consistories and church councils did in the Calvinist lands. Fatefully, however, the Lutheran churches gave to the princes the duty and power to manage and protect the church, which then led to more compliant state churches.

that mistake repeatedly. The most egregious was when Mao Tse-tung's murderous revolution in China was likened by some mainline Protestant elites to the coming kingdom. Or when the same group mistakenly fell for liberation theology as authentically Christian. Or when current forms of militant environmentalism are seen as "redeeming" the earth.

If what Mark Noll has written is true (p. 66, n. 13), that America's soul is deeply permeated by the Reformed vision, then it is certainly true that those who have held it have a lot to be proud of, but at the same time a lot to be concerned about. "Transformation" can be a covert form of "conformation."

BRUCE L. FIELDS

James K.A. Smith's treatment of the Reformed tradition regarding the church and politics is concisely summarized in his final statement:

> The church is not the state, but the church bears witness to the state and sends saints from its formative space to be a leavening organism in the political realm, hoping (against hope) to bend the kingdom of this world toward the kingdom of God (p. 162).

Although he brings forth helpful commentary through voices like Nicholas Wolterstorff and James Skillen, his incorporation of Kuyper's thought is particularly informative for understanding this view. I will begin my response by giving attention to a suggestion Smith makes regarding the church and culture and will then focus on a few particular theological insights and applications. I will close with a suggestion of how the church can derive helpful guidelines from the Reformed tradition while avoiding the possibility of theological constructs contributing to situations like South African apartheid, or justifying a certain brand of "manifest destiny" as in the United States.

I truly appreciated Smith's comment on the relationship of culture, politics, and the ideal impact of the church. Incorporating Kuyperian thought, he correctly observes that politics is a product of the values, traditions, and practices of a given community (p. 162). The political is shaped by the culture. Culture is the sphere in which the church can have impact by exercising pervasive presence and service in a social setting under the auspices of the gospel of Jesus Christ.

The Reformed transformative project is built upon certain theological pillars. Of the five that Smith discusses, two particularly resonate with the Black church tradition. First, the Reformed tradition insists on the sanctity of all aspects of life, a position that directly challenges the two-tiered existence motif (priests and church officials, then everyone else) that was operative under the auspices of the Roman Catholic Church around the time of the Reformation. This also emphasizes the value of all work:

> All of life is to be lived *coram Deo*, they would say — that is, before the face of God. *All* vocations can be holy, for *all* of our cultural labors can be expressions of tending God's world. There is no "secular" because there is not a square inch of creation that is not the Lord's (p. 141).

Institutions such as the political and the economic, Smith rightly observes, are features of a "good creation" (Gen. 1:31) and contribute to actualizing creation's potential. Yet a major problem in all this is the pervasive presence and effects of sin. As the experience of the Black church powerfully reminds us, structures of accountability for the people functioning in these systems are absolutely critical.

The matter of sin provides a natural bridge to the consideration of structural and systemic sin (p. 144). As Michael O. Emerson and Christian Smith demonstrate in their book *Divided by Faith*, evangelicals are less adept at identifying systemic sin, focusing most of their attention on individual sin because of the call for personal faith responses to the gospel.[79] Making a point long understood in the Black church tradition, Smith appropriately argues that "sin weaves itself into systems and structures *beyond* individual choices and decisions" (p. 145). Remedies of injustice in any sociocultural environment must also be systemic, calling for informed engagement in multiple spheres alongside preaching the gospel.

The connection between the maintenance of the nature and function of societal "spheres" and just government should dramatically draw our attention. Kuyper used the term "sphere sovereignty" to describe the "multiple modes of social relationship" (p. 149). These spheres include the family, the school, and the government; each has its own integrity, and ideally, God ultimately orchestrates their interactions. Smith does not treat the identification of spheres as a call for separation between the "secular" and the "sanctified." "Thus politics, government, and 'the

---

79. Michael O. Emerson and Christian Smith, *Divided by Faith: Evangelical Religion and the Problem of Race in America* (New York: Oxford University Press, 2000).

state' in particular are all understood to be aspects of a good but fallen creation" (p. 151). He advances the Reformed position that government is not the overarching way to achieve *shalom*.

The state, then, is to accomplish two tasks. First, the state must protect the integrity of the spheres of societal organization. It should protect "legitimate human vocation, institution, and organization" (p. 156). Second, the state should not penalize groups for their religious convictions. Such protection should extend to *all* religious traditions, not just individuals. Christians can impact the political sphere in a number of ways, but certainly one of them under the advocacy of Calvin, Kuyper, and Bavinck is the Word of God (p. 156).

Thus, there is much within this view that the Black church can embrace. Yet Smith also cautions, "This Reformed impulse to reorder and reform could easily give license to a draconian, almost fascist agenda: *We* are the reordered, regenerate elect; *we* know what God wants for society; therefore, *we* impose it" (p. 146). This caution rings true for many in the Black church who have been wronged by Christians using religious justifications for oppression. One of the ways to avoid this type of perspective, in which we confuse our churchly agenda with the norming norm of the Bible itself, is to read Scripture and to study theology cross-culturally, cross-racially. This is not a call to abandon the centrality of the gospel and God-honoring biblical exegesis, but it is a call to an ecclesiology that recognizes that members of different backgrounds who are all part of the body of Christ can and should contribute to these spheres.

As a Black man, I am aware of the historical and, to a certain extent, the contemporary view that Black church members should be "taught" by members of the dominant culture. We can then be condescendingly smiled upon when we try to make serious theological statements. God moves in his church, in total. Black and other racial/ethnic members of the body of Christ also bring something to the biblical/theological table along with members of the dominant culture.

A CATHOLIC (SYNTHETIC) RESPONSE

The Reformed view of the relation between the church and politics, as presented by Professor James K.A. Smith, has a great deal in common with Catholic social teaching. This can be seen by examining the five themes developed by Smith to present the essence of the Reformed view: the sanctification of ordinary life, government and political life as products of our ingenuity, the structural/systemic nature of sin, the effect of eschatology on political engagement, and the inevitability of pluralism because of the array of social institutions in a civil society.

The first theme refers to the obligation of all Christian "saints" to hallow their family, "social, economic, and political lives" (p. 141). Christians are to seek holiness in every aspect of their daily lives, not just when they are worshiping in church. The Catholic embrace of this approach is clearly explained in Vatican II's *Lumen gentium* (*The Dogmatic Constitution on the Church*).

The second theme means that God does not reveal the form of government under which people should live. Human beings must use their own ingenuity in order to set up the kind of government that will best enable them to live "in accordance with what God desires for his creation" (p. 142). Two of the most respected thinkers in the Catholic tradition, St. Augustine and St. Thomas More, looked to Cicero for guidance in the elaboration of their political thought. Contemporary Catholic social teaching looks to the tradition of political theology and other disciplines in order to come up with suggestions for public policy.

The third theme, dealing with the origin and impact of structural sin, reveals a sharp difference between the Reformed and Catholic traditions. Smith says,

> The Reformed tradition ... emphasizes the way in which sin weaves itself into systems and structures *beyond* individual choices and

decisions. In other words, sin is not just attributable to individual agents and actors; there is also a sense in which systems and structures and policies can be disordered — that sin can take on a life of its own in structures that transcend individual choices. (pp. 144 – 45).

While Catholicism recognizes the reality of structural sin, it does so in a way to highlight the personal responsibility of individual actors. That the Reformed tradition is downplaying individual responsibility of structural sin is further indicated by the following comment on social reform: "The solution to political injustices is not individual conversion but systemic reform" (p. 145). Catholic teaching would argue that systemic reform needs to take place, but will only have a chance of happening if enough individuals abandon vice for the practice of virtue. For example, in his first encyclical, *Deus caritas est,* Pope Benedict said that "just structures are neither established nor proven effective in the long run" unless the church helps to purify reason and moves people to act ethically in all areas of their lives.[80]

The purification of reason is necessary so that it might attain knowledge of what is just. Consider the Civil Rights Act of 1964. A remarkable coalition of numerous conservative and liberal Christians came together to support the structural change to be wrought by the 1964 Act. Many individual Christians were disposed by the virtue of justice to give Black Americans their due. Without that just disposition in the souls of so many individuals, one could argue, structural change would not have taken place.

The fourth theme is the effect of an eschatological orientation on political engagement in the service of justice. Reformed Christians are highly motivated to love their neighbors by "righting wrongs and reordering disordered laws and policies.... This Reformed impulse to reorder and reform [both the church and the world] could easily give license to a draconian, almost fascist agenda" (p. 146). This could be a temptation, because Reformed Christians, argues Smith, are tempted to believe that they know exactly "what God wants for society; therefore, [they] will impose it" (p. 146). Smith gives as an example of the Reformed imposition of an unjust regime: South African apartheid.

---

80. Pope Benedict XVI, *Deus caritas est,* no. 28.

As a protection against this and other draconian measures, Reformed Christianity cultivates an eschatological orientation that "serves as a kind of Augustinian check-and-balance on any pretension that [it is] going to institute 'the kingdom.' It is this eschatology that curtails any utopian activism" (p. 147). Catholicism is also protected against utopian schemes when it pays attention both to its teaching on eschatology and to what it has learned from classical political philosophy about the necessity of reconciling wisdom with consent. It is ironic that one of the most cogent rational arguments against utopian thinking is St. Thomas More's *Utopia*, which makes clear how horrible utopias can be.

The fifth and last theme is the desirability of multiple associations in a society. Typical associations are "the family, the corporation, the church, the school.... the array of social institutions are all subject to God's sovereignty while also sovereign 'within their sphere'" (p. 149). In Catholic thought the principle of subsidiarity corresponds to this theme.

Smith next discusses what Reformed Christianity expects from government. The Reformed expectations mentioned by Smith are also shared by Catholic Christianity: Moderate expectations of what can be done by government, limited government so that private associations can make their contribution, respect for the freedom of the church, allowing the church to be a leaven in society and a reforming influence on the government, and respect for the rights of every individual. If accepted by the body politic, Catholic social teaching would also allow and even encourage the government to form the character of citizens to a limited extent and to promote a public morality.

Smith addresses the problem of poverty though the lens of Abraham Kuyper's thought. Kuyper (1837–1920) was a Dutch statesman and very influential Calvinist theologian who developed a comprehensive approach to reducing the incidence of poverty, very similar to what Catholic social teaching embraces today. Besides private charity, he relied on government intervention that avoided both utopian or revolutionary strategies and insufficient action. Kuyper had moderate expectations from government action because he astutely realized that government officials, because of their error and sin, could be manipulated by the powerful classes to do their bidding. Therefore, Smith went so far as to say,

If inequality and poverty are generated, to some extent, by the greed and disordered desires of the wealthy and those who legislate policy, then shaping and re-forming those desires is not irrelevant to the macro problem of poverty, even if such focus is not adequate to fully address the problem (p. 162).

This recognition is celebrated over and over again in Catholic social teaching. Forming the character of both citizens and their rulers is crucial for the resolution of all social problems, including poverty.

Another staple of Catholic teaching, seemingly not discussed by Kuyper, is relying on good family life and a sound education from kindergarten through college or trade school as the most efficient way out of poverty. Of course, statecraft must also do enough to keep open the paths of economic opportunity and to provide financial help when needed. Because the government may play such important roles, Kuyper went so far as to say that the "problem of poverty is, in a significant sense, a failure of statecraft" (p. 160).

THE CATHOLIC (SYNTHETIC) VIEW

J. BRIAN BENESTAD

Introduction

This chapter explains how the Catholic Church understands its relation to the political and social order and how it can benefit temporal life while pursuing its salvific mission.[1]

I. Catholic Social Doctrine

A. The Origin of Catholic Social Doctrine (CSD)

The contemporary Catholic view on the relation between the church and politics can be discerned in that body of teaching known as Catholic social doctrine (CSD). The *Instruction on Christian Freedom and Liberation,* written by Cardinal Ratzinger for a Vatican teaching office before he became Pope Benedict XVI, explains that Catholic social doctrine emerged from the practice of the Christian faith. "The Church's social teaching is born of the encounter of the gospel message and of its demands [summarized in the supreme commandment of love of God and neighbor in justice] with the problems emanating from the life of society."[2]

CSD gives valuable guidance by helping people come to know what love and justice require in the various circumstances of life, knowledge

---

1. This chapter includes excerpts from my book *Church, State, and Society: An Introduction to Catholic Social Doctrine* (Washington: The Catholic University of America Press, 2011). They are used by permission of the publisher.

2. Congregation for the Doctrine of the Faith, *Instruction on Christian Freedom and Liberation* (March 22, 1986), no. 72.

that would escape many people without instruction. St. Augustine underscores the difficulty of carrying out the commandment to love one's neighbor: "From this commandment arise the duties pertaining to human society, about which it is difficult not to err."[3] For example, many Catholics have difficulty seeing that love requires that their faith should affect the way they do business and that all people should refrain from killing embryos by extracting embryonic stem cells for research purposes. Since CSD seeks to overcome the split between Christian teaching and daily life, it is addressed not just to scholars and other well-educated people, but to the whole people of God and even to all people of good will. The latter can be addressed because many elements of CSD can be grasped and appreciated by reason alone.

B. CSD Is Based on Faith and Reason

The *Instruction* calls social teaching a doctrine because it uses "the resources of human wisdom and the sciences."[4] More precisely, it discerns the permanently valid ethical principles in the treasury of human wisdom and applies these principles to the many and varied situations arising in the life of any society. CSD is also a doctrine, in my opinion, because it relies on the truths of the faith in conjunction with right reason to make ethical judgments on human affairs.

That CSD can be rightly based on both faith and reason is confirmed by the teaching of Vatican Council II in its Declaration on Religious Liberty:

> For the Church is, by the will of Christ, the teacher of the truth. It is her duty to give utterance to, and authoritatively to teach, that truth which is Christ Himself, and also to declare and confirm by her authority those principles of the moral order which have their origins in human nature itself.[5]

3. St. Augustine, *The Catholic and Manichaean Ways of Life* (*De moribus ecclesiae Catholicae et de moribus Manichaeorum*) (Washington: The Catholic University of America Press, 1966), no. 49, p. 40.

4. *Instruction on Christian Freedom and Liberation*, no. 72.

5. *Dignitatis humanae*, no. 14. Vatican Council II (1962–65) was a meeting of Catholic bishops from around the world to discuss ways in which the Catholic Church could be more effective both in communicating the Catholic faith and promoting its acceptance. Pope Paul VI formally approved the sixteen documents issued by the Council on December 8, 1965.

Vatican Council II, of course, is indirectly referring to the role of the church in interpreting the natural law. Pope Benedict XVI has been particularly eloquent on the church's role in promoting the use of reason. Addressing the Muslim community of Cameroon, he said, "My friends, I believe a particularly urgent task of religion today is to unveil the vast potential of human reason, which is God's gift and which is elevated by revelation and faith."[6]

Given the heavy reliance on reason in CSD, no one should be surprised that it encourages Catholics to dialogue and cooperate with non-Catholic Christians, with members of the world's religions, and with civil and political authorities on matters pertaining to the common good.[7] The assumption, of course, is that Catholics have reason in common with everyone else on the planet. Pope Benedict, not surprisingly, touched on this theme in his trip to Africa:

> May the enthusiastic cooperation of Muslims, Catholics, and other Christians in Cameroon be a beacon to other African nations of the enormous potential of an interreligious commitment to peace, justice and the common good.[8]

C. The Basic Principles of CSD

The *Instruction* next makes the very important point that CSD contains both permanently valid principles and "contingent judgments." The latter is the case because, "being essentially oriented towards action, [CSD] develops in accordance with the changing circumstances of history." Of course, it will not always be easy to discern what is permanent and what is contingent in CSD.

In addition to the permanently valid principles, the church's social doctrine also presents "criteria for judgment" and "directives for action."[9] The Vatican *Compendium of the Social Doctrine of the Church* says these three aspects of CSD "are the starting point for the promo-

---

6. "Meeting with Representatives of the Muslim Community of Cameroon" (March 19, 2009).

7. *Compendium of the Social Doctrine of the Church*, nos. 534–537.

8. "Meeting with Representatives of the Muslim Community of Cameroon" (March 19, 2009).

9. *Instruction*, no. 72. Cf. Pope Paul VI, *Octogesima adveniens*, no. 4, where the pope speaks of "norms of judgment."

tion of an integral and solidary humanism."[10] The *Instruction* mentions as examples of fundamental principles the dignity of the human person, solidarity, and subsidiarity and then adds that these principles (explained in the last part of this chapter) "are the basis of *criteria for making judgments* on social *situations, structures* and *systems*."[11] Correct judgments, however, cannot be made unless people keep in mind that

> the first thing to be done is to appeal to the spiritual and moral capacities of the individual and to the permanent need for inner conversion, if one is to achieve the economic and social changes that will truly be at the service of man.[12]

Otherwise stated, a society will not be just unless individuals are virtuous, a central point of CSD.[13] Virtues can only be true and effective if supported by divine grace.[14]

Besides the dignity of the human person, solidarity, and subsidiarity, other fundamental principles of CSD are as follows: the common good, the sacredness of life, the social character of the human person (families and political communities are part of the natural order), rights and responsibilities, the option for the poor and vulnerable, the dignity of work, international solidarity (meaning commitment to the international common good), and care for the environment. In the main body of this chapter I explain the two most fundamental principles of CSD: the dignity of the human person and the common good.

D. Authoritative Sources of CSD Not Well Known by Catholics

A survey of the Catholic laity as a whole and of Catholic clergy would, no doubt, reveal that most Catholics could not give an adequate account of the church's position. This widespread ignorance stems largely from lack of education. Seminaries have, for the most part, not done a good

---

10. *Compendium*, no. 7.

11. *Instruction*, no. 74.

12. *Instruction*, no. 75.

13. *Compendium*, no. 19. The humanism of Catholic social doctrine "can become a reality if individual men and women and their communities are able to cultivate moral and social virtues in themselves and spread them in society."

14. *Gaudium et spes*, no. 30. "Then, under the necessary help of divine grace, there will arise a generation of new men, the molders of a new humanity."

job of preparing future priests to think about the relation of the Catholic faith and politics.

Only a few of the laity would study the subject in a Catholic university or hear about it in a Sunday homily. The laity would, perforce, gather most of their information in fragments from secular sources such as *The New York Times*. There is no place like the Nicene Creed, the Ten Commandments, or the Lord's Prayer that would provide a ready summary of the church's nuanced view. Yet, there are authoritative papal, episcopal, and conciliar documents that inform both priests and laity about CSD.

Many encyclicals, which are authoritative papal documents, provide insight into the relation between church and politics. Pope Leo XIII's *Rerum novarum* (1891) and Pope John Paul II's *Centesimus annus* (*On the Hundredth Anniversary of Rerum novarum*, 1991) are two important social encyclicals. Others such as Paul VI's *Humanae vitae* (*Of Human Life*, 1968) and John Paul II's *Evangelium vitae* (*The Gospel of Life*, 1995) add crucial insights.

Episcopal documents refer to pastoral letters written by individual bishops or by the United States Conference of Catholic Bishops, an organization set up to speak for all the Catholic bishops in that country. Conciliar documents refer to those produced by the Vatican Council II (1962–65), especially *Gaudium et spes* (*Pastoral Constitution on the Church in the Modern World*) and *Dignitatis humanae* (*Declaration on Religious Liberty*). Two other sources of authoritative teaching are statements from the Vatican Congregation for the Doctrine of the Faith and the Pontifical Council for Justice and Peace. The latter published its *Compendium of the Social Doctrine of the Church* in 2004.

Lastly, Catholic social doctrine relies on the natural law, especially as explained by St. Thomas Aquinas. The Catholic Church believes that all people can, in principle, discern the basic meaning of the natural law, the moral obligations attached to our nature as human beings. For example, the second tablet of the Decalogue is regarded as natural law teaching in addition to being part of the revealed Word of God. Every person of good will senses that legally enforced racism must contradict a higher law, namely the natural law.

The application of CSD to the contemporary scene—using Christian principles for guidance in making policy choices—requires a good knowledge of the society, government, and the history of one's country, and sometimes knowledge of major problems in the nations of the world. A complete education in CSD is a daunting task, requiring a thorough liberal education in addition to serious formation in the faith as a whole. Catholics sometimes take the shortcut of following their political ideology or some truncated version of social justice.

Before exploring what contemporary Catholic social doctrine has to say about the church's relation to the political order, I will turn first to the historical roots of its position in the writings of St. Augustine and St. Thomas Aquinas.

II. The Historical Roots of Catholic Church's Position on Faith and Politics

A. St. Augustine

1. Augustine's Reliance on Cicero

In the *The City of God* Augustine comments on the Roman politician Scipio's definition of a republic in the Roman statesman Cicero's *De republica*. Scipio says that a republic is "the affair of a people" and defines a people as a "fellowship of a multitude united through a consensus concerning right and a sharing of advantage."[15]

Augustine explains that there can be no "consensus concerning right" without justice. In Augustine's radical formulation, justice requires order in the soul of citizens: Reason rules the vices and in turn is subject to God through practice of the Christian virtues. If there is no justice in individuals, "without doubt neither is there any in a fellowship of human beings which consists of such men."[16] So, without just souls there can be no communal consensus concerning right and, thus, no real republic. Augustine's modification of Cicero's republic describes a common good that would be as close to perfection as one can imagine on earth.

Augustine's second and more realistic definition of a republic is "a fellowship of a multitude of rational beings united through a sharing in and agreement about what it loves.... It is a better people if it agrees in loving better things; a worse one if it agrees in loving worse

---

15. St. Augustine, *The City of God*, book XIX, chapter 21.
16. Ibid.

things."[17] Otherwise stated, there can be various levels of agreement in any particular regime. Citizens inspired by a Catholic vision of the common good have a paradigm in Augustine's first definition of a republic by which to take their bearings in prudently working to refine and elevate the agreement about what the political community loves. Individual citizens must be educated to love virtue because, as Augustine argues in the *Confessions*, "My love is my weight: wherever I go my love is what brings me there" (book XIII, chapter 9).

For a long time Augustine was carried along by contradictory loves such as his love of wisdom and love of lust. Eventually, his good loves drove out his bad loves.

2. Educating Citizens to Take Justice Seriously

What does all this mean for educating students and other citizens to take justice seriously? Simply stated, their souls must be free to receive the love and knowledge of justice, as well as the knowledge and love of faith and the other virtues. If people are all carried by their loves, Augustine is logical in arguing that Christians must be educated to know and love all the virtues. The personal experience of suffering by the innocent can generate a love for justice and therefore can be a form of education.

Two other approaches to the same end are indispensable: an education to know and love the whole faith, including the creeds, the church and the sacraments, morality, and prayer; and an education to ponder the thoughts of great authors on matters pertaining to justice and injustice. As John Paul II has argued, the way to the heart is often through the mind. Think of the influence of Aleksandr Solzhenitsyn's *Gulag Archipelago* in weaning French intellectuals from their love of communism.

According to Augustine's understanding, if the mores are corrupt, citizens will not support social reform at home or abroad unless their self-interest is somehow engaged. Citizens who have a disordered love of goods and freedom will not be inclined to support public initiatives requiring self-sacrifice or to undertake works of justice. So, anything done to elevate the loves of citizens will be a contribution to justice in a particular society. This means that individuals, families, schools,

---

17. *The City of God*, book XIX, chapter 24.

universities, voluntary groups, political persuasion, wise laws, and especially churches can all contribute to forming the loves of citizens. Whatever these citizens love will decisively affect the attainment of justice in a particular society. Educating men and women to love justice is no easy task because, as Augustine argues in the *Confessions*, we want what we love to be the truth (cf. book X, chapter 23).

3. The Core of Augustine's Political Teaching

Because of what Augustine says about the requirements of a true republic, scholar Ernest Fortin comments, "The core of Augustine's political doctrine may be said to his teaching concerning virtue, a teaching that has its roots in both the philosophic and biblical traditions." Augustine agrees with Plato's and Aristotle's view that no society can be just unless individuals are virtuous. He differs from them in arguing that they were unable "to bring about a just society," not having the remedy for the congenital weakness of humanity. The two classical philosophers had no way to educate the majority of citizens to a life of virtue. Consequently, Fortin draws this conclusion:

> Man's salvation, including his political salvation, accrues to him, not from philosophy, as Plato had intimated, but from God. Divine grace rather than human justice is the bond of society and the true source of happiness.... In the actual state of humanity, the task of securing the good life devolves specifically upon the Church as the divinely instituted and visible instrument of God's grace. The scope of civil society is drastically limited in comparison with that assigned to it by classical philosophy.[18]

This Augustinian position supports the indirect influence of the church on the political order of which Pope Benedict XVI wrote in his first encyclical. That influence will be more or less deep, depending on people's receptivity to church teaching and to divine grace. With the advent of Christianity, the world of politics will not necessarily get better. Progress will depend on the education people receive and on whether they use their freedom well.

---

18. Ernest Fortin, *Classical Christianity and the Political Order: Reflections on Theologico-Political Problem*, Vol. 2 of *Collected Essays*, ed. J. Brian Benestad (Lanham, MD: Rowman & Littlefield, 1996), 8.

B. St. Thomas Aquinas

1. Aquinas on the Various Meanings of Justice

In order for the laity and the clergy to benefit the political order, they not only need grace, but also have to know what justice requires of them. Many people speak endlessly of justice, especially social justice, without saying what it is or without even feeling the need to ask about its nature. The church's social doctrine can profitably rely on Thomas Aquinas for assistance in clarifying the nature of justice and its various dimensions. He may not have said everything we need to know today, but he made many illuminating observations about justice in general, legal justice, distributive justice, and commutative justice.

Aquinas gets to the heart of the matter with the basic definition of justice: "a habit whereby an individual renders to each one his due [or right (*ius*)] by a constant and perpetual will."[19] This may be the most oft-quoted definition of justice. It shows that justice is about those things that have to do with our relationsip with one another. The word "right" in the definition, of course, is not synonymous with the modern concept of "rights," but refers to "the just thing itself." While justice properly speaking governs the relations of one person or entity to another, it can also be understood in a metaphorical sense as the virtue regulating relations among the various powers of the soul, such as reason and the appetites. Reason, then, is in turn subject to God's will known through faith. This is the justice of which Augustine spoke in *the City of God*.

This concept of justice as order in the soul of individuals needs to be rediscovered today for several reasons. First, it enables us to understand better the meaning of justification and justice in the New Testament. Aquinas explains,

> [T]he justice which faith works in us, is that whereby the ungodly is justified: it consists in the due co-ordination of the parts of the soul.... Now this belongs to justice metaphorically understood, which may be found even in a man who lives by himself.[20]

We capture this sense of justice when we speak of the just person in our ordinary speech.

---

19. *Summa theologiae* II-II, qu. 58, a. 1.
20. *Summa theologiae* II-II, qu. 58, a. 2, reply to obj. 1.

Second, the political and social significance of justice as order in the soul can be readily perceived by turning back to Augustine's influential teaching that the attainment of justice in a political community depends on the presence of justice in the souls of individuals. And justice must be understood as order in the soul, which is only achieved by the practice of all the virtues.[21]

Today there is a lot of talk about giving people their due, usually under the rubric of "social justice." There is not, however, a corresponding enthusiasm for achieving order in our souls, even though many people readily understand that some don't receive what is just because others don't want to give it to them. The reluctance to give, if it doesn't proceed from ignorance, is caused by disordered passions in the soul. People with disorder in their souls will not be inclined to give others their due.

Ordinary speech makes this same judgment when it blames an unjust situation on the "corruption" of leaders. Aquinas clarifies this point in his treatment of the connection among the virtues. He makes the common sense observation that fear and desire, if not governed by fortitude and temperance, can often lead people to injustice. He says in *Disputed Questions on Virtue*:

> But the principles of morals are so interrelated to one another that the failure of one would entail the failure in others. For example, if one were weak on the principle that concupiscence is not to be followed, which pertains to desire, then sometimes in pursuing concupiscence, he would do injury and thus violate justice.[22]

In other words, excessive love of pleasure and money can lead people to harm others, as in committing adultery or defrauding them of their goods. Similarly, people may have to overcome their own fears in order to protect others from being harmed in some way. For example, a teen may know that his friends are wrong to pick on a weaker boy, but hesitates to speak up for fear of being excluded. Advisers to a president may hesitate to speak the truth in front of their boss about some injustice for fear of losing influence or their job. Patience, a dimension of fortitude, enables a person both to control anger in the face of provocation and

---

21. St. Augustine, *City of God*, book XIX, chapter 21.
22. *Disputed Questions on Virtue*, ed. and trans. by Ralph McInerny (South Bend, IN: St. Augustine's Press, 1999), 120.

to persevere in the face of opposition. Without sufficient patience a person may not persevere in the struggle to make sure that others receive their due. For example, a school principal may lack the patience to find and train the best teachers or to ensure that the school really delivers a quality education.

The connection of prudence with justice is especially pertinent. Aquinas distinguishes ordinary prudence from political prudence. He says that everyone in the state of grace has sufficient prudence to do what is required for their own salvation, but not everyone has the political prudence to discern the requirements of the common good. Prudence is acquired over time with the right kind of experience and instruction. Wise older people with much experience of the world are apt instructors of the young. Books written by those who have wisdom on matters pertaining to the common good offer excellent guidance for the acquisition of political prudence.

Aquinas also offers us a commentary on particular justice that is directed to the private individual in two ways and, appropriately, has two different names. "The order of one private individual to another" is governed by *commutative justice*.[23] What is owed (the *debitum*) is two-fold. First, Aquinas says, "it is necessary to equalize thing with thing, so that the one person should pay back to the other just so much as he has become richer out of that which belonged to the other."[24] This form of commutative justice is also called "contract justice" because the parties agree to some fair exchange, for instance, a certain sum of money in exchange for a house or a car.

Commutative justice also takes the form of restitution. Aquinas says restitution is in order when one person has what belongs to another, "either with his consent, for instance on loan or deposit, or against his will, as in robbery or theft."[25] People have a very serious obligation to restore what has been taken unjustly. Such restitution is even necessary for salvation. Commutative justice also applies to penal justice. Offenses against the citizens of a nation call for proportionate punishment.

The other form of particular justice, *distributive justice*, governs "the order of the whole towards the parts to which corresponds the

---

23. *Summa theologiae* II-II, qu. 61, a. 1.
24. *Summa theologiae* II-II, qu. 61, a. 2.
25. *Summa theologiae* II-II, qu. 62, a. 1.

order of that which belongs to the community in relation to each single person."[26] The community distributes common goods proportionately to individuals as they are deserving because of some excellence or need. Arguments always arise as to who is more entitled to receive the common goods, but often nearly everyone will agree that a particular group of people will justly receive more material goods or services than others. For example, there is widespread agreement that the political community should spend much more money on the education of children than that of adults, so developed nations like the United States provide primary and secondary education for free.

The attainment of distributive justice depends very much on the prudence and moral virtue of those responsible for distributing common goods. Since citizens in democratic regimes can bring pressure to bear on rulers to act justly, they share in the responsibility for distributive justice. But they need sufficient knowledge and virtue to fulfill this role. For that kind of transformation to happen, democratic citizens must be suitably educated by the institutions of civil society, especially by the family, the church, and the university.

Distributive justice requires the practice of *legal justice*, the virtue that Aquinas says "directs the acts of all the virtues to the common good."[27] Legal justice inclines a person to perform actions useful to another, to the community, or to the ruler of the community. It consists in the exercise of every virtue having to do with another. Every moral virtue directed to the common good is called "legal justice." In 1931 Pius XI introduced the concept of social justice into his encyclical *Quadragesimo anno,* and he seems to have meant for the most part what Aquinas described as legal justice. Through examining the virtue of legal justice, Aquinas makes clear the essential link between personal virtue and justice, as well as the obligation of all citizens to find a way to contribute to the common good either by fighting injustices and/or by promoting an ever more just society.

---

26. *Summa theologiae* II-II, qu. 61, a. 1.
27. *Summa theologiae* II-II, qu. 58, a. 6.

2. The Use of Law and Governmental Persuasion to Provide a Moral Education

Besides explaining the various dimensions of justice, Aquinas makes a persuasive case for using the law to provide a moral education to both the good and the bad. The educational role of law follows from its definition: "an ordinance of reason for the common good, made by the one who has care of the community, and promulgated."[28] The common good, as understood by Aquinas, ultimately requires that all people in a political community come to live a life of virtue. The law can play both a negative and positive role in respectively restraining bad people and guiding those who are basically good.

Thomistic scholar Mary Keys puts it this way: For Aquinas, "the law is necessary to restrain and reform the 'bad man,' to open up for him the possibility of cultivating virtues and to diminish his corrupting influence on others."[29] In addition, "the well-framed law assists the basically good person in acquiring the social virtues he or she already wishes to possess."[30]

Aquinas said that because some are "depraved, and prone to vice," they must

> be restrained from evil by force and fear in order that, at least, they might desist from evil doing, and leave others in peace, and that they themselves, by being habituated in this way, might be brought to do willingly what hither to they did from fear; and thus become virtuous.[31]

For Aquinas fear, force, and habituation are the key motivating factors for the depraved.

In addition to the depraved, every political community has people "inclined to good, either from nature or from custom, or rather from grace; and the like have to be taught and improved by means of the precept of the law."[32]

---

28. *Summa theologiae* I-II, qu. 90, a. 4.
29. Mary Keys, *Aquinas, Aristotle, and the Power of the Common Good* (New York: Cambridge University Press, 2006), 205.
30. Ibid.
31. *Summa theologiae* I-II, qu. 95, a. 10.
32. *Summa theologiae* qu. 101, a. 3.

Keys discerns three reasons these good people need guidance from the law. The first is as a remedy for moral ignorance. In a culture where erroneous beliefs have been widely embraced, even good people will have trouble discerning the truth in all situations. For example, when the natural law is obscured under the influence of the culture, many Catholics in the Western world no longer believe that marriage requires a male and a female or that physician-assisted suicide is always wrong.

The second reason why good people need the law is its "contribution to the habituation necessary for ethical virtue's acquisition."[33] In a wide variety of circumstances the law can be framed so as to build up habits in individuals — both good and bad — that incline them to become virtuous.

The third reason that the virtuously inclined need the law, argues Keys, is to guide the practice of virtue so that it is "proportionate to the common good."[34] This is necessary because human beings are social and political animals with an obligation to promote "social and civic flourishing." Properly framed law can require or persuade citizens to practice virtue in such a way as to promote the common good.

Keys offers as an example the inculcation of gratitude by the observance of Thanksgiving Day in the United States. This national holiday began as a celebration of the original Pilgrims — "and was later sanctioned by George Washington's proclamations at Congress's request and finally by Abraham Lincoln's executive order."[35] Lincoln's order, issued in October 1863, didn't require American citizens to celebrate Thanksgiving Day, but invited them to do so. He also invited them to look after widows, orphans, mourners, and other sufferers. Further, Lincoln invited Americans to pray and show gratitude to God on Thanksgiving Day, thereby recommending that citizens maintain a strong connection and friendship with God. Inculcating gratitude by persuasion is an especially appropriate way of proceeding in a liberal democracy where the emphasis is on the protection of rights rather than the promotion of virtue.

While Aquinas rightly argues that the law should promote the acquired moral virtues, he goes to an extreme in advocating for the use

---

33. Keys, *Aquinas, Aristotle, and the Power of the Common Good*, 211.
34. *Summa theologiae* I-II, qu. 92, a. 1, ad 3.
35. Keys, *Aquinas, Aristotle, and the Power of the Common Good*, 220.

of law both to punish "obstinate heretics" and to "foster religion." The church should typically not ask political authorities to promote the legal enforcement of theological and infused moral virtues. "Politics' highest function," according to Keys's interpretation of Aquinas,

> is rather to promote ethically virtuous living among the people, nobly but also realistically and moderately, for the sake of the common good … as well as to provide the base of physical, social, and economic security that tends to facilitate virtuous living. Human law can and should therefore assist humans in combatting vice and encouraging the inculcation of virtue; it *cannot* guarantee or achieve this goal absolutely speaking, and it errs considerably when it attempts to do so.[36]

This Thomistic position on the use of law to promote virtue is central to contemporary Catholic social doctrine, but is not widely known or accepted by many contemporary Catholics.

III. Contemporary Catholic Social Doctrine on Faith and Politics
A. The Role of the Church and Its Laity in Promoting Charity and Justice

Having highlighted the basic thought of Augustine and Thomas Aquinas on the relation of faith and politics, we are ready to begin our analysis of contemporary Catholic social doctrine.

A helpful way to get at the essence of the contemporary Catholic view is to take a look at Pope Benedict XVI's first encyclical, *Deus caritas est*, in which he outlines the threefold responsibility of the church: "proclaiming the word of God (*kerygma-martyria*), celebrating the sacraments (*leitourgia*), and exercising the ministry of charity (*diakonia*)" (no. 25). The third aspect of the church's nature requires the institutional church to engage in works of mercy and summons individual church members to follow the teaching of the parable of the Good Samaritan, "which imposes universal love towards the needy whom we encounter 'by chance' (cf. Lk 10:31), whoever they may be" (no. 25).

Does Christian love, then, require individual Catholics to participate in the political process? Pope Benedict responds that the "*direct* duty to

---

36. Ibid., 229.

work for a just structuring of society ... is proper to the lay faithful" (my emphasis).[37] Under the influence of love they have the responsibility to work for the policy that will best contribute to the protection of human dignity and the realization of the common good. For example, on the basis of more or less limited knowledge, the lay faithful will endorse various positions on issues such as health care, taxes, immigration, and foreign policy.

The church acting as Church should not endorse debatable policy options, but the laity must do this to fulfill their responsibilities as citizens. The church should intervene to point out clear evils harming the body politic. For example, the church can direct Catholics' attention to the evil of abortion and physician-assisted suicide, but should not endorse a particular tax bill if it is one about which reasonable Catholics could disagree. The laity will also contribute to the just structuring of society by practicing the virtues in their family life, at work, and in their relations with neighbors.

Does the church as Church have an obligation to bring about justice in society in order to fulfill its ministry of charity? Pope Benedict XVI responds, "The Church cannot and must not take upon herself the political battle to bring about the most just society possible. She cannot and must not replace the State" (no. 28). At the same time, however, the church "cannot and must not remain on the sidelines in the fight for justice" (no. 28).

What, then, is the role of the church and its social doctrine with respect to justice? The aim of the church's social doctrine "is simply to help purify reason and to contribute, here and now, to the acknowledgment and attainment of what is just" (no. 28). Because people are blinded by their interests and love of power, they have difficulty reasoning about justice and seeing what it requires in particular instances. To be an effective instrument, reason "must undergo constant purification." As a part of the work of purifying reason, the church forms the conscience of people, builds their character, and motivates them to act justly by reawakening their spiritual energy. In this perspective the church *indirectly*, but powerfully, contributes to the realization of justice in society and the state.

---

37. *Deus caritas est*, no. 29.

The church has indirectly influenced work for justice in the secular realm by fulfilling its threefold mission of teaching, sanctifying, and serving through works of mercy. Especially relevant in the realm of teaching is the church's perspective on the following matters: the dignity of the human person, the common good, the sanctity of life, rights and duties, the virtues, the various meanings of justice, marriage, family life, education, the economy, work, poverty, the environment, religious liberty, subsidiarity, solidarity, just war principles, development, and the common good of the international community.

B. The Dignity of the Human Person

With these principles in mind, let us examine the two principal themes of CSD: the dignity of the human person and the common good. According to Catholic teaching, people have dignity because they are created in the image and likeness of God, redeemed by Jesus Christ, and destined for eternal life in communion with God. In Pope John Paul II's words,

> The dignity of the person is manifested in all its radiance when the person's origin and destiny are considered: created by God in his image and likeness as well as redeemed by the most precious blood of Christ, the person is called to be a "child in the Son" and a living temple of the Spirit, destined for eternal life of blessed communion with God.[38]

The threefold foundation for human dignity is both unshakable and instructive. No act of the human person can remove this foundation. Even when people commit the worst sins and crimes and suffer diminished physical and spiritual capacities, they retain human dignity. While this Christian teaching about the permanent character of human dignity is often mentioned and acknowledged by informed Christians, rarely do Catholics hear that human dignity is also a goal or an achievement. But this is the clear implication of the threefold foundation of human dignity and the explicit teaching of Vatican Council II and John Paul II.

The Council makes the point when discussing the obligation of all to obey their conscience. "Man has a law in his heart inscribed by God,

---

38. Pope John Paul II, *Christifideles laici*, no. 37.

to obey which is his very dignity, and according to which he will be judged."[39] The text implies that people diminish their dignity by not obeying their rightly formed conscience. Everyday speech captures this human possibility in the expression "to act beneath one's dignity." In sum, all people continually *achieve* or realize their dignity by seeking the truth, obeying conscience, resisting sin, practicing virtue, and repenting when they succumb to temptation. In other words, dignity is not just a permanent possession, unaffected by the way we live. All people have to obey their informed conscience, both to avoid acting beneath their dignity and to develop it.

So there is a sense in which dignity may be continually diminished by a life of sin or progressively appropriated over a lifetime by seeking perfection. In *Rerum novarum* Pope Leo XIII made the same point using language characteristic of Thomas Aquinas: "True dignity and excellence in men resides in moral living, that is, in virtue."[40] Saint Leo the Great's famous Christmas sermon states this point in a memorable way: "Christian, recognize your dignity, and now that you share in God's own nature, do not return by sin to your former base condition."[41] It is significant that this quotation stands as the first sentence in the section on morality in the new *Catechism of the Catholic Church*. It immediately directs attention to the necessity of achieving human dignity by living without sin and practicing virtue. What constitutes the perfection of human dignity for Catholics is determined by natural law and the teaching of the church, reasonably well summarized in the *Catechism of the Catholic Church*.

Without teaching the twofold character of human dignity, the very keystone of CSD is not accurately described and therefore not quite up to the task of informing the elaboration of other important themes in the discipline. As John Paul II said in *Centesimus annus*, "From the Christian vision of the human person there necessarily follows a correct picture of society."[42] That picture is one in which all elements of society should find ways to help people perfect their dignity.

---

39. *Gaudium et spes*, no. 16.
40. Pope Leo XIII, *Rerum novarum*, no. 37.
41. *Catechism of the Catholic Church*, no. 1691.
42. Pope John Paul II, *Centesimus annus*, no. 65.

The conclusion of *Gaudium et spes* states that the *whole conciliar program* for all people is to help them "so that perceiving more clearly their integral vocation, they may conform the world more to the surpassing dignity of the human person."[43] A world so conformed would not only reflect the eminent dignity of human beings, but also be an instrument in helping people to achieve that dignity. A world not so conformed leads people astray, making the achievement of dignity more difficult.

Every element of society should promote respect for human dignity and its perfection. As Vatican Council II specifically says, "[I]t devolves on humanity to establish a political, social, and economic order which will to an even better extent serve man and help individuals as well as groups to affirm and perfect the dignity proper to them" (*ad dignitatem sibi propriam affirmandam et excolendam*).[44] This means that the family, mediating institutions, the law, and the church all have a role to play in helping individuals perfect their dignity. For example, parents educate their children in the family to help them recognize and achieve their dignity. Schools, a primary mediating institution, form the character of students so that they might be inclined to act in accordance with their dignity. The law encourages people not to act beneath their dignity by driving while drunk or acting in a discriminatory manner toward racial minorities.

In *Centesimus annus* Pope John Paul II says that the church contributes to the enrichment of human dignity when she "proclaims God's salvation to man, when she offers and communicates the life of God through the sacraments, when she gives direction to human life through the commandments of love of God and neighbor."[45] These examples show that a correct conception of the human person provides guidance to all educators and to legislators and also enables all people to recognize that they must strive to perfect their dignity in order to be good persons and, even, good democratic citizens.

---

43. *Gaudium et spes*, no. 91. "*ut, suam integram vocationem clarius percipientes, mundum praecellenti dignitati hominis conforment....*"
44. *Gaudium et spes*, no. 9, modified translation and my emphasis.
45. *Centesimus annus*, no. 55.

C. The Common Good

Understanding the permanent character of human dignity and what it means to speak of its perfection, we can more readily appreciate the Catholic concept of the common good. Let us call to mind Pope John XXIII's famous definition of the common good, as slightly reformulated by the *Catechism of the Catholic Church*: "the sum total of the conditions of social life which allow people, either as groups or individuals, to reach their own perfection more fully and more easily."

CSD recommends that certain social conditions be established so that individuals will be able to seek perfection without too many obstacles and with appropriate help. The perfection of *each* citizen, or the perfection of human dignity, is the goal of civil society and is, therefore, an essential part of the common good. The virtue of solidarity "is a firm and persevering determination to commit oneself to the common good: that is to say to the good of all and of each individual, because we are really responsible for all."[46]

Establishing the requisite social conditions and educating individuals to perfection are the shared responsibility of government, the church, voluntary associations, and individuals themselves. In other words, the government must not attempt to realize all elements of the common good, but respect the principle of subsidiarity. The classic description of this principle is found in Pius XI's *Quadragesimo anno* (1931):

> Just as it is gravely wrong to take from individuals what they can accomplish by their own initiative and industry and give it to the community, so also it is an injustice and at the same time a grave evil and disturbance of right order to assign to a greater and higher association what lesser and subordinate organizations can do. For every social activity ought of its very nature to furnish help to the members of the body social, and never destroy and absorb them. The supreme authority of the state ought, therefore, to let subordinate groups handle matters and concerns of lesser importance, which would otherwise dissipate its efforts greatly.... Therefore, those in power should be sure that the more perfectly a graduated order is kept among the various associations, in observance of the

---

46. Pope John Paul II, *Sollicitudo rei socialis* (*On Social Concern*, 1987), no. 38.

principle of "subsidiarity function," the stronger social authority and effectiveness will be and the happier and more prosperous the condition of the state.[47]

When that principle is observed, there is less chance of improper government intrusion and more chance of success in the combined efforts to achieve the common good. *"On the basis of this principle,"* explains the *Compendium of the Social Doctrine of the Church, "all societies of a superior order must adopt attitudes of help ('subsidium') — therefore of support, promotion, development — with respect to lower-order societies."*[48] This means that Catholic social doctrine wants to see everyone contributing to the well-being of civil society: individuals, families, the church, voluntary associations, and the state. The larger entities are to support and encourage the smaller ones, so that the initiative, freedom, and responsibility of all will be in play. This important principle of political philosophy promotes contributions of everyone to the common good of society.

"The principle of subsidiarity ... is imperative," says the *Compendium, "because every person, family and intermediate group has something original to offer to the community."*[49] The participation of all in the life of society is not just a democratic essentiality, but a logical implication of human dignity. Men and women realize their dignity by contributing to the common good of society through their active participation in its life. Of course, the active participation of citizens also ensures the smooth working of democracy and *"one of the major guarantees of the permanence of the democratic system."*[50]

Catholics recognize that government at any level in a liberal society will have a limited role in promoting the common good as articulated by Vatican Council II and the CCC because a liberal society is not authorized by its constitution to use the law in pursuit of the perfection of human beings. Catholics would necessarily understand perfection as the imitation of Jesus Christ and union with God, but would recognize other religious and philosophic understandings of perfection as a preparation for, or partial realization of, the way taught by Jesus. Some

---

47. Pius XI, *Quadragesimo anno*, nos. 79–80.
48. *Compendium*, no. 186. Italics are in the *Compendium*.
49. *Compendium*, no. 187.
50. *Compendium*, no. 190.

understandings of perfection would surely be at odds with the Catholic view. Even so, Catholics are always bound by the ideal of Christian perfection and would rely on the family, church, educational institutions, other voluntary associations, and the law to promote perfection as they understand it.

What the law could and should achieve in a liberal society will always be a subject for debate, in which Catholics have the right and duty to participate. It is little noticed that government does form the character of citizens to some extent by the law. Think of all the character formation that takes place in a public school: no bullying, no cheating, the good of service to others, and dedication to school work. Perhaps Aquinas is not off the mark in recommending the use of law to deter bad action and to encourage good actions. Catholics would, however, disagree among themselves about how much the law could do to deter evil and promote good.

The social conditions "which allow people ... to reach their proper perfection" may, at first glance, seem too difficult to name or describe. Perfection is not a common term in a liberal society. Citizens and theorists would more readily speak of social conditions conducive to the attainment or preservation of liberty and equality. The attainment of perfection would require a special set of social conditions hardly limited to instrumental goods. According to Catholic social teaching, some of these conditions are as follows: respect for life (e.g., no abortion, euthanasia, or destruction of embryos), religious freedom, the fidelity of the Catholic Church to its salvific mission, fidelity in marriages between one man and one woman, sound family life, character education in families and schools, comprehensive liberal education in the universities, high ethical principles in workplaces, true friendships, concord or harmony among citizens, forgiveness of injuries and reconciliation among citizens who have committed and suffered wrong, education and care for the poor, and more. Arguing how precisely these goals could be attained through persuasion and law is a matter of internal Catholic debate.

D. Why Does the Church Have a Teaching on the Common Good?

How practical is the church's teaching on the necessity of pursuing a substantive common good in every society? This teaching doesn't mean that Christians have to engage in utopian political reform. As we have already seen, Augustine offers advice about how to proceed when circumstances do not allow the establishment of a full common good — which is actually all the time because of ignorance, human imperfection, and human depravity.

Ultimately, the church presents a teaching on the common good of the political community because the realization of the common good facilitates the attainment of salvation. Since good laws and mores dispose people to receive Christian teaching and live a Christian life, and bad laws and mores do the opposite, the church attempts to persuade political communities to establish and maintain good laws and mores, or in the language of classical political philosophy, a good regime.

Pius XII made this point in his 1941 Pentecost message, in which he says that the church "must take cognizance of social conditions, which, whether one wills it or not, make difficult or practically impossible a Christian life in conformity with the precepts of the Divine Lawgiver."[51] He says that people need to "breathe the healthy vivifying atmosphere of truth and moral virtue" and not "the disease laden and often fatal air of error and corruption."

As a precedent and proof of his position, Pius XII cites Leo XIII's encyclical to the world, *Rerum novarum,* which "pointed out the dangers of the materialist Socialism conception, the fatal consequences of economic Liberalism, so often unaware, or forgetful, or contemptuous of social duties." Pius XII clearly does not limit his understanding of social conditions to instrumental goods. He must also be talking about those substantive elements of the common good that dispose people to be receptive to the gift of salvation.

Another reason for the church's social teaching is that the realization of a subordinate common good is a partial expression of the way human beings ought to live together. The dignity of the human person not only requires freedom for each individual, but a life dedicated to the practice of virtue and harmony among people based on truth. The church's teaching on the common good provides guidelines, not only for political authorities and the mediating institutions of civil society, but also for individuals living in every kind of regime. The latter can always practice virtue in view of the common good, even if they live under a corrupt government.

---

51. *Acta Apostolicae Sedis 33* (1941): *218–219.*

IV. Catholics and Poverty

A. The Obligation to Help the Poor

Let us now turn to one of the social conditions demanded by the common good: care for the poor. CSD is crystal clear about the obligation toward the poor. Christians are obliged to have a preferential option for the poor, which Pope John Paul II defined as a *"special form* of primacy in the exercise of Christian charity."[52] St. John Chrysostom expressed this Christian teaching in two memorable sentences: "Not to share one's wealth with the poor is to steal from them and to take away their livelihood. It is not our own goods which we hold, but theirs."[53] Mother Teresa of Calcutta and the congregation of sisters that she founded are perhaps the most well-known example of a Catholic commitment to the relief of the poor in India, especially in Calcutta. She inspired millions to remember the poor.

Father Raniero Cantalamessa says that we must keep the poor before our eyes and let them "get under our skin."[54] We must take notice of the poor with our heart. "The question is to let them into our hearts, so that they stop being someone else's problem rather than ours and become a kind of family problem."[55] In order to acquire the proper attitude, people should develop the habit of self-denial and keep constantly in mind that to welcome the poor is to welcome Christ. "For parents, children are a constant reason to do without things, to give up something, to make savings — in a word, to be poor."[56]

When we are poor in some way, we are more likely to perceive the poor with our heart, to see Christ. If we pray for guidance, the Spirit will let us know what we are to give up and how we might benefit the poor in our state of life. Father Cantalamessa tells the story of a rich businessman who went to a cloistered nun and asked how he might serve the poor. After praying for a time, realizing that he had the money, she said, " 'Well, go and open another factory and give jobs to some more workers!' And that's what he did."[57]

---

52. *Sollicitudo rei socialis*, no. 42.
53. Pope Francis, *Evangelii gaudium*, no. 57, quoting St. John Chrysostom.
54. Raniero Cantalamessa, *Poverty* (New York: Alba House, 1997), 3.
55. Ibid., 4.
56. Ibid., 56.
57. Ibid., 86.

B. The Importance of Education, Marriage, and Family

The provision of education to the poor may be the most important means of getting vast numbers out of poverty. Special attention should be given to public schools in areas of poverty so that poor children may receive the kind of education that will free them from the cycle of poverty. Whether governments do or do not assume any responsibility for educating the poor, individuals, associations, and churches should always try to find ways to do so. For example, private programs have arranged for college graduates to devote several years teaching the poor in inner-city schools. Catholic schools in the big cities have educated a great number of poor children, both Catholic and non-Catholic. Everyone knows that Catholic schools and other religiously affiliated schools can and do help the poor. It is high time, therefore, for more accommodation in church-state laws. At the very least, government should find a way to provide funding to poor children whose families want them to attend a private school, religiously affiliated or not.

Because divorce often plunges children into poverty, another effective measure to overcome it is to help people marry well and stay together. This is especially the role of the churches, but properly framed laws can also help. For example, laws that diminish the incidence of divorce will prevent some children from slipping into poverty. As things stand, the marriage laws in the states do not discourage divorce at all. Since the law is a teacher, it should tell stories of fidelity between spouses and loving care of children, and it should make divorce more difficult. With some nudging from the law, more couples will work out their difficulties and thereby give their children a better chance to avoid becoming mired in poverty.[58]

C. The Government Plays a Role

A genuine love of the poor must include not only individual and group efforts to help people move from and stay out of poverty, but also effective government action. Cash assistance is important as a temporary measure for those on the road to self-support and as a permanent

---

58. Mary Ann Glendon's book, *Abortion and Divorce in Western Law: American Failures, European Challenges* (Cambridge, MA: Harvard University Press, 1987) is eloquent and informative on this subject.

subsidy for people who cannot, for various legitimate reasons, obtain or hold a job. In addressing the economy as a whole, CSD has consistently defended a basically free economy along with appropriate regulation of the economy by the various levels of government. The Catholic Church realizes that reasonable people will legitimately disagree on the kind of government intervention that will most effectively regulate the economy in a way that benefits the greatest number of people, especially the poor.

D. The Limits of Government Action and of the Free Market

In his third encyclical, *Caritas in veritate*, Pope Benedict XVI describes three prongs to a viable and just economy: a free market in which people enjoy equal opportunity and respect contracts, political action to redistribute wealth, and most importantly, the spirit of gift or the principle of gratuitousness (no. 37). This means that economic behavior in a free market is regulated by law, commutative justice, and the personal virtues of the participants.

The pope highlights the point that the presence of gratuitousness, or freely embraced solidarity, is necessary for the *attainment* of justice. Neither the free market nor the laws, therefore, can assure justice, especially commutative justice, but only the virtuous qualities of the economic players. Pope Benedict is really saying that the market-plus-state binary model is not sufficient to produce a just and productive economy. Otherwise stated, the economy cannot function well simply on the basis of self-interest and state intervention, however intelligent. The market and politics absolutely need virtuous participants.

In addition to stressing the importance of virtue for a sound economy, Pope Benedict also suggests that businesses adopt a fundamentally different mode of management.

> [B]usiness management cannot concern itself only with the interests of the proprietors, but must also assume responsibility for all the other stakeholders who contribute to the life of the business: the workers, the clients, the suppliers of various elements of production, the community of reference (no. 40).

Attentiveness to all stakeholders increases the long-term sustainability of businesses. The pope questions the justice of business managers answering only to the shareholders. He also encourages businesses to benefit the local communities where they operate.

Otherwise stated, business should not just be about the bottom line. Of course, any business has to make a sufficient profit to take care of all the stakeholders. A business, however, must not harm the community in which it is located, but benefit it in any measure possible. It must not take advantage of its poor clients and must find ways for the poor to be so trained that they can competently fill jobs that pay enough to support a family.

Conclusion

The teaching of contemporary Catholic social doctrine on faith and politics will not be fully grasped unless it is read in the light of points made by Augustine and Thomas Aquinas.

Augustine argues persuasively that justice in the political and social order ultimately depends on the order of the soul of individual citizens, which, in turn, depends on receptivity to church teaching and grace. Augustine's reflections on love as the motivating factor in people's lives help Christian educators understand what they must do to move their students and listeners to make a contribution to the common good.

Aquinas's systematic explanation of all the virtues, especially justice and prudence, makes clearer what it means to work for justice. His reflections on the law as an instrument to restrain the bad and guide the good are especially needed today.

Thomas More, another important figure, offers powerful personal witness and persuasive exhortation to work for whatever, albeit limited, good that is possible. His *Utopia* shows clearly that people are inclined to withdraw from political life and commitment to the common good when they run into opposition.

All three authors argue persuasively against a central contention of modern political philosophy that institutional solutions can make up for the character defects of citizens and leaders. Finally, they help church leaders realize what they must understand and teach to move the clergy and laity to integrate faith into every aspect of their lives.

Contemporary Catholic social doctrine explains that the church acting as Church does not have the ultimate responsibility to bring about a just social order, but contributes to that goal by educating members in the faith, by explaining Catholic social doctrine, and by helping the faithful to use their reason well. People who live their Catholic faith well integrate it into every aspect of their lives: for example, into family life, work, relations with friends and neighbors, participation in the public square as engaged citizens, and recreation.

The understanding of human dignity as both a permanent characteristic of human beings and as a goal to be achieved introduces principles that can serve as guiding lights in a liberal democracy, even when they are partially implemented using different language. The physical, psychological, intellectual, and spiritual development of individuals promoted in families, churches, and schools is another way of talking about perfecting the dignity of the human person.

The proper development of every human person is the goal of every initiative to promote the common good. Of course, many think that respecting human dignity means primarily establishing social conditions that enable individuals to have more autonomy. The Catholic Church has great respect for human freedom, but believes that many citizens of various faiths or no faith can achieve some agreement on what social conditions promote the dignity of the human person.

Ultimately, the Catholic Church does not seek to impose its views, but to persuade people to see some wisdom in its social teachings. The role of the church, in politics as in all realms, is faithful witness to Jesus Christ.

AN ANABAPTIST (SEPARATIONIST) RESPONSE

THOMAS W. HEILKE

Much of what I might say in response to Professor Benestad I have already said in the responses to Professors Benne and Smith. The argument will not improve from repetition. Instead, I will turn to one or two specific aspects of Benestad's argument for comment.

There is much in this essay that an Anabaptist could politico-theologically affirm. That "Christians are obliged to have a preferential option for the poor," for example, is widely accepted among contemporary Anabaptists. So, too—with a strong exception to the laity-clergy distinction and some questions about the precise origins, meaning, and content of "the virtues"—few Anabaptists would object to the claim that "the laity [believers?] will also contribute to the just structuring of society by practicing the virtues in their family life, at work, and in their relations with neighbors." My Anabaptist concerns with the approach of Benestad reside elsewhere.

In my own essay, I imply that one's socio-political status may have conscious or unconscious effects for one's ethical concerns and formulations and that these effects are not illegitimate. This assertion is a core premise of certain current Anabaptist approaches to ethics, and Fields has shown how that has certainly been true for the American Black church. Despite the seemingly universalist approach of Benestad's explication of Roman Catholic social doctrine (CSD), the problem of the *Sitz im Leben* is nowhere more evident than in his presentation. Benestad seems firmly to assume power (the church with its institutions, resources, and socio-political influence) speaking truth to power (the political authorities and/or the state).

Yet, so characterizing this chapter seems less than fair. Benestad is all-too-aware of our post-Christian, "secular" context, and his typically (and justified) Catholic assumption of the church as a strong institution does not seem in many passages to imply strictly Constantinian or neo-Constantinian arrangements between church, political authorities, and society.

He is explicit that he is speaking of "contemporary Catholic social doctrine," and if he does make repeated reference to historical thinkers in the Roman Catholic tradition, especially Thomas Aquinas and Aurelius Augustine, that does not make him a proponent of having a church that co-rules society with the political authorities. If I were to utter yet another common Anabaptist complaint against much Christian social theory—where is Jesus in all this?—he could point out that his beginning point includes "that truth which is Christ Himself," and that he does not neglect to note that we are redeemed by Jesus Christ (and not political institutions or processes), and that he ends with a comment that any Anabaptist could affirm: "The role of the Church, in politics as in all realms, is faithful witness to Jesus Christ." The problem here is the same as between Protestants and Anabaptists: What is the socio-ethical *content* of "the truth which is Christ himself," and what are the ecclesiological, social, and political implications of that truth and of our redemption by him?

Benestad's approach is in part a testimony to the rich philosophical and liturgical heritage of the Roman Catholic tradition from which other traditions represented in this book—especially, in my opinion, Lutherans and Anabaptists—might do well to profit. But in Benestad's presentation, this voice—despite the many historical references to philosophical voices in Roman Catholic history—has a peculiarly ahistorical cast that stands in decided contrast to the other four chapters of this book. This peculiarity is not necessarily a rejection of my argument concerning one's *Sitz im Leben* and one's assumption about that "seat," its merits, and its relative permanence or transience (which is *in no way* an argument for situation ethics). Rather, it seems to emerge from an assumption that human reason is universal and transhistorical and that Roman Catholic doctrine is more or less universally accessible.

Consider this statement, cited from *Centesimus annus*: "from the Christian vision of the human person there necessarily follows a correct picture of society." Historically speaking, unless a "correct picture of society" is so general and broad as to be useless for practical application, this statement is simply false. Monarchy, aristocracy, and democracy (each in several varieties); toleration, persecution, and banishment;

pacifism, just war, and crusade have all been derived, in some cases by Roman Catholic authorities whom Benestad cites, from "the Christian vision of the human person."

Benestad argues further that CSD "relies on the truths of the faith in conjunction with right reason to make ethical judgments on human affairs," and that it "can be rightly based on both faith and reason," as argued in *Dignitatis Humanae*. I have indicated elsewhere at length that the language of justice, dignity, and rights is contested within the Roman Catholic tradition itself, and that it often emerges in documents like *Dignitatis humanae* from secular sources, not the gospel. That does not make such language wrong, but especially in light of historical (both recent and long past) church approval for various kinds of regimes we would now reject on the basis of rational argument, and in light of other abuses, the claims of a close relationship between the gospel and Enlightenment notions of freedom and dignity are less than convincing. Without deep historical elaboration and explicit mechanisms of repentance and forgiveness for past wrongs and mistakes, it also makes any ethic claiming dependence upon a union of the two inherently unstable.[59]

The intent here is not to point a wagging finger and say, "Look at all the bad things you have done!" as though that settles any imaginable ethical debate. Rather, it is to face one's mistakes and account for them and to say how one intends to do better in the future. So, I have suggested, Anabaptists (and any utopian Christian) must do with respect to Münster and, I would add here, with respect to Anabaptist abuses of the ban of patriarchal authority in rural communities, and other historical mistakes.

Without an equivalent accounting, however, Benestad's preferred doctrine remains deeply unstable: Was the persecution of heretics and the church-sanctioned prosecution of religious wars a mistake of reason, a mistake of scriptural interpretation, a mistake in historical perspective, or something else? And out of this selection of causes, which choice provides the best chance of a correction that is not merely expedient, but speaks with integrity and honesty from the community of believers to the watching world?

---

59. See my "The Promised Time of *Dignitatis Humanae*: A Radical Protestant Perspective," in Kenneth L. Grasso and Robert P. Hunt, eds., *Catholicism and Religious Freedom: Contemporary Reflections on Vatican II's Declaration on Religious Liberty* (Lanham, MD: Rowman & Littlefield Publishers, Inc., 2006), 87–113.

A LUTHERAN (PARADOXICAL) RESPONSE

Brian Benestad's account of the Roman Catholic view of the church's role in the political realm is attractive and persuasive. There is much I as a Lutheran want to embrace. Benestad argues that the current Catholic emphasis is on the formation of the laity—not only on inculcating virtue, but on awakening conscience through Catholic Social Teaching, or "purifying reason," as he puts it. The laity are then encouraged to engage in the political process, employing both their conscience and their virtue in that involvement. He notes a reluctance on the part of the Catholic Church to intervene in the political process except in cases where Christian teachings are either clearly affirmed or violated by government policy. He also presents well the Catholic doctrine of subsidiarity that resists an omnicompetent state that threatens free associations. Catholic concern for the poor and the common good are given clear emphasis.

However, this account is so beguiling because it doesn't deal with the historic propensity of the Roman Catholic Church to intervene vigorously in the political process, which in an earlier day led many Americans to distrust Catholics in political office, especially that of President. To diminish their distrust, it took a John F. Kennedy to tell Protestants that his Catholicism had absolutely no effect on his politics. The propensity of the church to use the earthly sword of power in the political sphere led to one of the central objections of the Reformers of the sixteenth century. Its deep involvement in political power has led to extreme reactions to that role in France, Spain, England, Mexico, and most recently in places like Quebec and Ireland. I would have appreciated a bit more self-criticism of the church's historic political role as well as some reflection on why and how great changes in that role have taken place.

Nevertheless, I believe the Catholic Church is Christianity's main bulwark for promoting authentic Christian values (sanctity of life, marriage, the natural family, care for the poor, religious freedom) in the public sphere. Protestantism simply cannot speak clearly and strongly, partly because it often lacks a body of social teachings and partly because it is so diverse in what it has to say. Among Lutherans, the public witness of the Evangelical Lutheran Church in America and the Lutheran Church—Missouri Synod would clash dramatically.

As Benestad observes, an important strength of the Catholic Church is its strong doctrine of natural law to back up those values mentioned above. Though natural law arguments convince few in the secular world these days, they may become increasingly persuasive as the culture unravels in spasms of libertarian chaos and confusion. The Catholic bishops, even though hampered by earlier scandals, must continue their witness to those values in the public sphere in the face of widespread resistance. The future of America may depend on such a clear witness. I wish that Benestad had emphasized that role even more than he did.

So, yes, the Roman Catholic Church must continue its promotion of virtue and Catholic social doctrine (CSD), as Benestad avers. This will no doubt mean a renewal of catechesis in Catholic churches and institutions to an extent that will be daunting. It will probably mean fewer but more intense Catholics, as casual cultural Catholics depart for an easier life away from such a call to discipleship. But it will also mean the continuance of the strongest public Christian witness in the political sphere.

A BLACK CHURCH (PROPHETIC) RESPONSE

BRUCE L. FIELDS

The stage for my response to Benestad's work is set using his words on Augustine, a foundational contributor to Catholic social doctrine (CSD):

> Augustine argues persuasively that justice in the political and social order ultimately depends on the order of the soul of individual citizens, which, in turn depends on receptivity to Church teaching and grace. Augustine's reflections on love as the motivating factor in people's lives help Christian educators understand what they must do to move their students and listeners to make a contribution to the common good (p. 203).

Benestad shows how CSD is based on faith and reason. The church's task in relationship to a sociopolitical order is to be a witness to the faith and a pervasive presence in the social setting, through various means affecting the reasoning capacities of the people to move toward virtue. He ably demonstrates that the Catholic tradition is the product of centuries of reflection, and he makes convincing claims for at least a guarded confidence in the common ground of reason, albeit still needing to be strengthened by grace. This greater confidence in reason's abilities clearly sets the Catholic view apart from the others. In this response, I will mention a few themes that are particularly helpful in understanding this synthetic view of the church and the political realm. Then I will close with some questions in light of Benestad's applications.

Benestad encapsulates some key contributing thoughts from Augustine and Thomas Aquinas. Two elements from Augustine's thought particularly resonate with the Black church tradition. The first is that justice requires an ordering of the souls of the citizens (p. 182). Benestad writes, "Augustine agrees with Plato's and Aristotle's view that no society can be just unless individuals are virtuous" (p. 184). The difference between them was that Plato and Aristotle could not address the inherent weakness of sin in the soul of human beings. Benestad also notes the role of love in Augustine's thought in light of a call for the citizens to be taught to love virtue. Love essentially draws the person to a value, an attitude, a course of action.

Benestad's discussion of Thomas Aquinas offers helpful categories for understanding justice (p. 185). It therefore makes a timely connection with Augustine's thought by concluding that people with disordered souls cannot extend justice to others (p. 186). Aquinas's categories offer guidelines for societies and name the factors needed to enhance the appropriate dispensation of justice. Aquinas's insistence on the use of law to restrain and reform violators is timely, but Benestad notes that the Thomistic position on the use of the law to develop virtue is not "widely known or accepted by many contemporary Catholics" (p. 191).

The Catholic view challenges our thinking concerning human dignity through recognizing the multiple factors at its foundation. Although many traditions focus on human beings being made in the image of God, the Catholic tradition's emphasis on Christ's blood shed to offer the hope of salvation for the world advances further the case for human dignity. This tradition offers an additional challenge to consider dignity as a developmental process; as Pope Leo XIII, revealing Thomistic influence, wrote, "True dignity and excellence in men resides in moral living, that is, in virtue" (p. 194).

Although the Catholic tradition contributes greatly to Christian political thought, a few issues need further attention. In particular, in light of liberation theology among other factors, Benestad's essay raises questions about the application of subsidiarity, the relationship of reason to grace, and the role of government.

First, the principle of subsidiarity seems to share some commonality with sphere sovereignty in the Reformed tradition. My focus, however, is on the statement made in the *Compendium of the Social Doctrine of the Church* that includes reference to "societies of a *superior* order ... therefore of support, promotion, development—with respect to *lower-order* societies" (p. 197, emphasis mine). Although the pursuit of the "common good" is central for all societies, how are *superior* and *inferior* determined? An understandable fear from many in the Black church is that apart from exploring the foundations of such labels, much dehumanization can occur despite noble intentions. The process of dehumanization can begin with the entertainment of unidirectional help: The idea that there may be something to learn from those who are being helped does not cross the mind of the helpers.

Second, what is the relationship of reason to grace? Benestad mentions how CSD can speak "even to all people of good will. The latter can be addressed because many elements of CSD can be grasped and appreciated by reason alone" (p. 178). Yet, the Vatican's *Compendium* can speak of the "need for inner conversion, if one is to achieve the economic and social changes that will truly be at the service of man" (p. 180). In a similar vein, Pope Benedict XVI spoke to the Muslim community of Cameroon: "I believe a particularly urgent task of religion today is to unveil the vast potential of human reason, which is God's gift and which is elevated by revelation and faith" (p. 179). I wholeheartedly concur with the latter part of this statement. As important as the latter affirmation may be, the experience of the Black church is a sobering reminder of how the power of sin can corrupt reason and how intensely humans and their institutions need grace.

Third, then, what if government proves to benefit only a select few or a particular class? Does grace mean that the marginalized simply maintain the status quo, or is there room for more direct responses on the part of either Christian citizens or churches? And how far may such responses go? For obvious reasons, the Catholic tradition's previous tendency to uphold governmental authority and to oppose resistance embodies an area of great personal struggle for members of the Black church tradition. As modern Catholics often acknowledge more clearly, these questions of grace and government should concern all Christians.

JAMES K.A. SMITH

Let me begin with a slightly petulant protest: I, too, am "Catholic." What Brian Benestad has articulated is a *Roman* Catholic view of the church and politics. But Rome does not own the "Catholic" tradition — it is an august, enduring, dominant expression of it, of course. But I take it that those streams of Christianity that affirm the ancient creeds (including the affirmation of "one, holy, catholic church") and the Spirit's continued work throughout history are equally "catholic."[60]

This isn't just a tetchy protest; it has important implications for how we think about the church and politics. In an increasingly secularized, post-Christian culture, it is crucial that "the church" be understood "catholically" — as a transnational body that finds its commonness in the Scriptures, the sacraments, and the Nicene tradition. In short, catholicity has political implications: Christians should be looking for allies in the public square, and our shared catholic faith should unite us in our public witness.[61]

I don't envy Benestad's task: to summarize "the" (Roman!) Catholic view for a tradition that is ancient, variegated, and contested. I would say Benestad has offered "a" Catholic view, not necessarily "the" Catholic view. Indeed, I think there are important aspects of Roman Catholic teaching and habits with respect to government and politics that are not addressed in his essay. I would like to highlight a couple of those briefly.

But first, let me heartily affirm Benestad's link between virtue and the common good and the crucial synergy between the formative space

---

60. Thus, in *Letters to a Young Calvinist* (Grand Rapids: Brazos Press, 2010) I have said that for me, becoming Reformed was a way of becoming Catholic. As I suggest there, one could describe the Reformation as an Augustinian renewal movement within the church catholic.

61. This will admittedly be most challenging for those streams of evangelicalism that are "primitivist" rather than catholic, tending to denigrate all post-apostolic fruits of the church. For a relevant discussion, see Timothy George, ed., *Evangelicals and Nicene Faith: Reclaiming the Apostolic Witness* (Grand Rapids: Baker Academic, 2011).

of the church (along with families) and the public good of the *polis*. More specifically, the Reformed view shares the Roman Catholic sense of a *common* good. Furthermore, the Reformed view resonates with Thomas's case for "using the law to provide a moral education." Pictured here is a synergy between different layers and spheres of society—the family, the school, the parish, the market, the state—that work in concert for the common good. Catholic social teaching describes this as "subsidiarity." This affirmation of a robust civil society resonates with the Kuyperian articulation of "sphere sovereignty."[62]

But Benestad's emphases are telling. While he makes reference to Pope Leo XIII's key encyclical, *Rerum novarum*, in the end he sounds like an advocate of a much more minimalist state than Leo envisioned.[63] Whereas Pope Leo emphasized the importance of labor—including organized labor—in his encyclical, we hear little of that aspect in Benestad's presentation. Instead, Catholic social teaching seems to amount to a rationale for small government.

I think Benestad has given us a fairly selective picture of the Roman Catholic understanding of the relationship between the church and politics, ignoring a long track record of how this worked itself out in the past (precisely what my forebears in the Reformation protested). If he had given us a more descriptive history of the Roman Catholic understanding of the relationship between the church and "the state" (a term that can only be used anachronistically in pre-modern contexts), we would have seen configurations in which the state was swallowed by the church, models wherein the pope was effectively seen as a Holy Roman emperor—that was one of the historic expressions of "synthesis" that the Reformers rightly protested against. Why, in the past, did the Roman Catholic view yield an undifferentiated amalgam of church and state?[64]

---

62. See Kent A. Van Til, "Subsidiarity and Sphere Sovereignty," *Theological Studies* 69 (2008): 610–36, and Richard Mouw, *Abraham Kuyper: A Short and Personal Introduction* (Grand Rapids: Eerdmans, 2011), 26–27.

63. I heard echoes of something like Samuel Gregg's minority report, *Tea Party Catholic: The Catholic Case for Limited Government, a Free Economy, and Human Flourishing* (New York: Crossroad, 2013). In this respect, I would say Abraham Kuyper is much closer to the spirit and program of *Rerum novarum* than Gregg is. For a relevant discussion, see Brian Dijkema, "Is Catholic Social Teaching the Same as Individual Contract Theory?" in the *Journal of Markets & Morality* 17, no. 2 (Fall 2014): 517–24.

64. For a relevant discussion of "differentiation" as a principle of Reformed social philosophy, and one historically absent from Roman Catholic accounts of the relationship between

Benestad outlines a division of labor that accepts the distinction between the church and the state and then seems to assume that "reason" and "nature" disclose that the state should be "liberal." This is without a vibrant stream of Catholic thought on the state, perhaps most influentially articulated by John Courtney Murray.[65] However, there is a different strain of Catholic political thought—dubbed "radical Catholicism" by Notre Dame political scientist Patrick Deneen—that takes a more fundamentally suspicious stance without respect to liberalism. Influenced by the work of Alasdair MacIntyre, thinkers like Deneen and William Cavanaugh articulate a more radical critique of the assumptions underlying American liberalism and assess them negatively in light of Catholic doctrine.[66]

While we might share an affirmation of government per se, there must be room for a trenchant Christian critique of the specific configurations of government. The antithetical side of the Kuyperian tradition leads me to be more sympathetic to this radical Catholicism that Benestad ignores.

---

the church and the state, see Jonathan Chaplin, *Herman Dooyeweerd: Christian Philosopher of State and Civil Society* (South Bend, IN: University of Notre Dame Press, 2011), 246–54.

65. See the influential classic, John Courtney Murray, *We Hold These Truths: Catholic Reflections on the American Proposition* (1960; reprint, New York: Sheed & Ward, 2005).

66. See, for example, William Cavanaugh, *Theopolitical Imagination* (London: T & T Clark, 2003).

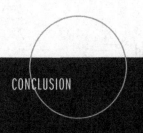

CHRISTIAN WITNESS IN THE PUBLIC SQUARE

AMY E. BLACK

In contemporary politics, one need not look far to find examples of Christians aligning themselves on different sides of major political debates. One Christian organization argues passionately for government action on a public policy, even as another argues loudly against it. How should Christians approach political debates over divisive issues such as health care, the environment, immigration, and more? Instead of calling all followers of Christ to speak with one political voice and claiming to resolve political debates definitively, this book highlights different Christian approaches to politics and the principles that animate them.

As the contributors to this volume have demonstrated, Christians throughout the centuries have debated the extent to which church and government should interact and have wrestled with divisive political issues. Each of the five views represented in this book introduces concepts and vocabulary useful for discussing the proper role of government, the place of political participation, and the purposes and foundations of the law. Interaction with these rich theological traditions can help guide those seeking to think more deeply about their Christian witness in politics.

Politics and Government in a Complex World

The contributors have offered a range of perspectives on the role and purpose of government, the formal political and institutional *structures* of a state, and politics, the informal *process* for addressing social and economic problems. Like everything in our fallen world, government and politics are broken and incomplete. When most corrupted, governments insulate leaders from the people and promote tyranny and oppression. When designed well, government institutions divide power and authority, provide internal and external checks on political power, and connect the people with their leaders. At its best, government serves the common good and makes positive contributions that benefit many people.

Political scientist Harold Lasswell famously described politics as determining "who gets what, when, [and] how."[1] A wide range of people — elected officials, government bureaucrats, representatives of business, labor, and special interest groups — compete in the political arena, raising their particular concerns as they make collective decisions. When working well, the political process makes a way for everyone in society to flourish. At its worst, self-interest reigns and the process grinds to a halt. So long as societies continue to face collective problems and decisions, government will be necessary, and political issues will divide people.

Modern governments have accomplished many great things. Most industrialized democracies have solved the simplest problems affecting society. For example, few people living in these countries worry about access to clean water, utilities, public education, fire and police protection, and infrastructure like roads and bridges. Their governments have assessed the needs and developed plans for providing these public goods.

Most of the easy work has been accomplished, but important and difficult work remains. The remaining social problems that government might address are the most complicated and entrenched, and they rarely have clear or easy solutions. Thus the issues under public debate become sources of significant disagreement and conflict. Policy experts honestly disagree about what path government should take and the extent to which government can help at all. To complicate matters further,

---

1. Harold D. Lasswell, *Politics: Who Gets What, When, How* (New York: Whittelsey House, 1936).

elected officials keep a constant eye on reelection, so they tend to focus on the short term and postpone making politically difficult choices.

Given the wide range of perspectives within the Christian tradition and the complex and divisive nature of politics, it shouldn't surprise us that Christians also disagree about how to approach politics and government. The late Congressman Paul Henry explained the dilemma:

> If orthodox Christians practicing charity toward one another cannot come to agreement on matters where there appears to be direct biblical teaching (such as the administration of the sacraments or eschatology), it can hardly be expected that they will come to agreement on those matters where biblical teachings are arrived at only indirectly and inductively.[2]

The historic traditions of Christian thought we have explored in this book offer tools for navigating the complexities of politics and government and present distinctive ways to apply biblical teaching to these questions. Examining some of the key areas of agreement and disagreement can help shape our understanding of how we, individually and in our churches, should interact with the political sphere.

Historical Traditions, Contemporary Applications

In the preceding chapters and responses, the contributors have identified fundamental principles and raised questions that inform political discussions. A final task remains: placing these traditions in the context of contemporary American politics. Given the diversity within the five traditions presented in this book and the complexity of issues debated in the public square, this is no simple task. Even so, the distinctive principles and emphases from each tradition tend to pull adherents in different partisan directions.

Unlike many other modern democracies, the United States is dominated by a two-party system. Although the nation's founders thought they had created a system free of political parties, they have been in place since 1796. A combination of tradition and various structures of the constitutional system has created an equilibrium in which two, and only two, major parties vie for power against each other at any given time.

---

2. Paul Henry, *Politics for Evangelicals* (Valley Forge, PA: Judson Press, 1974), 75.

Since so few parties compete in the American system, the two parties are broad-based and address a wide range of issues. Party leaders, elected officials, and local activists within each party do not act in lockstep; the diversity within the two major parties leaves room for much inter-party disagreement. Despite this, the two parties are politically distinctive from each other. The Democratic party is the most natural home for those with liberal or progressive views, whereas the Republican party is known for its ideological conservatism.[3] Republicans typically favor a smaller government that provides fewer services and are more concerned that the government protect morality. Democrats are more likely to favor a larger government that offers more services and are more skeptical of governmental protection of morality.

To what extent do the views presented in this book correlate with the politics and goals of the Democratic and Republican parties? As we will see, none of the perspectives compared in this book overlaps completely with the dominant positions of either of the two major parties. The teachings of some traditions will fit more naturally with one or the other party, some will agree more with one party on certain issues and the other party on others, and some traditions are internally divided between their more politically—and theologically—conservative and liberal branches.

Catholics and Contemporary American Politics

Of the five views we have discussed, the Catholic tradition is the most open to interaction between church and state. As J. Brian Benestad explained, the unified structure of the church allows her to speak directly to the divisive issues of the day. Papal encyclicals, statements from the Vatican Congregation for the Doctrine of the Faith and the Pontifical Council for Justice and Peace, and other authoritative teachings of the Church direct Catholic priests and laity in ways to apply their faith to politics. Individual parishioners, of course, are free to disagree with the church's official teaching on certain matters, and evidence suggests this is rather common. Even so, the church has

---

3. Inter-party disagreement is an important aspect of the American party system. For the purpose of this discussion and the need for brevity, I will compare the two parties by focusing on the dominant positions each party takes on key political issues.

institutional authority unparalleled in Protestantism and consequently speaks to her people and the world with a much more unified voice than any Protestant tradition can offer.

Catholic teachings address a wide range of political issues that do not fit neatly with either major party's priorities, so Catholics are unlikely to find a natural political home as Republicans or Democrats. Different principles of Catholic Social Doctrine pull adherents in opposite partisan directions. The emphasis on the dignity of the human person and the sacredness of life, for example, translates into strong positions against the practices of abortion and euthanasia, views most commonly held by Republicans. In stark contrast, these same principles lead the Church to oppose capital punishment, a position more commonly held by Democrats. As an extension of the principle of the preferential option for the poor and vulnerable, Catholic leaders have tended to support Democratic policies and proposals in their advocacy for public safety net programs. Yet, Catholic leaders have been critical of recent Democratic-promoted regulations that threaten their religious freedom. As these examples demonstrate, different aspects of official Catholic teachings line up with each of the two major parties. Catholic voters face the dilemma of choosing which set of issues they believe is most relevant to earn their support.

The Black Church and Contemporary Politics

The chapter on the Black church detailed how this tradition wrestles directly with the tension between "the already and the not yet." Forged from experiences of great oppression and suffering, the church seeks transformation in the here and now, confronting evil and calling for correctives that will combat injustice and help her people. At the same time, the church brings comfort with the gospel message of ultimate redemption and restoration in the life to come.

As Bruce Fields described in his chapter, the African-American experience with politics and government has been "complex and perplexing." At times, government actions have oppressed and marginalized African Americans; at other times, government has been a forceful agent of empowerment and righting societal wrongs. Their experiences with government—both positive and negative—have helped them realize the power political systems can wield. Despite government attempts at redress and in no small part as a consequence of racism and discrimination, African Americans continue to face significant economic disadvantages. Leaders in the Black church have been at the forefront of social movements demanding change, and many pastors incorporate political themes into their preaching.

In the decades immediately following emancipation, most Blacks identified with Republicans, the party of Abraham Lincoln. But the issue positions and allegiances of the two major parties shifted over time. By the 1960s, the Democratic party had become the champion of civil rights and government programs designed to alleviate poverty and combat discrimination, and most African Americans switched their party allegiance.[4] In contemporary politics, most African-American elected officials are Democrats, and most worshipers in the Black church identify as Democrats, especially on economic issues and civil rights. This alliance is not without tension, however, as the more conservative social and cultural views associated with the Republican party align more closely with the typical teachings of the Black church. In most election cycles, Democratic elected officials and candidates actively court Black voters as an essential part of their political base, whereas few Republicans make concerted efforts to win their support.

The Reformed and Lutheran Traditions and Contemporary American Politics

As we have seen, the Reformed and Lutheran traditions share roots in the magisterial reformation, yet they have different theological perspectives on the interaction between faith and politics. The dominant strain of Reformed thought emphasizes government as part of God's created order, a conviction that, as James K.A. Smith outlines, "propels believers into government and politics" (p. 151). The state is one of many societal institutions that can serve as an agent of transformation, and believers can and should participate in it. Integration is an overarching theme. The Lutheran tradition, in contrast, envisions government as a post-Fall reality, needed to restrain evil, and draws sharp distinctions

---

4. For a more detailed discussion of this shift, see Edward G. Carmines and James A. Stimson, *Issue Evolution: Race and the Transformation of American Politics* (Princeton, NJ: Princeton University Press, 1989).

between the temporal and eternal kingdoms. Much of the tradition, as Robert Benne notes, has tended toward quietism.

Although these two traditions differ sharply in their political theology, their behavior in contemporary American politics connects closely with trends in other Protestant traditions. Denominational differences matter, but they have been eclipsed in recent decades by theological differences. Most American Protestant denominations are split between their historic mainline, often more "liberal," churches and their evangelical, more theologically conservative, counterparts. Evangelicals emphasize the authority of Scripture, the centrality of the cross, and the importance of individual conversion; mainline Protestants are more communitarian in focus, have a more optimistic view of human nature, and tend to interpret the Bible with more influence from modern reason and contemporary experience.

Mainline denominations are larger and more established, so they tend to be more theologically diverse than their evangelical counterparts. In recent decades, theologically conservative congregations from a range of mainline denominations have moved to evangelical branches, often breaking away over contentious issues such as the ordination of gays and lesbians and recognition of same-sex marriage.

Most of the large mainline Protestant denominations have offices in Washington, DC, that advocate on a range of social justice issues, and their official political stances most often align with the Democratic party. Evangelical churches are less likely to have a denominational presence in Washington, but many of their members are politically engaged, and several national interest groups advocate on their behalf. Evangelicals tend to hold views opposite those of their mainline counterparts, especially on cultural issues, and identify strongly with the Republican party.

As the cleavage between evangelical and liberal Protestantism has become more politically significant, evangelical Lutherans and Presbyterians are more likely to find political common ground than mainline Lutherans and Presbyterians. This cleavage also holds true within other Protestant groups that have less cohesively distinctive political traditions, such as Methodists and Baptists.

Anabaptists and Contemporary Politics

As Thomas Heilke's essay highlighted, the Anabaptist tradition is less recognized for its political thought than for its ethics. The movement emphasizes the teachings of Jesus, lay leadership, nonviolence, and communal practice. The Anabaptist focus on radical discipleship often translates into separation from mainstream culture and distancing from formal politics.

The complexities and emphases of this tradition make it an uneasy fit with contemporary politics. Separatist tendencies and suspicion of governmental authority pull many away from direct political activity, so very few Anabaptists seek elected office or other forms of formal participation. The tradition's commitment to nonviolence does not fit well with the mainstream of either major political party and offers a sharp contrast to many elements of American foreign policy. An analysis of data from the Pew Center shows that contemporary Anabaptists favor more government protection of morality and prefer a smaller role for government, views that align best with the Republican party.[5] Even so, some Anabaptists prefer the Democratic party due to its emphasis on combating poverty and promoting social justice.

Anabaptists have political concerns, but such matters are typically secondary to other areas of focus. Ultimately, the hallmark of the Anabaptist tradition is its distinctive witness, modeling an alternative community that demonstrates love for neighbor and points people to Christ.

Religion, Partisanship, and Voting

As we have seen, the central teachings and emphases of these five traditions do not align perfectly with the American two-party system, but they tend to pull their adherents in particular political directions. Although most political surveys do not break respondents into categories that overlap perfectly with all the five traditions explored in this volume, the data reveal interesting patterns of how different religious groups vote.

---

5. Tobin Grant, "Politics of American Churches and Religions in One Graph," Religion News Service blog, August 27, 2014 (data from Pew's Religious Landscape Survey, http://tobingrant.religionnews.com/2014/08/27/politics-american-churches-religions-one-graph/, accessed June 5, 2015).

National surveys typically ask questions that allow for comparison of the political behavior of Catholics and three different groups of Protestants. In recognition of their unique history and distinctive religious traditions, African-American Protestants are typically separated into their own category.[6] Survey researchers usually divide the remaining Protestants between evangelical Protestants, those who say they attend churches affiliated with evangelical denominations or those who describe themselves as "born again," and mainline Protestants, the other Protestants in the sample.[7] Depending on their particular denominational affiliation, believers from Anabaptist, Lutheran, and Reformed churches are dispersed between the mainline and evangelical groups, mingling in with other Protestants from a wide range of denominations.

Particular religious beliefs and behaviors cannot always predict the way a person will vote. Instead, the translation of these positions into the support of a particular political disposition varies by tradition. For example, white evangelicals and Black Protestants look very similar on many questions about religious belief. Members of both groups are theologically conservative, say that religion is very important in their lives, and report high levels of church attendance. As we will see, however, they apply these religious convictions to the political realm quite differently.

Religious Groups and Party Affiliation

Analysis of survey data reveals distinctive patterns that persist across time and election cycles. Religious affiliation is an important factor that influences voting decisions, and religious groups vary in their partisan leanings.

Two religious groups have strong allegiances with political parties. Much like African Americans in the general population, very large percentages of Black Protestants identify with the Democratic

---

6. Scholars of religion and politics sometimes face criticism for distinguishing Black Protestants from other religious groups. Given the robust and significant role the Black church has played in American history, this distinction not only makes theoretical sense but turns out to be an empirical necessity.

7. Researchers disagree about the best way to classify evangelical and mainline Protestants, and the limited number of religious questions on some surveys complicates the process even further. It is prudent to view these classifications as constructive but rough and somewhat limited determinations of the different populations.

party. In the Pew Center's 2015 U.S. Religious Landscape Survey, for example, 82 percent of Black Protestants said they were Democrats or leaned Democratic, a pattern that has been quite consistent for decades. White evangelicals, in contrast, identify as Republicans by a strong margin: more than two of three (68 percent) say they are Republicans. Although majorities of white evangelicals have described themselves as Republicans for several decades, the gap between the parties has widened in recent years as the percentage of evangelicals who identify as Democrats has decreased.[8]

The party allegiance of Catholics and mainline Protestants is more evenly divided. In the Pew survey cited above, equal percentages of both groups were somewhat more likely to identify as Democrats (48%) than as Republicans (40%). When looking at data since 1994, however, the two groups show some differentiation over time. Catholic Democrats have consistently outnumbered Catholic Republicans by small margins each year, but the gap has narrowed slightly in recent years. The party identification of mainline Protestants, on the other hand, has been rather evenly distributed between the two parties over time, with Republicans occasionally outnumbering Democrats.

Religious Groups and Voting Behavior

As one might expect, party preferences are reflected in voting patterns. In recent decades, mainline Protestants and Roman Catholics have been swing voters, dividing their vote rather evenly between the two parties. Although Catholic voters historically tended to be more heavily Democratic, in the last few elections they have tended to divide their votes more evenly between the two parties. In the 2004 presidential election, George W. Bush won a slim majority (52%) of the Catholic vote; Barack Obama won a slight majority (54%) in 2008 and half the Catholic vote (50%) in 2012.[9] The voting patterns in Congressional elections have also been reasonably evenly split and look quite similar to

---

8. "Trends in Party Identification by Religion," The Pew Forum on Religion and Public Life, http://www.pewforum.org/2012/02/02/trends-in-party-identification-of-religious-groups (accessed June 2, 2015).

9. "Trends in Party Identification by Religion," The Pew Forum on Religion and Public Life, http://www.pewforum.org/2012/02/02/trends-in-party-identification-of-religious-groups (accessed June 2, 2015).

national outcomes: The percentage of Catholics voting for Democratic congressional candidates ranged from 55% in 2006, to 44% in 2010, and 45% in 2014. In recent presidential elections, the mainline Protestant vote has leaned slightly Republican. In 2004, George W. Bush won 59% of their vote. John McCain won 54% in 2008, and Mitt Romney won 57% in 2012.

In contrast, Black Protestants and white evangelicals comprise important and secure voting blocs for their respective parties. Black Protestants vote solidly Democratic. John Kerry received 86% of the Black Protestant vote in 2004; Obama won 94% of this group in 2008 and 95% in 2012. On the other hand, white evangelicals have been an important part of the Republican base in recent decades. In the 2004 election, 79% of self-identified white evangelicals voted for Bush; McCain won 73% of their vote in 2008; and Romney won 79% in 2012. In Congressional elections, super-majorities of white evangelicals chose Republican candidates; they won 70% of the vote in 1996, 77% in 2010, and 78% in 2014.

Politicians and political consultants are quite aware of these patterns, of course, so many candidates tailor messages to reach out to particular religious groups. Republicans routinely craft appeals that they hope will inspire white evangelicals to increase voter turnout, even as Democrats reach out to African-American voters to shore up this important base. Candidates from both parties seek ways to appeal to Catholic and mainline Protestant voters in attempts to swing them toward their side.

Enduring Principles, Enduring Questions: Reaching Across Borders

As we have seen, the political behavior of American Christians varies quite dramatically between and even within traditions. But questions about the role and nature of government extend far beyond the United States and the particularities of its political system. The rich theological traditions we have explored in this book reach back across centuries — all but the Black church tradition predate the founding of the United States — and span across the globe. Even the Black church, a uniquely American tradition forged in the midst of tragedy and oppression, connects themes of liberation and prophetic witness that speak to many other contexts. Each of these five traditions speaks far beyond the contemporary American scene, identifying core principles and raising questions that challenge us all to be citizens of the global kingdom of God.

Agreement on Core Principles

All of the views represented in this book share important core principles that animate their political theology. In our exploration, several common themes have emerged:

The centrality of the church and its witness to the gospel. Each tradition differs about the specific location of this witness, but they all share this common goal. Anabaptists look primarily to the church as a community of discipleship, set apart as a witness to the outside world. The Catholic and Reformed views hold a broader interpretation of the role of the church in the culture, seeking to transform law and society.

The importance of governing institutions. Governments have significant power both to further the common good and to oppress. Most traditions view government as a potential source for good, and each wrestles with how to guide, limit, or control its power.

The importance of civil society/free associations. These must be allowed the freedom to flourish. The Catholic doctrine of subsidiarity and the Kuyperian notion of sphere sovereignty offer two specific ways of thinking about these relationships, but all traditions agree that churches, families, schools, and other important institutions play essential roles in society and deserve protection.

A concern for cultivating virtue in individuals and working toward a more virtuous society. As the authors have demonstrated, the traditions are divided on how to define virtue: Are true virtues knowable for all, as the Catholic tradition of natural law attests? Or is virtue only revealed through Scripture? Despite these significant differences, all views agree that God is the source of all virtue and that virtue is essential to human flourishing.

Enduring Questions

The discussion has also revealed many points of tension and disagreement, raising central questions about the relationship between the Christian faith and politics:

- When addressing societal problems and making collective decisions, what are the proper roles for individuals, churches, and political authorities? How and to what extent should they relate to one another?
- What is the proper level for Christian political engagement? In what ways should individual Christians participate in the political community? Do churches have a proper political role?
- In what ways should Scripture (and its interpretation), reason, historical perspective, and contemporary experience guide Christian political thought?
- In what ways does sin corrupt government, politics, and Christian interaction in the public sphere? What are the best ways to counteract the effects of individual and systemic sin?

It is not always necessary to find common answers to these questions. Instead we can use them as starting points for rich and meaningful conversations about the nature of politics and its relationship to Christian life. As Bruce Fields reminds us, such conversations need to include voices from all members of the body of Christ, and we should value the contributions of those too often deemed the "other."

Political-Theological Difference and Christian Unity

By design, this book highlights the differences between five traditions of political theology. We have focused on these differences to help readers think more deeply about the dynamics of Christian witness in the public sphere and consider alternative perspectives. But the purpose of this book is not to convince readers they must choose a side as if in the midst of a raging debate. Instead, we invite readers to compare and contrast central ideas and themes from each tradition to help them develop a more thoughtful, careful, and Christ-centered approach to politics and government.

Readers need not belong to one of the church traditions presented in this book to learn from them or to embrace their principles and ideals. As the dialogue between the authors has revealed, conversations about the role of church and state are dynamic, not static. These traditions overlap in many significant ways, have borrowed from each other's teachings over time, and continue to learn from one another and change from within.

As long as societies face collective problems and decisions, government will be necessary, and political issues will divide people. Cultural and political battles will continue to rage, and faithful Christians from all traditions will get caught in the crossfire. As James K.A. Smith astutely remarks in his response to the Catholic tradition, we are all part of the church universal: "In an increasingly secularized, post-Christian culture, it is crucial that 'the church' be understood 'catholically' — as a transnational body that finds its commonness in the Scriptures, the sacraments, and the Nicene tradition" (p. 213). The nature of how we engage politically and how we disagree with each other is an aspect of our discipleship. By working together across boundaries of denomination and nation, we can seek unity in Christ as we share the gospel message with a broken world.

CONTRIBUTORS

J. Brian Benestad is the D'Amour Chair of Catholic Thought at Assumption College in Worcester, Massachusetts, where he currently teaches in the Department of Theology. From 1976 to 2013 he taught theology at the University of Scranton, a Catholic, Jesuit institution in northeastern Pennsylvania. His publications include *Collected Essays* in three volumes by Ernest Fortin (1996); *The Pursuit of a Just Social Order: Policy Statement of the U.S Catholic Bishops, 1966–1980* (1982); and *Church, State, and Society: An Introduction to Catholic Social Doctrine* (2011). He has served as editor of the *Fellowship of Catholic Scholars Quarterly* since the spring of 2007. Professor Benestad has also lectured widely throughout his career on many aspects of Catholic social doctrine.

Robert Benne was Jordan-Trexler Professor of Religion and Chair of the Religion and Philosophy Department at Roanoke College for eighteen years before he left full-time teaching in 2000. He founded the Roanoke College Center for Religion in 1982 and continues at Roanoke College as a Research Associate in its Religion and Philosophy Department. Before going to Roanoke College he was Professor of Church and Society at the Lutheran School of Theology at Chicago for seventeen years. His graduate degrees are from the University of Chicago. He has written and lectured widely on the relation of Christianity and culture. The most recent of his twelve books are *Good and Bad Ways to Think About Religion and Politics; Quality with Soul: How Six Premier Colleges and Universities Keep Faith with Their Religious Traditions; Reasonable Ethics*; and *A Christian Approach to Social, Economic, and Political Concerns*.

232 • FIVE VIEWS ON THE CHURCH AND POLITICS

Bruce L. Fields is Associate Professor of Biblical and Systematic Theology and Chair of the Biblical and Systematic Theology Department at Trinity Evangelical Divinity School in Deerfield, Illinois, where he has taught since 1988. Prior to coming to Trinity, Dr. Fields was on staff for six years with Campus Crusade for Christ. There he served in a variety of roles, including Athletes in Action, the Indian ministry in Colorado, and the staff of the University of Michigan. He earned a BA at the University of Pennsylvania, an MDiv and ThM at Trinity Evangelical Divinity School, and his PhD at Marquette University. He is the author of *Black Theology: 3 Crucial Questions for the Evangelical Church*, and his areas of expertise include the Epistle to the Philippians and liberation and black theology.

Thomas W. Heilke is Associate Dean of Graduate Studies and Professor of Political Science at the University of British Columbia, Okanagan. He holds BA and MA degrees from the University of Calgary and a PhD from Duke University. He was previously Dean of Graduate Studies and Professor of Political Science at the University of Kansas, where he held various posts, including Director of the Center for Global and International Studies, Associate Dean of International Programs, and a courtesy appointment in the Humanities and Western Civilization Program. He is author, co-author, or co-editor of more than 40 publications, including *Voegelin on the Idea of Race; Nietzsche's Tragic Regime: Culture, Aesthetics, and Political Education;* and *Eric Voegelin: In Quest of Reality.*

James K.A. Smith is Professor of Philosophy at Calvin College, where he holds the Gary & Henrietta Byker Chair in Applied Reformed Theology & Worldview. He is the award-winning author of *Who's Afraid of Postmodernism?* and *Desiring the Kingdom*, and his most recent books include *Imagining the Kingdom* (2013); *Discipleship in the Present Tense* (2013); *Who's Afraid of Relativism?* (2014); and *How (Not) To Be Secular: Reading Charles Taylor* (2014). His popular writing has appeared in magazines such as *Christianity Today, Books & Culture*, and *First Things* and periodicals such as *The New York Times, Wall Street Journal*, and *Detroit Free Press*. He is a Senior Fellow of Cardus and serves as editor of *Comment* magazine. Jamie and his wife, Deanna, have four children.

Amy E. Black is Professor of Political Science at Wheaton College. She earned her BA at Claremont McKenna College and her PhD at Massachusetts Institute of Technology. Her books include *Honoring God in Red or Blue: Approaching Politics with Humility, Grace, and Reason; Religion and American Politics: Classic and Contemporary Perspectives*, edited with Douglas Koopman and Larycia Hawkins; *Beyond Left and Right: Helping Christians Make Sense of American Politics; From Inspiration to Legislation: How an Idea Becomes a Law*; and *Of Little Faith: The Politics of George W. Bush's Faith Based Initiatives*, with Douglas Koopman and David Ryden. She is the author of many articles, reviews, and commentary that have appeared in publications such as *Christianity Today, Books & Culture*, and *The Christian Science Monitor*.

AUTHOR INDEX

SUBJECT INDEX

SCRIPTURE INDEX